THE FURNITURE GUYS® BOOK

The FURNITURE GUYS® Book

Joe L'Erario
and
Ed Feldman

WILLIAM MORROW AND COMPANY, INC.   NEW YORK

Photographs by Peter Lien
Line drawings by Barbara Steadman
In color photograph of Mid-century Modern chair: painting by Joe L'Erario
In color photograph of Mid-century Modern table: sculpture by Abraham Rothblatt

It is the policy of William Morrow and Company, Inc., and its imprints and affiliates,
recognizing the importance of preserving what has been written, to print the books we
publish on acid-free paper, and we exert our best efforts to that end.

ISBN 0-688-13766-0

Printed in the United States of America

BOOK DESIGN BY OKSANA KUSHNIR

WE PROUDLY DEDICATE THIS BOOK
TO THE MEMORY OF RICHARD BOONE

(because no one else has ever dedicated a book to him)

Joe's Acknowledgments

Obviously, there are a lot of people to thank when you put a book like this together, and not necessarily "thanks" only to those people associated with the book, like our editor, Toni Sciarra, who has stuck with us and allowed us the ability to be us, and Michael Mouland, who took what we wrote, said, "Huh?", and who now may be in a home somewhere in Toronto. . . . So I'd like to start by thanking my parents for imbuing me with the sense of wonder and appreciation for life that keeps them alive and with me always; my son, Zane, for being the loving and talented boy I always dreamed of having; my dearest and incredibly wonderful partner in life, Heidi Higgins, whose understanding, strength, and inner grace rescued me from myself; her talented and beautiful daughters, Avalon, Avonlea, and Paris, truly angels in the flesh; my brothers, Pat and Frank, and their wives, Rita and Rosemary, for their always constant encouragement; my aunts Ellie and Chris and my uncle Bud, for having always been there; my aunt Dolly, once there, now gone, always remembered, always loved; Deborah Haig for being the mother of Zane and a beautiful human being; Pete and Dee Stevens; my cousin Marty and his wife, Janet; my aunt Mickey, who someday will reveal to me the secrets of the family; John Overmeyer; Glenn Goldstein for his friendship and crack-shot workmanship; Susan Goldstein for loosing us upon the different cities we have been to and shall go; all the people from our PBS days at Channel 12 in Philadelphia, most notably Eileen Lucas, who came over to my shop one day and put a home video camera on a couple of jerks just to see what we had; Eric (Horsehaar) Sennhenn; Fred Ficke for his constant reminder that "tape was cheap"; Banyan Productions; everyone at Center City Video, especially Jordan Schwartz; Mr. Milton Feldman, my high school art teacher, one of the most dedicated teachers I have ever known, who taught me what art was not; Dorian Chitani, who left too soon; Jack Gallant, who's still with me from those good old days when Dorian was; Ed Fink and Ted Artz for being great friends and inspirers who had the sense to hire me because I was one of the best workers they ever had; Ted's wife, Diane Zatz, for laughing at me when I told her stories about my youth, especially about Mrs. Bleschman; my childhood friend Billy Loskeiwitz for being the kind of friend I hope for and wish I had in life now; Bill Headley for hiring me on the first woodworking job I ever did; Donald Gilligan: mighty giant, "ginger-colored ape" felled too early in life; Gil Cohen, a teacher I had in art college, for having come from the same mold as Mr. Feldman when it came to teaching; for his impeccably soothing sound and knowledge of jazz and the great musicians that inspire him to his own greatness as well as his talent for comforting as a loving friend I'd like to thank Ted Gerike, who has probably taught me more about what's weird about this world than anyone else; Caroline Cook Storer and her husband, Richard Storer, for being Heidi's and my adopted parents and for allowing us the benefits of knowing how much love really heals; Michael Donnelly for being the kind of friend I really need; Pat Sanagan out there somewhere, always remembered; Kate White and Robert Miller, new friends along for the ride in my new world; Michael and Tara Zahab; Joe Grey for his laughter; Abe Rothblatt for his lovable whining; Bob Barnett for his genuineness; Cathy O'Connell for her soul love; Lon Chaney Sr., who taught me sympathy for those who are different; Abbott and Costello; W. C. Fields, The Marx Brothers, and Moe, Larry, and Curly—also Shemp, for filling my youth with laughter; *The Dick Van Dyke Show* for just having been; Boris Karloff for his "monster" and eternal "grinch"; Bela Lugosi for his style; Martin Yan for his guidance; Dean Martin and Jerry Lewis; Charles Brennan for having been the best bartender/writer/person I ever sat before in my "old world"; George Frank, master finisher, whose books I devoured; Frank Frazetta, still the only and the best; Salvador Dali, ditto; Padgett Hopkins, for giving me a chance at Architectural Antiques Exchange in Philadelphia and for showing me what finishing was all about; Mark Charry for hiring me; Sam Mauriello for his lasting friendship and boyish wonder and fascination at what I do for a living; John Greco for feeding me at Stan's, King of Sandwiches; John, Paul, George, and Ringo; Bird, Duke, Count, Mingus, Lester, and Coltrane and Django; Picasso; Lou and Sam Brood, two of the nicest guys you'd ever want to meet; Sid Caesar's *Your Show of Shows* and everyone associated with it; David Auspitz, Famous Delicatessen; Grandpa Al Lewis and Mr. John Voight for appearing on our show; the Amazing Randi; The Banana Man; Carl Balantine; Jonathan Haze for his "Seymour Krelboing"; Steve Arbitman; Alan at National Hardware in Philadelphia; Tony D'Agostina, newfound friend; The Pythons; Stanley Kubrick; Scorsese; Clayton Moore and that damn prospector he always disguised himself as because I didn't know it was him; Benny, Burns, and Berle; and mostly thanks to Ed, who came to my shop one day with an idea and an offer to buy me dim sum at Joi Tsin Lau if I'd help him with a touchup that day—"Bastard!"

Ed's Acknowledgments

First, I thank my parents, Jack and Bella Feldman, who never threw me out of the house—although I gave them cause—and whose achievements and work ethic are an example to me (I'm still trying to get the hang of that work ethic stuff, though). To my sister, Marcia Feldman, whose talent and capacity for love is, as far as I can see, infinite.

To my friends, who have shown me what it is to be a friend—supportive, loving, yet honest enough to say when I'm being a jerk (don't they ever get tired of that?): Lenny Loev, Gary Richter, Barry Glasser, Michael Petkov, Susan Ziman, Clare Kane, Emedio Sevieri, and Ted Artz.

To South Street, where in the 70s, anything was possible.

To Kitti Watts, one of the nicest people on earth, who supported me in every way in lean times; and to our daughter, Amanda Watts-Feldman, who is a young supernova of beauty, talent, and goodness, and who truly possesses the better angels of both our natures.

To Sandy Radich, who always showed me that relationships may change but love and respect are the foundation. To Constance Long, who taught me to fix furniture and who didn't get frustrated when I couldn't.

To Carol Anne Reilly-Prusich, who showed us that our production company name was right under our noses, and that acceptance was right under mine.

To Allan Hurt, who gave me my start in construction. To Bill Headly, who hired me to work on a job in Chestnut Hill, where I met the guy to whom I am now linked inextricably.

To the Mount Airy Learning Tree, where I got the idea for the show—and where ideas are coin of the realm. To WHYY Channel 12, where Ilene Lucas showed us how to make TV. To Mike Quattrone, who said, "I won't forget you guys," and didn't. To Glenn Goldstein, our attorney, who has wrestled with more adversaries on our behalf than Hulk Hogan has for Vince McMahon. To Susan Goldstein, who struggles daily to get our live bodies before the unwary public.

To Ted Gerike, our music master, whose encyclopedic knowledge of all notes, jazz or otherwise, makes our show instantly recognizable. Simply the best music on television, "Fonebone, old buddy."

To The Learning Channel, where John Ford took a chance on weirdness. To Nancy Lavin, who allowed that weirdness to grow.

To our crews: Lisa Marie Russo, Eric Sennhenn, Lynn Cates, John McInhenny, and John Knapp at Channel 12.

To Banyan Productions: Susan Cohen Dickler, Ray Murray, and Jan Dickler.

To Dave Bowers, Don Vitello, Anthony Yuro,

Jim Mullen, John Shupin, Dave Figenshu, Bill Santoro, and Joe Kennedy.

To Kelly Ryan, that rare combination of tenacity and kindness, and our current cast: Christine Urbanski, Gillian Rye, Steve West, Valerie Rusk, Alicia Jacobson, Kevin Maraza, Lee Cado, Juanita Bennett, Joe Pleviak, J. R. Arsenault, Colleen Casey, and Lisa Calianno.

To everyone at Center City Film and Video: Jordan Schwartz, Chris Foster, Damon Alberts, Steve Cipollone, Tito Santiago, and Mark DiBartolomeo.

To our editor, Toni Sciarra, whose belief in us and patience with us really made this book possible.

To Michael Mouland, whose skill made this book readable.

To Steve Arbitman, whose expertise made the above people's jobs bearable.

And finally to Dr. John Cotter, my favorite professor at Penn, who gave me the best career advice I ever got: "Put your life experience together and create a job only you can fill." I did it, Dr. Cotter—thanks.

Contents

One WHY OLD FURNITURE?   1

Abundance of Styles • Availability • Individuality • Fun • Adventure • Price • Quality • Setting Up Your Workplace, or You're Really Serious About Doing This • Finishing Supplies and Tools
Project 1: Pine Hoosier   10
Peeling Paint Electrically • Professional Strippers • Selecting Strippers • Preparing to Paint • Color Matching • Painting Basics • Painting Hardware • Stenciling • That's All, Folks

Two INTRODUCTION TO UPHOLSTERY, *or Mallets Toward Everyone*   20

Remembrance of Springs Past • Couch Springs Eternal • There's Nothing Like a Frame • What Kind of Tool Am I? • Now Cut That Out • Guns Along the Mohair • Mallets • Needles and Thread • Tack Strips • Finding Supplies: A Walk on the Wrong Side of Town • Choosing Fabric • Estimating Yardage • Yipes! Stripes! • The Final Touch
Project 2: Victorian Renaissance Revival with a Touch of Gothic (and a Bit of Chippendale with Marlborough Legs) Throne Chair, or You Sit on Me All the Time   26
A Little Bit of History • Of Things Shakespearean • Our Throne Chair and How We Acquired It • To Burn or Not to Burn? • Preparing the Chair for Refinishing • Sanding Is a No-no • The Plot Begins to Unravel • Thank Heaven for Little Coils • Playing with Slinkies: Those Damn Coil Tops • The Cover-up • Victory at Seat • Cambric or Dustcover?

Joe's Introduction

Hi, I'm Joe L'Erario.

People always ask me, "Hey—where's the other guy? Where's Ed?" Like I know his every move—or we live together like Felix and Oscar. I always say the same thing: "I killed him!" And that usually makes them laugh.

But everyone also always wants to know the whys and wherefores of furniture stripping, refinishing, and restoration, and that's exactly why we've assembled this book. (Well, to tell you the truth, we just shuffled around a lot of loose pages; the binding was done at a big factory with giant machines that could hurt you.)

We wanted to put together a textbook for everything you've seen us do on television, and that's exactly what we've accomplished. We even threw in some history as we went along, so you'd learn lots of new facts with which to regale your friends when they think they're coming over for a simple cookout. "Hey, Harry, did you know it takes about one hundred thousand lac bugs to make a gallon of shellac?"

Understand, there are a lot of people in the woodworking trade who are far more knowledgeable than I, but they're not funny and they don't have a TV show. I am happy to share some of the tricks of the trade with you: the quick fixes, remedies, and solutions that I've amassed over the past sixteen years, which have cost me lots of sore knees from kneeling in front of things while applying stain, burned nose hairs from the inhalation of chemicals—and I can't even begin to count the splinters. Do you know how much hand cream I've gone through?

But it's paid off, right? I mean, I scrimped and saved and struggled and slaved, and now I get to tell you how *not* to make those same mistakes! That alone is worth the price of the book.

So, where to begin? I worked for a lot of people in the woodworking and finishing trade. Some were nice and some were not so nice. I remember one of the great gigs I had was mixing colors for a furniture manufacturer. The manufacturer's staff included a guy who sprayed on finishes, but he didn't know how to mix colors. So I'd go in: a specialist—a color consultant. In the course of three hours I'd mix up the exact color they needed to match the sample they presented to me, for which I charged them thirty dollars an hour. When I left after three hours, they'd present me with a check and I was ninety bucks ahead.

Easy money. I was blessed with an eye for color. I can look at something and match it exactly (which is something I have been doing a lot longer than finishing, since I have been drawing and painting for most of my life). I worked for two cabinet makers and at an antiques exchange that specialized in bar and restaurant interiors before I worked up enough steam to start my own business in 1984. I called it Refinishing by Vincent—because Vincent is my middle name and sounds a lot better than Refinishing by Joe, don't you think?

I can hear you saying, "But where did it all begin?"

Well, can I thank my parents? Seriously. They were in show business. My dad's name was Frank Page. He was a tap dancer/comedian. My mother's stage name was Helen Lane. She played "swing" Hawaiian steel guitar and had been on the road from the time she was seventeen. I used to go with them to the clubs and sit backstage, watching them perform.

I remember the first time my father made me a part of the act. I was about nine. He used to do a drunk act in which he shoved this beat-up old fedora on his head and staggered around onstage, puffing on a cigarette and telling a story. One night before he went on, he told me to throw him his hat when he called for it. Well, you can imagine my excitement. I sat on a chair backstage curling the brim of that hat in my little sweaty palms until it was time.

When I threw it out, it didn't go far enough, so he told me to come out and get it for him. When I walked out onstage, that was it. I stood there in my brand-new suit, staring into the crowd—and I could see only the first few rows because the house lights were down, the stage lights were bright in front, and the smoke was incredibly thick—but I saw those ivory crescent smiles and heard the flesh of the audience's hands meeting and clapping for me . . . and you know, every time I see the little red light on top of the camera when we're about to tape a scene for the show, that one moment from my youth flashes through my mind.

Yes, those were the good old days. And they got even better—but I'll refrain from telling you about the time my dad took me to a stag show without his knowing it, because this is not that kind of book.

So we flash forward in time to 1980, and Ed and me working construction together, mixing concrete. We also tied steel and did carpentry, but mostly our jobs seemed to be making everyone else on the site laugh. People call it chemistry—well, I flunked chemistry. Go figure. All I knew was that with Ed it was quite easy to go off on wild tangents and act out skits in front of a crew of fourteen.

By 1989, my refinishing business was somewhat established. Ed was doing in-home repair for various furniture stores. On occasion, if he was in my part of town, he'd stop in and we'd go out to lunch. One time he came in and told me he had had a dream that we were on TV being funny and fixing furniture. Now I could have been knee-deep in stain and drowning in bills, and politely asked him to hand me the rope I had so conveniently made into a noose. I don't remember.

Eventually, though, I relented, and we wrote an eight-page script on stripping and refinishing an old bureau. We presented this to the local PBS affiliate, which liked it. After we did fourteen shows with PBS between 1990 and 1991, The Learning Channel found out about us and asked if we'd like to come and make shows there. Of course we did, and then we went national, and then we wrote the very book you are holding in your hands. (And if you're just reading it at the bookstore to pass the time, why not buy it?)

I could go on and on, but I already like you, so I'm going to give you the real low-down. OK?

When I first met Ed, he was wearing a big fluffy owl costume and standing outside a newly opened restaurant, handing out flyers to passersby along with complimentary crullers. He didn't last too long at this job, though, because for some crazy reason, he felt compelled to work in his snappy "button routine" between his "Hello's." This was a tired routine in which he would demonstrate how to sew buttons on a throw pillow using a needle big enough for shish kebob. He was supposed to be waving people into the damn restaurant, for cryin' out loud, and there he was goofing around. (The owl costume, just in case you were wondering, was a marketing device the restaurant had devised to herald its twenty-four-hour service.)

So there he was: big old bird costume, glasses that didn't fit under the headpiece so he was blind to boot, and feathers—colored feathers everywhere! Did you ever see a big owl trying to sew a button on a fat pillow with an eight-inch needle? He kept dropping the buttons because it was difficult to hold on to them with the padded fingers of the suit, so he'd lean over and scurry about, trying to stop the rolling buttons with his orange rubber-clawed feet. Was it hilarious!

Once I watched a kid push him: A button fell, and when he bent to retrieve it, another kid rode by on a bike and shoved him good with a foot in the rear. Down he went, struggling on his back in that big owl suit, going back and forth, to and fro, until finally he had rocked himself to sleep and I could hear the gently purring sound of his breath blowing through his mustache hairs.

I moved in and helped him up. He took off the owl head because I asked him to, and he thanked me for saving him. I suggested he try the routine without the costume and also suggested that we work together on something new and unique. "Television!" I said. "Will we show them how to make shows!" (Just that day I had had an offer from a network.)

Well, that's how it all happened. So help me.

It never occurred to either of us that someday we would be able to utilize the ingredients of our chemistry to create the national fungus known as The Furniture Guys.

So there you have it. I suppose now you're going to read Ed's Intro, which is all made-up stuff with not a bit of truth, unlike mine. Go ahead. See if I care. Go ahead, turn the page. . . . See if I care. . . . Gahead. . . .

Ed's Introduction

The moon, slivered to toenail size, fought valiantly against the assaults of fast-moving, knife-edged clouds asserting their will on the moor below.

Alone I wandered this verdant landscape—which undulated like the rippling back of a huge crouching beast.

More than fear of aloneness or of the unknown, I felt a fear of becoming part of this beast, because as I wandered deeper into his world, I felt less a part of mine, as if his power were claiming me, calling me to his wildness.

And then I heard these words from the bushes: "You, boy!" Was the beast calling me—finally calling me home?

The green wall parted and I saw it—a face. Fearful, wan, yet kind, entreating me to draw closer. I did not hesitate . . . I moved toward him. And as if the words I spoke had been in me always, I asked, "What are you doing—do you need help?"

The reply came back sure and certain, every bit as measured as my question: "I'm marbleizing. Take this rag and get the edges."

This may or may not be the way I met Joe L'Erario.

An alternate, slightly less evocative version takes place in a posh neighborhood in Philadelphia called Chestnut Hill—the area in which I now live. But in 1979 the closest I got to this lifestyle was mixing concrete in a trough, which would then be poured into the foundation of an exceptionally expensive house in said 'hood.

There was another guy mixing with me. As we mixed, we talked and talked—and joked—and did impressions—and tried to stump each other with erudite queries like "What was Allen Brady's secretary's name?" or "Who was Thelonious Monk's sax man?" (Answers: Marge and Sahib Shihab.)

Others on the crew joined occasionally in this nonstop comedy musical quiz show act. But they couldn't keep up. They had obviously wasted their youth on unimportant matters—like listening in class. But this guy, he had it in the blood. Just like me.

I grew up in Philadelphia. My dad was a jazz drummer, as well as having a real job. My sister became an actress and singer, and my mom—well, let's just say that she's a sitcom all by herself.

I always devoured every bit of information I heard or saw, memorizing everything from Lenny Bruce records at age five (often I listened over and over till I learned them phonetically—I didn't understand all the phrasing cognitively) to reading the *Encyclopaedia Britannica* (my favorite entry: "Anatomy," featuring a naked woman on translucent color plates).

Bored by school, I learned on my own, reading and watching the glowing box in the living room that had become a best friend to all of us.

Which is why we got to write this book, let's face it.

I dropped out of college at eighteen, tried to foment urban insurrection, failed, and relaxed for a while. Drove trucks, ran with carnivals, sold ice cream, chauffeured, ran a food co-op, and in 1978, at age twenty-five, said, "Time to get moving." So I talked my way into the University of Pennsylvania and got two jobs. One was washing dishes in a restaurant at night, and the other was on a construction crew—they gave me a broom and I swept up. Eventually I worked my way up the tool chain to hammer.

I worked on crews until 1983, when my friend Constance broke her ankle cross-country skiing with her husband. She worked for a company that fixed furniture that had been delivered from stores and damaged in transit, or that had a manufacturer's defect. Constance would go to the owner's home and fix the piece while the customer watched suspiciously, complaining all the while, "I'll never buy anything from that store again. Why don't they just replace it? This is not acceptable," blah, blah, blah.

Constance asked if I wanted to take her place at the company while her ankle healed. I was then the world's worst contractor, underestimating jobs to the extent that my profits, after paying my workers, were in the single digits. I told her that while I knew how to fix broken furniture frames because of my carpentry experience, and had done some finishing, I had never done touch-up repairing scratches to wood, and I knew *nothing at all* about upholstery. (The cry goes out across the land, "I knew it!")

She said, "Fake it." So I did, sometimes phoning her in the middle of a house call for advice. (It was reminiscent of movies about bomb squads: "Cut the red wire—no, the blue one"— BOOM!)

After a year of faking it, I started my own business. It wasn't hard. (Feldman's career advice: Fake it till you know how to do it, and the customer can always be fooled.) I was doing forty to fifty house calls a week, and every customer had bad credit.

In 1985 I started teaching furniture repair at a night school in Philadelphia called the Mount Airy Learning Tree. The school had courses in everything from car repair to yoga. My motive was to teach enough people to find some talented apprentices whom I would hire to expand my business. Then I could stay in the office more and not be as tempted to kill my constantly complaining clientele.

Although the class was popular, I never did get any workers from it, because my teaching technique included rants about what a horrible job it was—dirty houses, surly customers—but as I became more relaxed in my rap, I came upon a very simple thought (worlds turn on such thoughts): People were learning and laughing about *fixing furniture*.

I watched how-to shows on TV. They showed how to put up a nine-level deck—complete with Ferris wheel and petting zoo—all in a half-hour program. But who builds such things?

On the other hand, everyone in my class—and almost everyone I knew—had an old, inherited or trash-picked piece of quality furniture that needed repair. The time was right— boomer/yuppies were yard-sale, flea-market, and swap-meet crazy. They needed to fill their idle hours with sweat equity projects lest they try to pry their kids away from the glowing box—an unrewarding endeavor.

I also saw TV cooking shows with personality-driven themes—cooks are natural extroverts— but the how-to shows had hosts who were slightly "dry," to be kind; craftspeople often work alone and are more introverted by nature.

So, two new concepts: Teach some new stuff that a lot of people are interested in, and do it with comedy—and personality.

Could I do it myself? Who else knew this stuff and was funny? There was one guy, Bertrand Russell, but he was dead. That left but one other on earth: the guy in the bushes, Joe L'Erario.

Through tenacity, hard work, some bribery, and blackmail we got the hang of the glowing box—and now it's on the printed page. I hope you enjoy it. If not, put the book on the folding table at your next yard sale—next to the bureau they'll want to refinish—and send us some of the resale money.

THE FURNITURE GUYS® BOOK

One

WHY OLD FURNITURE?

The eternal question has always been: Why? Innumerable books have started with these words. Why do we exist? Why does humankind commit heinous, unconscionable acts? And worst of all, why didn't those animal-like friends of yours at my party last night use their coasters? Now I have white rings all over the tabletops and a cigarette burn in the arm of the love seat. There are scrapes in the floor caused by the chair that had no rubber cap on the end of one leg. The cap kept falling off and I wound up throwing it in the drawer filled with rubber bands from the newspapers, bottle caps, and coupons for products that aren't made anymore. And now look at the damage: They drink my liquor, eat my canapés, and ruin my furniture while they're at it. . . . Why? Why? Why? Why? Why?

There really is no answer to this question, and aren't you glad we didn't string you along for forty chapters exploring this question and all its ramifications? But here is a question that we really can answer: Why get involved with fixing old furniture?

Here's why: abundance of furniture styles to choose from, availability, individuality, fun and adventure (or therapeutic value), price, and, most important of all, quality. So, let's start from the top.

Abundance of Styles

Furniture has been around for a long time. From the very first rocks that cave dwellers sat on while dangling their muddy tootsies in a natural hot spring, to the $10,000 polystyrene boulder with stereo speakers that sits at the edge of the $40,000 in-ground hot tub today, humans have been in search of comfort, style, and durability. Thus, in between the dawn of civilization and 2001, we have seen thousands upon thousands of style changes. Most of these styles are still available today in various states, both geographic and structural. Even many of the aforementioned prehistoric rocks are in excellent condition and have suffered only slight wear and tear caused by the odd cudgel blow (the result of an early attempt at recliner design).

Typically, when you venture into a retail furniture store, you are offered a limited choice of the styles that are deemed popular at the time. Even the largest furniture manufacturers sell only a handful of lines at any given moment, especially in their high-end outlets. A sample selection of choices is typically limited to pieces described as "colonial" (dark pine festooned with eagles), "Queen Anne cherry," and whatever contemporary look has been deemed "in" or "hot" at the moment. This could include an eclectic assortment of styles with names like "Southwestern Lodge" or "Adirondack Twig." And if these styles don't move out the door fast enough, they're dropped like hot potatoes by the manufacturer. Woe betide the poor buyer who needs a replacement part or fabric panel after the Adirondack Twig has vanished from the face of the earth. Now there's service for you!

In contrast, the abundance of styles available to the used furniture buyer is almost unlimited, and largely determined by the quality and the ability of the piece to withstand unspeakable acts of abuse. Take, for instance, dressers that have been painted purple or kitchen tables that have been used as workbenches. This is Darwinist furniture theory in action: The more strongly made furniture has survived these abuses over the years and is now yours for the taking. Remember that under a ghastly coat of paint there may lurk walnut, oak, or mahogany. No matter how many owners and wild and wacky paint jobs this furniture may have had, underneath its soul survives, waiting for you to expose it again.

Most furniture that you find will be American-made—assuming you're reading this in America. Furniture styles through the 1800s went through dozens of changes, from Federal, at the beginning of the century, to the Arts and Crafts movement at the dawn of the twentieth century, which begat Gustav Stickley's Mission style, which in turn begat the so-called Modern style, which begat Cole Porter's beguine.

In between these big moments in furniture styles were the endless "neo" designs of the nineteenth century: Neo-Classical, Neo-Gothic, Neo-Renaissance, and Neo-lithic, or rock revival. The twentieth century gave us many other styles to choose from, including Mission, Nouveau, Deco, and Mid-century Modern. The latter can still be seen worldwide each night on TV reruns, reposing in the homes of Rob and Laura Petrie, Samantha and Darrin Stephens, and Tim and his favorite Martian uncle who, incidentally, seems to be staying with him for quite a long time. All of these styles were produced in great abundance, and all it takes to acquire them for yourself is a little cash, some investigation, and some nerve.

Availability

We've been living in a throwaway culture for at least a generation now. Styrofoam, plastic wrap, and flakeboard have made it so. Unfortunately, our throwaway habits have caused us to throw away things that were made before the things that were meant to be thrown away. To clarify: People throw away good stuff because they've gotten into the habit of throwing stuff away. Sometimes they sell it on their lawn, or they pay somebody to come and haul it away, or they give it to their ungrateful children, who repeat the aforementioned pattern. In order to get good stuff, you have to be there at the right moment. Not before or after, because the good stuff will be gone or it will not have arrived yet. You get the picture: Timing is very important.

We've discovered what we call the furniture food chain: A piece of furniture begins with the original owners, then passes to trash pickers, then to estate sale specialists, and finally to auctions and used furniture stores. Very often there are many levels of ownership within these categories. To get closest to the original source, one needs cunning and knowledge. In this book we will tell you tales of an auction that is held every other week on a site the size of a football field where thousands of pieces of furniture can be had for the right price, and we'll spin yarns of the high-tech trash pickers who prowl the streets at dawn in search of the perfect iron column, tin cornice, ghoulish gargoyle, or piece of furniture.

Why so much furniture? (Notice we are back to the big question: Why?) America has been turning out furniture for four hundred years now, and producing it on a really grand scale in factories for more than one hundred and fifty years. In the old days we had a country full of happy, unwary, and defenseless trees. Had they been able to anticipate the swinging of axes and seesaw of sharp saw blades, they might have evolved into more wary trees. But because trees are trees, they weren't able to escape the onslaught of the Bunyanesque saw and axe.

The Industrial Revolution saw the emergence of enormous furniture-making empires, some of which still exist today. Millions of pieces of furniture have been made over the last century and a half, and much of it is still in excellent shape. Unlike a house or a car, furniture isn't usually exposed to the vagaries of the elements. Rather, it may have reposed under a tattered sheet for many years, forlorn in its aloneness, waiting for a nice grandchild to come to the rescue with a new home where it can stand tall and proud again, usually as a quality centerpiece amid ready-to-assemble furniture made of plastic and slowly swelling flakeboard. And as luck will have it, the old piece of furniture will probably outlive its new owner, just as it outlived the likes of McKinley and Roosevelt, Lindbergh and Dillinger, Liz Taylor and Hilton, Liz and Wilding, Liz and Todd, Liz and Fisher, Liz and Burton, etc., etc.

Individuality

Today's on-the-go lifestyles are, in a word, eclectic. So why get locked into living with a four-teen-piece leather, glass, and chrome ensemble featuring lamps with enormous aluminum shades that hit you in the head every time you turn around to grab a drink from the minibar—which also dispenses postal stamps from the concealed Pitney Bowes direct-drive stamp machine? In most furniture showrooms, the furniture sales-person begins by sizing you (or your wallet) up and then presents you with page after page of mind-numbing pictures from a brochure illus-trating an array of ghastly furniture ensembles. Do you really want twelve pieces of furniture that all look the same? Do you want twelve kids that all have red hair and freckles? Wouldn't it be bet-ter to create your own environment that reflects your unique personality and tastes? If you prefer the fast-food approach to home furnishing, you'd better put this book down now. *You read it right: put the book down, and go over to the How-Not-To aisle in the bookstore!* By the way, if you're still reading this book in the public library you can help us out with sales if you take the book home and report it stolen. By doing this the library will have to order another one, and we'll get more royalties.

Fun

A large part of the fun of furnishing your home lies in discovering which styles go well together, and which styles best complement your attitude. How many attitudes do you have? If you're feel-ing a bit monkish, try Mission. Coy and maid-enly? Opt for Victorian. Sparse and celibate? You gotta go Shaker. And once the whole family catches the used furniture bug, loved ones will inevitably want to design and fill their own living spaces with restored pieces: Grandma may want Rococo; English Hunt with its deep green walls and bulky mahogany and leather furniture goes to Papa; French Deco with its frosted glass shades and sleek chrome designs is claimed by and complements Aunt Mini, who is frosted most of the time at the all-night bar; while your retro teens will focus on the ever-popular black leatherette, plaid, and shag because they didn't live through the 1960s (which, let's face it, they consider ancient history).

Adventure

Some heed the call of the sea. But you can get nauseous at sea, or a large fish could bite you. You can hang off the side of a cliff suspended by steel clips and nylon ties, or dive off a crane con-nected by a giant rubber band. And if that isn't adventure enough for you, for a real thrill you can get married. None of these options compares to the thrill of accomplishing a lovely refinishing or upholstery job. And you'll get a full-body workout in the process.

You'll have to start by doing a bit of detective work locating furniture auctions and flea mar-kets. First, go into larger bookstores that sell magazines and you will probably find high- and low-end magazines on antiques. Go into any antique store and you will find newspapers that list auction after auction and scores of flea mar-kets in your area. Check the classifieds in your local newspapers, which list furniture for sale.

Next comes map reading and driving skills—essential for getting you to the motherlode. If you're not good at driving or map reading, bribe someone who is with a free lunch. Once you get to the furniture-buying venue, you'll need a cou-ple of qualities to outmaneuver your adversaries for any precious item you want. You'll need the discerning eye of Peter Falk's *Columbo*—which is right on since he only has one real eye; the other is glass—and the steely nerves of Diamond Jack, the river boat gambler. You also have to know what you want. Sometimes furniture has been altered or cut-down. For instance, a piece will have its ball and claw feet sawed off, or original hardware will be replaced by new hardware. If you tip the piece, you can clearly see that the legs have been sawn away because you'll notice fresh saw marks. It's very hard to hide replacement hardware. If the hardware was originally large and knobby, which you can tell from the dark outline it left on the wood, and in its place is a small cheap glass button you cannot even grasp, you know the furniture's not original. And if the piece you have your eye on is big, remember to bring someone strong to do the hoisting if you can't move the item yourself.

The first physical workout in your furniture-buying adventure involves getting the item to the vehicle in one piece. You may need a roof rack, a van, or a pickup truck to transport your purchase home. And once you're back at the homestead, it's time for the full-body workout we mentioned—taking apart what comes apart, cleaning, sanding, stapling, stitching, pulling, and hammering (these activities work the upper and lower muscle groups). With the inevitable attendant screaming and hollering (expletives deleted), the sinuous and tender throat muscles are treated to some of the excitement. The payoff for all this work is that your ego gets an enormous boost when all your friends and relatives turn green with envy when they see what you've accomplished. You'll have to decide what posture to take: will you let hubris rule, or will you ooze unctuous modesty?

No matter what, you'll have managed to work both sides of the brain along with the quads, hams, lats, delts, traps, and the id without wasting a lousy, stinking dime on any 1-800 numbers hosted by singers with multiple dentures dispensing advice. By keeping busy refinishing furniture, you won't have time to think about your problems. And you'll end up with a nice rolltop desk, settee, or chifferobe when you're done.

Price

Buying new furniture causes the same kind of anxiety as buying a new car. The salesperson knows the wholesale price of the item you're interested in, what the wholesale price was at the store you just left, and what the price will be at the store you're going to visit next. That means that the salesperson has to do a high-pressure sales job on you to get you to buy on the spot. It works like this: There is always an outrageous price tag pinned on floor models—something we call the UHRTNOEP, which stands for "the Unbelievably High Retail That No One Ever Pays." In any event, the drill is always the same: The salesperson will tell you he must consult with some unseen store manager. He will tell you to wait just a second and then wander off to a small stockroom. He will enter this room, pause momentarily next to an old water cooler that hasn't worked for years, chew on a broken nail and count to twenty. As he returns, you will see his smile grow as he tells you he can give it to you cheaper—which is the same price any schmuck would get it for anyway! You'll finally get the Price That Everyone Gets, or the PTEG.

Furniture salespeople know full well that you have no recourse. Their distributors distribute only to them, and manufacturers won't sell so much as a nightstand to the public. And, despite the so-called factory-direct-to-your-home ads you see on storefronts and in newspapers, the "factories" aren't offering bargains much beyond what you get in regular furniture stores. Sure, their markup might be less than a store's, but there's zero room for any kind of negotiation. Let's face it, they have you by the nether regions.

There are ways to get out from under the control of retail furniture mongers: Turn to used furniture for quality and a myriad of choices. When you enter the game, you'll get closer to the source of old furniture. Where do local antique stores buy from? An auction house? Go there yourself and buy from the source. Trash pickers, called "pickers" in the business, can be cornered outside of stores where they do business. Don't be intimidated by the cellular phone and ominous-looking black pickup, ask if they will sell to you. You may be surprised. Just be sure you can pay cash right there and then. The closer you get to the source, the more relationships you'll cultivate. And the better the deals and the bigger the savings.

God bless this country of ours.

Quality

In the world of furniture buying, quality has as little to do with price as Elvis had to do with tofu. Words such as *composites* and *furniture solids* are code words for the nefarious flakeboard or particleboard, which are basically bits of wood all ground up and pressed into various shapes and bonded with formaldehyde glue. Where solid wood boards were once used, these glue-and-chip composites are now the standard. Solid cherry has been replaced by "cherry finish," which is usually a combination of cherry and maple, stained and toned to look like the real deal. Staples have replaced tacks, plastics have replaced woods and glass, and prices have still gone up. Why? There is that question again, and we feel compelled to answer it for you.

Has the quality plummeted solely for the profit of the manufacturers? Not necessarily. It's true that the planet's resources are dwindling and many trees are in danger, leaving some woods scarce or prohibitively expensive. So, here we rationalize our selfish quest for price and quality by claiming to make an altruistic gesture to the environment: Every time we buy old furniture we are recycling the planet's natural resources.

Moreover, by preserving old furniture, we're preserving the stylistic heritage of our nation, the memory of our craftspeople, and the various odors infused in the wood, which recall hearty breakfasts of yesteryear, when a bowl of steamy hot oatmeal was served instead of the tiny box of dry flakes with skim milk and no fruit that you usually get these days.

Setting Up Your Workplace, or You're Really Serious About Doing This

For almost every furniture refinishing project you're going to need a place to work in. You might want to deck out your work area with industrial-grade, explosive-proof lighting and ventilation systems, along with enough electricity to run thousands of dollars' worth of tools. But if you're like most people, you can carve out a more modest spot in your basement, garage, or backyard.

Ventilation

No matter where you set up, remember that there are many safety precautions to follow when working with furniture refinishing products. Ventilation is the most important consideration, especially when working with hazardous chemicals like removers and thinners. Why not keep your brain intact by donning a mask fitted with the right filters?

When we say mask we are talking about a respirator, not a tie-around cloth mask such as the one Clayton Moore fashioned from the vest of his dead brother after all them Texas Rangers were ambushed in the first episode of the *Lone Ranger*. Respirators are available in many sizes and vary in price. You can buy one for about thirty bucks. This type covers the nose and mouth and features replaceable charcoal micronite filters. If you have the money, you can splurge and get yourself a full face mask respirator with replaceable screw-in filters. Some of these can even be hooked up to an air supply system. They are also good for seeing tiny things crawling about on the ocean floor, but this is not recommended—looking at things on the bottom of the ocean, that is. A respirator should be worn along with rubber gloves to protect your hands and arms from chemical strippers and other harmful substances.

An ideal place for a work area is a garage that features a door that can be opened to allow fans to exhaust bad air. Such a setup provides both light and space, but cover the car with a tarpaulin of some sort because if you get lacquer thinner or stripper on it you'll have to drive to Shibe: ninety-nine ninety-five!

If your garage has a gas-fired water heater or furnace in the corner and you are going to work with any flammable product, *you must extinguish the pilot light before getting to work.* Wouldn't it be a shame if you had to join your dear departed Aunt Rose while you watched the prize antique that you inherited from her go up in a blazing fireball just before you started varnishing? A good alternative is to work outside, far away from pilot lights. There are situations where you're going to have to use strippers and chemicals in the house in the proximity of gas-fired appliances. For instance, you're not going to remove a bank of kitchen cabinets from the wall just to refinish them. In instances like this, just remember to extinguish pilot lights before you begin working and encourage ventilation by opening all the windows. If we have managed to scare you with these precautions, take heart in knowing that the number of casualties from home-finishing accidents is much smaller than those caused by everyday activities like driving a car, crossing the street, or eating your in-laws' overcooked meat loaf with the black egg in the middle.

Finally, remember that smoking is out of the question during any of these operations.

Moral: smoking and wood = no good.

Basic Needs

You need at least three basic areas in a well-set-up workshop: one for storage of flammables, another for tools and other supplies, and a third for doing the actual work. Flammables should be stored in heavy metal, flame-proof cabinets that can be closed and locked. You might be tempted to store important documents and valuables inside the cabinets, too. But think of your attorney smelling the will retrieved from your workshop cabinet and the bemused look on his face while he reads the lines: "being of sound mind and body," and realizes that the documents on his desk smell like varnish.

You should also have a metal trash can for throwing away soiled rags. Another idea is to have a bucket of water handy into which you can throw thinner- or oil-stain-soaked rags to prevent spontaneous combustion, which could do much damage to the nose hairs. And while we're on the subject of things that go boom and burn, common sense tells you that you should have a fire extinguisher that is easily accessible and fully charged at all times.

Introducing the Peg-Board

Now that you've been frightened by the above, let's move on to the tool table, over which you should hang a Peg-Board. You can hang most of your tools from metal hooks designed to fit into holes on the board, which will free the tool table drawers for odds and ends, old pinups, rubber bands, Q-tips, and bits of string. A Peg-Board will also help keep your worktable free of clutter and all your tools organized. Well, at least until you start losing your tools, and then you'll be left with a Peg-Board filled with hooks.

The Worktable

In the center of the room, you should have another table or platform to work on. This can be a stationary table, a movable one with wheels, or a large piece of plywood spanning a couple of sawhorses that can be dismantled and stored between projects. Placing the main worktable in the middle of the room gives you easy access to the piece you're working on. This is especially handy when the piece is wet and sticky with shellac, varnish, or paint. If you don't like the idea of being able to walk around the worktable, you can always construct a big lazy Susan to spin your project around on. The effort required to push the whole affair may be as daunting as having to walk around the worktable—unless you can hook it up to an elaborate and complex system of pistons, wire pulleys, and sprockets, which could in turn be connected to the kids' gerbil treadmill.

Finishing Supplies and Tools

Power Tools

Power tools are not really necessary for refinishing furniture. But a belt sander is handy for resurfacing tops, as is a "pad," or "orbital" sander. A 1/4-inch sheet sander or a 1/2-inch sheet sander will do the trick. A variable-speed, reversible drill is essential for any "take-apart" project, and it can double as a buffer when fitted with the appropriate attachment. If polishing is your thing, you should look into a dedicated polishing tool.

Depending on quality, plan on spending

between $200 and $450 for your power tools. Better-quality tools cost a little more, but they also last longer. There are many good brands, and we'll gladly recommend the one that sends us the biggest endorsement check. Thank you.

Hand Tools

If you're going to be taking things apart and regluing them, clamps are extremely important. You may need to use up to ten clamps per chair, depending on the scope of the job. There are many types of clamps—bar clamps, C-clamps, spring clamps, strap clamps, and the ever-popular Jorgensen (the type that the Addams family's Uncle Fester used when he had a headache).

Bar clamps are best used for joining boards together or for regluing chairs, because they can be set up to span a big distance. Bar clamps come in many different sizes, from 10 inches to 8 feet in length. A 10-inch clamp can cost about twelve bucks; the next size up, sixteen; and so on.

C-clamps also come in many sizes and can be used for joining boards together. Place wood pads between the piece you are working on and the clamp's rounded metal jaws to prevent the clamp from leaving a circular indentation.

Spring clamps, or pony clamps, work like spring clothespins. They cannot be adjusted, but they are available in a range of sizes. They're good for holding things in place while you work on them. For instance, if you have a small piece of molding that needs to be reattached to a drawer front, you couldn't possibly clamp it using a pipe clamp or a C-clamp, but a spring clamp gives just the right amount of pressure needed to effect the repair. You could even use clothespins in certain instances.

A strap clamp, also known as a web clamp, is a nylon strap attached to a metal cinching device. Strap clamps are used when curved shapes, such as picture frames or whole chairs, need to be clamped. These clamps encircle the piece to be clamped, acting sort of like a belt around its circumference. Strap clamps are capable of pulling together numerous joints simultaneously, and they can be used in conjunction with other clamps. They are reasonably priced and are about as large as Orson Welles's favorite paisley smoking-jacket belt.

The Jorgensen, or what we call the "Uncle Fester," clamp, with its fearsome wooden jaws and two adjusting pins, is used for "sistering," or gluing the face sides of two boards or planks together. If you turn the pins simultaneously, the clamp's jaws will open or close, depending on which way you twist. Jorgensen clamps are available in many different sizes.

The cardinal rule of gluing is that you must clamp joints together if you want them to be strong and to last. And you must leave the clamps on any glued piece for a good 24 hours (not a bad 24 hours). You can use white glue or yellow woodworker's glue, but you must clamp your job together. Both glues work well for all kinds of repairs. They set up slowly, permitting you to position the joined pieces just after applying the glue and before clamping them in place. Fast-drying epoxies are just that, fast-drying, so be careful when using them. While they are amazingly strong and effective, they do not allow you time to adjust your work. It's better to use them on clean breaks in wood, where you can easily see how the pieces fit together. Epoxies also stink like a barnyard, demand clamping like any other wood adhesive, and cost more than simple white or yellow glues.

Abrasives

Abrasives are not talk show hosts; rather, they are essential to any finishing job. Abrasives include sandpaper, steel wool, and powdered abrasives. Steel wool comes in different grades of abrasiveness. The roughest is single "0." Then comes "00," "000," and "0000," which is the least abrasive and is used for fine work. Files and rasps, wire brushes, and grinder attachments for drills also fall into the "abrasive" category. Every finishing project that you will ever tackle will require some amount of sanding and rubbing. You'll find abrasives vital in refinishing, or bringing out a highly polished gleam in your furniture projects.

Sandpapers comes in a range of grits, from 30

grit all the way up to 3,000 and above. Grits from 1,200 and above are not commonly used for furniture. The exception is for sanding highly polished nitro-cellulose lacquer, or polymer coatings. Grits of 2,000 or more are used in the automotive and aviation industries, so unless you are doing some work on your own private DC-10, stick with what we tell you. Generally speaking, in finishing wood you move from lower grits to higher grits of sandpaper (see below).

Another abrasive we forgot to mention, which is often used in the area of distressing furniture to make it look old, is the cobblestone. This is very good for making a brand-new piece of wood look very old. By using it like a bowling ball on a tabletop, you can achieve the look of years of wear and tear. This is called distressing and you should not be laughing, if you are, because it's no joke—although "cobble" *is* a funny word.

Types of Sandpaper and Their Uses

GARNET: Sandpaper coated with a dark red, semi-precious stone. Harder and tougher than flint, it is used exclusively in finishing and woodworking.

ALUMINUM OXIDE: Aluminum oxide sandpaper is identified by its reddish brown color. It will last a long time, even through the toughest sanding job.

SILICON CARBIDE: Silicon carbide sandpaper is a combination of silicon and carbide and ideal for wet- and dry-sanding between coats of varnish and other finishes on wood.

Sandpaper Grits

60 GRIT: Good for rough boards and tabletops—you can buy 60-grit belts for belt sanders, as well as purchasing them in sheet form for orbital sanders and for hand-sanding. Be aware that a grit this low should be used only on hardwoods such as oak, ash, and in some cases, walnut.

80 GRIT: To achieve a smoother finish, follow up sanding jobs with an 80-grit sandpaper. You can use 80 grit on yellow pine, which is harder than white pine or sugar pine, or on certain types of mahogany, but always test on an inconspicuous

location before sanding to avoid marring the surface.

150 GRIT: Safe on pine and most woods, 150-grit garnet or aluminum sandpapers are good choices for general-purpose sanding. A tip: coarser sandpapers get clogged with wood dust, so try scraping the sandpaper with a wire brush to renew it.

220 GRIT: Start sanding with 80-grit sandpaper, then wet the sanded wood slightly and allow to dry: you will notice that the wood ends up feeling "hairy." That's because you've raised the wood grain. Sand those fibers off with 150-grit sandpaper, wet again, and let dry. Then sand again with 220-grit paper, wet the wood, and allow it to dry. Then sand, varnish, lacquer, or polyurethane the wood. Doing this will result in a beautifully smooth finish like the one we achieved on the rolltop desk project (page 49).

Wet and Dry Sandpapers

Usually, silicon carbide papers that are paper-backed can be used for wet sanding. Newer varieties of wet/dry papers come cloth-backed so they last longer when wet. It's a matter of what you want and what you can afford. You can buy paper that's wet/dry and use more of it, or you can buy cloth-backed paper, which lasts longer per piece but which also costs more per sheet. A sleeve of 150 sheets of paper-backed paper can cost anywhere from $25 to $30; cloth-backed paper may cost twice as much.

The best lubricant for wet sanding is naphtha, or paint thinner if you are sanding a lacquer finish. Make sure the finish has cured for a day or so. Pour on some naphtha, or if you wish, dip your paper into a container of naphtha and begin sanding with even pressure, going round and round in circles. You will feel the paper "cutting" the finish; it may take a while for you to get the feel of it. If you are going to spray fifteen coats of lacquer, it's not really necessary to wet-sand before each coat unless you like to work out or are just plain particular—i.e., crazy! Joe always waited until his finish was built up, scuffing each succeeding layer with 320-grit silicon carbide paper before recoating. Allow the last coat to dry for a week or longer if you have the time to spare. The final coat can then be wet-sanded with naphtha and a 600-grit silicon carbide finishing paper of your choice.

Another lubricant that can be used is soapy water. This is the preferred liquid for rubbing out varnish finishes. Save all those little pieces of soap—you know, when the bar gets to be "wafer thin." Drop them into a container of water and just let them sit until they dissolve. This thick, soapy solution can be used in place of the naphtha as described above.

Finishing Papers

220 SILICON CARBIDE
320 SILICON CARBIDE
400 SILICON CARBIDE
600 SILICON CARBIDE

All of these finishing papers should be used in the same way as the general-purpose sandpapers described above, but only after varnish, lacquer, or polyurethane coatings have been applied and allowed to dry. For instance, to achieve a smooth finish, apply a coat of varnish, allow the varnish to dry, and then sand with 220-grit silicon carbide finishing paper. Then recoat the sanded wood with varnish and allow to dry. Then sand again with 320-grit finishing paper. Repeat this process one or two more times, graduating to finer finishing papers each time. Then apply one last coat of varnish (or whatever) and let dry. If looks could kill.

Powdered Abrasives

There are different powdered abrasives used in final finishes that we'll discuss in later projects. Here is a list of their properties and what they're called.

PUMICE STONE: Pumice is powdered volcanic lava from Sicily. It comes in grades from 1F to 4F, with 1F being the coarsest.

ROTTENSTONE: Rottenstone is decomposed limestone. It is very fine and soft, like a gray talcum powder.

TRIPOLI: Jewelers use this stuff for polishing diamonds, but it can be used with oils for polishing varnished or lacquered surfaces as well.

Accessories

Paintbrushes are essential accessories, because without them you would have to use your hands, or a small animal like a ferret or vole, to coat wood with liquid finishing products. (If you had a big job, and no paintbrushes, you might have to resort to a wildebeest.) Brushes come in many, many sizes and shapes and it would take a tremendous amount of time and space to describe every variation available. Basically, you'll need a selection of good Chinese bristle brushes in various widths, some cheap hog hair brushes that you can throw away, various nylon brushes for applying latex and water-based varnishes, as well as water-based polyurethanes, and some disposable foam brushes. If you want to splurge on a good varnish brush, you can spend about $80 to get a brush like the one that Joe used in a few of our shows to show off. Such brushes are made of badger hair that is individually planted strand by strand according to length along the brush, ensuring that whatever you're applying will flow on perfectly.

Since the nature of furniture refinishing means you'll be dripping and dropping stuff, invest in a few good canvas tarps that you can gather up at the end of the day and shake out. They'll protect your floor and help keep the work area clean.

Empty cans are good for storing and mixing things. You can either save the ones you use at home or purchase cans with lids from paint stores.

Finally, you'll want to get some gloves to protect your hands from spills and splashes from finishing products. Depending on the scope of the project and what you have available, you can try using dishwashing gloves, surgical gloves, or heavy-duty black rubber gloves designed to be acid-resistant. But whatever you choose, let's deal with all this later and get started on a project.

PINE HOOSIER

What is a hoosier, you might ask? It's basically a tall, two-piece kitchen cabinet. The hoosier is so named because a great many were made in Indiana, becoming a fixture in country homes and farm kitchens. They were often the only piece of furniture in the kitchen besides the table. The hoosier's design made it an ideal workplace for the preparation of baked goods: there are wire cooling racks in the lower section, and a nonstick porcelain top surface perfect for kneading and rolling dough. Many hoosiers came equipped with a flour sifter and a set of canisters that would be hidden away behind the tambour, a roll-up door. Typically, the lower, and largest, drawer had a sliding tin roof for bread storage.

Hoosiers are prized for their space efficiency and are ideal for small kitchens and apartments. On the hoosier we worked on, the upper section had two side-by-side doors and a large tamboured section. The lower section featured a large door on the left and three drawers on the right. The porcelain or enamelware counter top is typical of just about every hoosier you may run across, whether it is made of fine oak or is a cheap flea-market reject like ours.

There are dozens of different styles of hoosiers. An oak example in fine condition with all of the above features and including, possibly, a speckled worktop and glazed doors in the upper section could fetch between $1,000 and $2,000. We got ours for free! A deal, yes. And there's a story to go with it, too. A friend bought the hoosier for $50 and gave it to us as a thank-you gift for telling her what items were worth

Hoosier "before"

buying at an auction we all attended. Anyway, the hoosier sat and sat and sat until we managed to get permission at the auction grounds where the piece originally came from to place it in the lineup again. We did this in the name of TV, so that when the cameras rolled we could pretend we were seeing the hoosier for the first time. What acting! But that's what TV's about.

The hoosier we worked on is pine and probably dates to the late 1930s or 1940s. At that time it probably sold for less than what we said was paid for it. Structurally, it was sound, the hardware was all there, and it was functional. Original hardware often disappears. This happens from owner to owner until you own it, and by then there are sometimes nails or screws serving as handles. This is called bastardization (we're allowed to say that because we're authors) and it always lowers the resale value of any piece of furniture.

We knew that this piece was not made of any great wood. Its light color was a tip-off that it was pine. Also, on the back were stenciled the words PINE/MINT ON IVORY. Once we had it stripped, we knew that if we tried to put a wood stain on that cheap pine, it would have looked like hell. So we decided to match what we imagined the piece must have originally looked like, and therefore we went for an enamel finish.

We did find one, uh, interesting feature: someone had lined the drawers and insides of the hoosier with yards and yards of Mother Goose motif contact paper. This was the first thing we removed, not because we don't like Mother Goose, but because the paper was ugly, sticky, and disgusting. Anytime you find stickers, any other type of gum-backed paper junk, extraneous paper cloth, or plastic appliqués on a piece, just get rid of them.

Once we had peeled off all of the goose paper, we washed all the surfaces where it had been adhered with naphtha, a petroleum distillate used in the finishing business as a cleaner and degreaser. We scrubbed with 0-medium steel wool to get rid of the stickiness. Naphtha, or for that matter paint thinner, will remove stubborn stickiness from just about any surface. However, don't use naphtha on some surfaces: It can melt plastic, rubber, and foam.

Next we removed the hardware. On any finishing or restoration job, you should remove any pieces that can be unscrewed or otherwise removed.

Before going full-bore on a stripping job, consider a few things first. Not every piece of furniture needs stripping. Many people think that every old piece of furniture needs stripping. But if you have an old piece with an attractive patina, it's better to try and restore the existing finish. To clean existing finishes such as those on kitchen cabinets, scrub with a solution of TSP (short for trisodium phosphate) and water. For an extra-strong cleaning solution, add a bit of chlorine bleach. Whatever you do, however, don't use the solution as an eye wash—in other words, wear goggles or some other form of eye protection. Quite often an antique piece stripped of its finish is less valuable than if the original finish were simply restored. Many museum conservators specialize in reviving existing finishes on antiques. In their efforts to preserve paint and varnish layers of the past, they painstakingly analyze finishes with microscopes and computers to determine the exact makeup of antique finishes.

Needless to say, they watch our show and realize that we never work on projects that are bona fide antiques. Admittedly, our show caters to average homeowners who don't have original Chippendales in their basements or Hepplewhites in their attics. Expert restorers consider us friends because we're not aiming to take over their turf. And because we're not ruining priceless antiques before millions of viewers, the experts are more sympathetic to our methods than they would be if we were attempting to fix up museum-quality antiques. That's not to say that some restorers don't hate us, whether it's for personal reasons or out of sheer jealousy. But hey, we have a TV show and you can try writing your own book.

Materials List

- Lacquer thinner
- Chemical paint stripper
- Planer chips
- Denatured alcohol
- Naphtha
- Oil-based primer
- Shellac
- Alkyd, or oil-based, paint
- Spray-on metal primer
- Alkyd, or oil-based, spray paint
- 220-grit garnet and 320-grit silicon carbide sandpaper
- Acrylic paints (for detail stenciling)
- Tack rags

Tool List

- Screwdrivers
- Wire brush
- Electric paint remover or heat gun
- Work gloves
- Respirator equipped with appropriate filters
- Goggles
- Paint scraper
- Gong brush
- Scrub brush
- Paintbrushes
- Mohair paint roller
- 0000 steel wool

Removing hardware

We began by unscrewing the hardware on the hoosier and placing the metal pieces in a pail filled with lacquer thinner. Lacquer thinner will eat through almost anything, and that was our intention with the ugly green paint that was caked on the hardware. After letting the thinner go to work for about an hour or so we were able to remove the hinges,

Removing paint from hardware using wire brush

catches, and screws. We scrubbed them clean with a small wire brush, available from industrial hardware stores and larger home centers. The hardware turned out to be made from common white pot metal, but it was the original stuff.

When we laid the top section of the hoosier flat on its back, the tambour could be pulled right out, making it easier for us to work with it. All tambours work the same and they are seldom locked in place with screws or mechanical devices. For more details on working with rolltops, see the rolltop desk project (page 49). Always be careful when you strip something that is canvas-backed such as a tambour: You run the risk that the chemical paint remover will loosen and weaken the glue holding the canvas to the wood slats. Use chemical removers sparingly when dealing with tambours.

Peeling Paint Electrically

Electric paint remover (EPR)

We used an EPR, or electric paint remover, to burn the top layers of paint off the hoosier. EPRs have an electric element contained within a metal pan. They were the prototype of today's widely used heat gun, but they work faster and better—if you can find them on the market. The heat gun is safer to use but both can cause serious burns—how's that for

equal billing? Once plugged in, EPRs turn on immediately without a switch and can reach a temperature of 900° F. We prefer using an EPR over a heat gun because we find that EPRs work better despite the fact that they are less safe than their modern counterparts. EPRs used in conjunction with a scraper make removing 6 × 4-inch patches of paint at one time much easier. But remember: if you set an EPR down incorrectly, like on your rug for instance, there's going to be a fire.

Removing top layers of paint using EPR

You should take a few precautions when working with an EPR or electric paint stripper. Old varnish and shellac underneath the paint pose a fire hazard when the high-intensity heat created by the remover element ignites these finishes. If you have a flare-up, use your scraper to pat the flames into remission. Don't panic if this happens: it's not as though the piece you are stripping will explode. Just don't try dousing the fire with lacquer thinner. Avoiding burn marks on the piece is another reason to be careful.

You should also avoid marring exposed wood when you scrape off softened paint. As an alternative to a sharp paint scraper, try using a thin piece of wood or plastic to remove the softened paint. Or just take your time with the scraper. Start the removal process by burning off paint on all the flat surfaces first. Never try to burn the paint off carvings and other delicate details. These

Scraping softened paint

are best left to chemical paint removers.

The main reason for burning off the paint first is that you save on chemical remover, and if you've ever tried to remove nine or ten coats of paint from an old desk with a paste remover you know what we're talking about. It often takes three to four applications, and much scraping—though, of course, that's always an option if you have a lot of free time.

Professional Strippers

Of course, the easiest and safest way to remove paint is to have someone else do the dirty work for you. There are two main categories of establishments: those that do hand-stripping (which is what we do) and those that specialize in dipping. The latter dip the piece in huge tanks filled with chemicals (sometimes the chemicals inside the tanks are heated; others employ a cold-bath, or flow system). When shopping around for a place that will do dipping remember that stripping furniture this way is a bit risky: stripper can find its way into furniture joints and loosen the adhesion qualities of the glue there. Reputable firms will warn you about this. The danger of this happening increases tenfold if the piece is set into a vat and the proprietor leaves on a long fishing trip. Always determine the process used, price, and estimated time for completion. Remember that there are never any guarantees when you are dealing with old furniture, but any reputable person who works with furniture should know the difference between solid wood and veneer. In other words, if the piece is covered with veneer it can't be submerged in a hot bath of caustic soda, or for that matter, of warm Diet Sprite. You should check three or four places and compare prices, and if by the end you are completely exhausted, do it yourself, just like we do.

The following conversation between the proprietor of a paint stripping establishment and

> ### Technique Tactic:
> ### How to Have a Shiny Brass
>
> Old solid brass hardware can be cleaned using a number of methods. The first method involves applying commercially available creamlike metal polishes to the metal. After applying the polish, allow it to dry on the metal and then use a soft cloth to buff the metal.
>
> Our preferred method, especially when working with old brass fittings, is to gently rub the surface of the brass with a brass or wire brush. This gives the metal a burnished look. If you consider doing this, make sure that a clear finish hasn't been applied over the hardware. Sometimes a shellac or varnish may have been applied over the dirt, and to achieve a burnished look using a wire brush you need to clean off that clear finish first. In such a case, throw the hardware into a container filled with lacquer thinner and let the thinner go to work for an hour or so removing the coating. (Sometimes heated white wine vinegar is effective in removing tough tarnish, too.) Then scour the hardware with a wire brush. Usually, however, hardware wears only the usual grime associated with time.
>
> The final method used to clean metal hardware and fittings is by using commercially available tarnish-removal liquids. Apply or soak the fittings according to package directions to make metal look brand-new and super clean and shiny. Tarnish-removal liquids will help you achieve a highly polished look.

you, the consumer, is a tip-off that it's time to go someplace else:

YOU: I have an old desk that was my grandfather's.

HIM: OK.

YOU: I'm not sure if it's veneer or solid wood.

HIM: Whatever.

YOU: How long will it take?

HIM: What're we in, spring?

YOU: Do you leave it in overnight?

HIM: Depends on the wife's mood.

YOU: Do you have caustic soda?

HIM: Just grape, I think.

Once you've burned as much paint off the furniture as possible you'll inevitably be left with small patches, or "islands," of paint on various portions of the furniture. These stubborn patches need to be removed with a pastelike paint remover.

Applying chemical stripper to doors

Selecting Strippers

The main ingredient in a lot of chemical paint strippers is methylene chloride, a member of a dangerous family of chlorinated hydrocarbons. Whenever you use one of these strippers, be sure to provide adequate ventilation. Set up fans and open windows to expel the noxious fumes from the work area.

Remember, once methylene chloride is in the bloodstream, the body metabolizes it into carbon monoxide. If you have heart or lung problems, avoid using chemical strippers; have a professional handle this part of the job. If you're healthy, wear a respirator equipped with the appropriate filters, as well as goggles and gloves.

How do you choose from the range of chemical strippers on the market? One trick is to lift various stripper cans and choose the heaviest. Methylene chloride is heavy, and logic tells us that if the can is heavy then there is a lot of methylene chloride inside it.

Methylene chloride is a good remover, though it may discolor some woods such as oak. But such discoloration can be removed once the stripping is completed by dabbing the area with chlorine bleach. Remember to shake the stripper can vigorously before applying it. The stripper may have been sitting on the shelf for a while and you want to mix all the ingredients together to make them happy.

Brushing on chemical stripper

Applying planer chips

Pour a convenient amount of stripper into a can or plastic bucket and use a brush with an unfinished wooden handle to apply the stripper to the wood. (If there's paint on the handle it will come off after contact with the remover and stain your work.) Use the brush to pat the remover on; avoid brushing it on the wood.

Apply the stripper,

Rubbing planer chips

Removing planer chips with gong brush

Applying solvent, wearing gloves

wait about fifteen minutes, and then pat on another coat. When the finish has softened it is ready to come off. You can use a paint scraper to remove the finish, or use our favorite method—trusty "planer chips." (See Technique Tactic: Planer Chips Are Not Like the Chocolate Ones.)

Any chips that remain on the surface can be scrubbed away with a stiff-bristled brush called a "gong" brush in the industry. These brushes have been manufactured for many years. Ted Gerike, the pianist who does the music for our show and the odd cameo here and there, told us his grandfather had a brush factory in Philadelphia during the 30s. The bristles are made from heavy red straw, the same as the bristles on street sweepers' brooms. The better ones have wooden handles. It got its name because it looks like the implement used to strike a gong—J. Arthur Rank, take note.

Once all the chips have been brushed away, wash the finished wood with a solvent—a mixture of lacquer thinner and alcohol. The preferred mix for the job is made by combining lacquer thinner and denatured alcohol in a one-to-one ratio. Combine this solution with some steel wool and lots of hard rubbing, and you're on your way to a beautiful finish. Make sure to wear gloves for this process—lacquer thinner can be absorbed by the skin and find its way into the bloodstream.

After the lacquer-thinner-and-alcohol wash, we applied one last wash, this time with mineral spirits or naphtha. (We're pro naphtha—for Free Trade, that is.) Naphtha and mineral spirits are petroleum distillate products and will dissolve any remover that's left in wood. Use a scrub brush to remove it. If you're working on oak, you can use a brass or wire brush to scrub the wood pores clean.

Preparing to Paint

If your goal is to stain and clear-finish the piece, you're going to strip and wash, wash and strip, and sand and sand like crazy because when old furniture was originally painted, it was done with-

Sandpaper sheet

Sanding

out an undercoat of shellac or varnish. This permitted the paint to soak into the wood just as a sponge absorbs water. Once the stripper has removed the top layers of paint you'll be confronted with a chalky paint film so engrained in the wood that it can only be removed by sanding for endless hours. This is insanity of the highest order. So, we paint.

TECHNIQUE TACTIC: PLANER CHIPS ARE NOT LIKE THE CHOCOLATE ONES

Planer chips are wood chips that are by-products of plank smoothing after boards have been sent through a planer. The chips look like the stuff found on the bottom of a hamster cage. You can often get planer chips for free at large lumberyards where boards are surfaced. Such places may have piles or trash barrels filled with the chips, and because lumberyards must pay to have the chips taken away, more often than not they'll be happy to have you do the job for free. Of course, the lumber dealers who have seen our show know the true value of the planer chips and will offer to *sell* you a bag. If this turns out to be the case, go to a another lumberyard where the people are oblivious to our fame.

Make sure that the planer chips you get are clean. In some cases lumberyards use them to soak up everything from oil to coffee before they throw them out.

Planer chips are handy and easy to use. Just throw a handful into the middle of the project you've stripped and start scrubbing with them. Once the chips have absorbed the wetness of the stripper, brush them away and dispose of them appropriately following the instructions on the stripper's can. Always be sure to don work gloves, goggles, and a mask when you're scrubbing.

To begin the enameling job and to duplicate the paint job originally on the piece, we had to sand the wood. It isn't necessary to go into the intricacies of sandpaper here, but it's important to stress that the look of the finished project is only as good as the sanding job. However, preparing wood for painting is much easier than preparing wood for staining. The idea is to roughen or scuff the wood to give it a "tooth," so that the paint will adhere well. To achieve this, we sanded with a 120-grit garnet paper on all the surfaces, and then dusted all the surfaces clean.

After the sanding was finished, we sealed all the wood with a shellac spit coat. Faithful viewers of our show know how much we love shellac. Shellac is derived from natural origins: it is secreted by the lac bug (*tachardia lacca*), which feeds on the sap of

Applying spit coat

Indian plum trees. Shellac is sold as dried flakes and in liquid form. It takes 5 pounds of dry flakes dissolved in 1 gallon of denatured alcohol to make a 5-pound cut. Shellac flakes are available from woodworkers' supply catalogues and art supply stores. If you buy the canned liquid version, it's usually a 3-pound cut: 3 pounds of flakes dissolved in 1 gallon of alcohol. Because the canned versions are thick in consistency, it is difficult to apply a drip-free coat to wood. This is where the spit coat, or wash coat, comes in.

The spit coat sealer may be applied to any wood surface to protect and seal the wood, but shellac is especially good for surfaces you are going to paint. Bare wood may be sealed with shellac, but remember that shellac doesn't offer the same protective quality as varnish and polyurethane. On vertical surfaces such as paneling and door jambs shellac may be a good choice as a sealer because it dries fast and the surfaces take less punishment. For our hoosier, we used it as a sealer to create a smooth surface on which we could apply a paint primer. Use a China bristle brush to do the job.

TECHNIQUE TACTIC: SPIT COAT

Spit coat recipe:

1 part 3-pound cut shellac (clear or amber will do for this project because it will be painted) to five parts denatured alcohol.

Applying primer

Oil-based primers are good because they are durable and easy to sand. Painting wood is no different from finishing with varnish or lacquer: After each coat you must sand with higher and higher (finer and finer) grits to make the final finish smooth. We've seen too many jobs where the coats weren't sanded, and the finished surfaces looked a lot like the face of the late actor Richard Boone, whom you may have known as Paladin (first name Wire) from *Have Gun Will Travel*—of course then he did *Richard Boone Theater* for one season, and then, much later when his face was at its craggy best, Hec Ramsey, which rotated with *Columbo, McMillan and Wife,* and *McCloud* in the seventies. This face, which in his early career relegated him to the roles of heavies, contributed to the strong emotional pull of the Paladin character. Possibly the strongest delineation of the antihero of the television western—the bounty hunter dressed all in black, defender of the innocent—Boone easily outdistanced the baby-faced Steve McQueen of *Wanted: Dead or Alive,* and most certainly the adolescent, nay nubile, Nick Adams, who wasn't even close to being a rebel in our book . . . but we digress.

Stir your primer well because, like stripper, it's probably been sitting on the shelf a while. Or ask the paint store proprietor to place the can into an electric paint mixer.

We used Chinese bristle brushes to apply the primer. These are brushes that look like all other brushes except they're made with natural animal hair and generally are best for applying alkyd (oil-based) paint, varnish, and stain. On the larger areas, the flats of the door, and the case piece, we were able to use a roller. Buy the best roller you can and avoid the eighty-nine-cent varieties that feature flimsy handles. The roller itself should be made of mohair. Mohair

Applying primer using paint roller

is preferable because its small fibers will not come off in the paint—especially important when you lay on your finish coat.

When painting, try to position the piece you are working on so that it lies flat. This way, you can work above and over it. When we painted the doors, for instance, we removed them and laid them flat, reducing the chances of creating drips (which can wreak havoc with your paint job, as we'll discuss later). Also, with the piece lying flat, flaws in your work will show up more readily under most lighting conditions, enabling you to fix them before the piece dries.

Color Matching

Because we wanted to re-create the original paint job on the hoosier, and we knew that it had originally been painted mint and ivory (according to the stencil on the back of the piece), we took a chip of green paint off the piece and went to a local paint store to try and match it.

Electronic color matching is fairly new in the painting industry and has become very popular, especially when trying to re-create historical colors. It works like this: A paint chip is placed in a paint analyzer and processed by a computer that spits out a recipe for mixing paint pigments to match the color of the paint chip you've supplied (you only need a small chip). An open can of white base paint is placed under a pigment dispenser, a few controls are set, and the pigments shoot out in the right proportions into the can of white base paint. The lid is banged back on, the can is placed in a paint mixer, and the ingredients are shaken together.

Our goal with the hoosier was to match the edge color of the porcelain top, which was mint green. The ivory color was easy enough to find without analysis: We just needed to get one that was close to the original.

Both green and ivory paints were oil-based paints. Latex paints are better used on interior walls and ceilings, and oil-based paints on wood and furniture. Water-based paint tends to raise the grain on wood furniture and latex paint dries faster, with the result that brush marks don't have as much time to flow out as they would if oil-based paint were used. To paint the metal hardware, we purchased a metal spray primer and a can of ivory enamel that matched the alkyd, or oil-based, ivory paint we purchased. You can get away with painting the hardware with a brush, but we like to mix mediums because the network we work for has the money and we like to spend it for them.

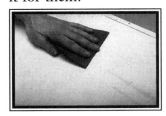

Sanding primed area before painting

Allow the primer to dry overnight, and before applying the first coat of paint over the primed area, sand the primer coat lightly with 220-grit garnet sandpaper. Be on the lookout for drips in the primer. They may not have fully dried and sanding over them will create a mess. If you notice some drips, or if you sand

---

TECHNIQUE TACTIC: TACK RAGS

Tack rags or cloths are used to pick up dust, lint, and sand particles that have accumulated on surfaces being prepared for refinishing. These particles are the bane of furniture refinishers. And guess what? No matter how much you wipe the surface there's still going to be some dust that gets by. Tack rags are a highly effective, though imperfect, solution to the problem. They are made of cheesecloth infused with resinous material that remains soft and tacky indefinitely. They are sold wrapped in plastic and should be stored in a sealed jar or other container. Don't worry about any fire hazard; they are guaranteed not to spontaneously ignite.

---

over them by accident, simply take some 0000 steel wool soaked in paint thinner and rub the spot. Because the drip is still wet, you should be able to remove it. In doing so, however, you may also remove primer from the area and you'll have to reprime that spot. In other words, try and be careful the first time around.

Painting Basics

As with most of our restoration projects, we decided in the case of our hoosier to preserve the same decorative touches that were on the original. We painted all the flats—the sides of both upper and lower sections, facades (fronts with doors and drawers off)—in ivory with a ¼-inch-nap mohair roller. The door frames, drawer fronts, and the tambour were painted mint green after they were primed. We allowed the paint to dry overnight between coats. If you want to wait longer you can, but

Painting tambour

always remember to sand each dried finish coat (except the last) with 320-grit wet/dry silicon carbide finishing paper, dust off the piece, and use a tack rag to pick up any excess dust. When you're coating stripped wood like that on the hoosier, you can't get away with applying just one coat. From a distance it may look good but, on closer examination or in brightly lit areas such as kitchens, it will look washed-out. You're going to have to apply at least two coats. Moreover, we needed a vivid, richly colored background to accentuate the stencil detailing we were going to apply later.

Painting Hardware

Before applying the stencils, we wanted to paint the hardware. With the various pieces of hardware laid out on newspaper, we used a can of

Using brush on trim

Stenciling brushes and supplies

TECHNIQUE TACTIC: PAINTING MOLDINGS

On a project such as this, painting along the rolled edges where the frames meet the center of the doors is a more challenging operation than painting flat surfaces. To successfully accomplish this feat, use a 2-inch brush with an angled, or chiseled, edge. Load the brush with paint on the side that will touch the molding; move the brush slowly down and along the inside edge of the molding. The basic concept here is to use the bristles on part of the brush to paint the molding on the inside edge, while using the rest to counterbalance the brush. The alternative to learning how to handle a paintbrush when coating trim is to tape the edges of the molding with masking tape before painting. There are a number of problems with this method, however:

1. It takes longer to paint.
2. It costs more.
3. It encourages you to slop on paint. Often excess paint will leak under the tape and you end up with disastrous results.

The moral of the story here is that you should really try and refine your brush-handling skills and develop a painting technique that you can use for the rest of your life.

spray paint to lightly coat the hardware with metal primer, holding the can at least 12 inches away from the hinges and knobs. Once the primer dried according to label directions, we sprayed on two coats of ivory enamel that matched the color of the ivory paint we used on the wood. Spray painting is easy, but for best results, start out by spraying beyond the subject and then aim the spray on the pieces to be coated. Do this because the spray may first emerge from the nozzle more thickly than later, or old dried paint particles in the nozzle's spray hole may get dislodged and speckle the pieces to be painted.

Using this technique, apply the paint with slow, even passes over the hardware. Strive for a thin coat rather than a thick one. When using any spray paint or finishing product, always wear a respirator with the appropriate filters. Do not rely on a simple dust mask. This advice bears repeating, and by now we assume you've purchased the proper respiratory protection. Right?

You naughty moose.

Stenciling

The hoosier, in its original condition, had stencils applied to the large bottom door and to the door frames. To recreate these decorative details using stencils, we called in a professional by the name of Margo Stitz (sometimes Joe and I tire of seeing each other, entrancing though we may be). The tools of her trade include a variety of acetate stencil sheets, circular stencil brushes, and a selection of acrylic paints. Most art supply stores carry the materials and tools you need for stenciling.

The stencils used for the hoosier were *compound stencils;* that is, in order to get more than one image and color in the design, the first stencil is taped down and the first color is applied with a stencil brush, moving in a circular motion. Then the same process is repeated using the second stencil and second color.

Applying paint on taped-down stencil

Use acrylic paint for stenciling because it dries very quickly and enables the second stencil to be laid over the image created with the first stencil in quick succession.

Strive to carefully center the stencils, even tracing them first with a pencil (which rhymes with *stencil*) to see how they will look once they are finished. (Other words that rhyme with stencil are *tensile* and *prehensile,* which we cannot work into this particular project but which are good to know regardless.)

The pattern created with the stencils around the door frames was of green leaves, or vines, with vermilion flowers bearing yellow buds. A yellow basket containing a variety of colored flowers was stenciled on the large bottom door. One good thing about painting with acrylics over oil-based paint is that if you screw up the stenciling, you can wipe your mistakes off the oil-based paint with a rag moistened with warm water. To make your finished stenciled designs stand up to everyday wear and tear, apply a clear varnish over the stenciled design.

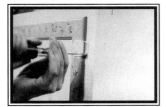

Reattaching door hardware

The last thing on the agenda was to re-secure the hardware and doors to their proper places on the cabinet. You re-

Reattaching door hardware

membered where and how everything was attached, right? Our photographer had taken "before" shots of the piece, so we could figure out where everything went. You can always take a snapshot with a Polaroid camera before you start working on a piece.

That's All, Folks

So that's our first project—a transformation from refuse into a beautiful centerpiece that would do any country kitchen proud. The total outlay for materials was about $125. The total work time was about five hours, minus drying times—or do a little bit every Saturday or Sunday afternoon. The original price of the piece at auction was $50. Selling price now? Between $900 and $1,600, depending on the swankiness of the shop.

So what are you waiting for? Upholstery?

Hoosier "after"

Two

INTRODUCTION TO UPHOLSTERY,
Or Mallets Toward Everyone

In layman's terms, upholstery is the soft stuff between you and the hard stuff. The earliest upholstery may have been moss, created by water dripping from stalactites onto rocks in early cave dwellings. And the cave dwellers who strategically placed those rocks became the first interior decorators, with as much insight and taste as many present-day ones (but with greener bottoms, no doubt).

Archaeological records reveal that small, sedentary furry animals were employed as footstools, supplying as much comfort and warmth as a pair of plush Hush Puppies. Nervous breeds offered the added benefit of a stimulating foot massage, as they vibrated when emotionally taxed.

To be serious for just a moment, the first materials used in upholstery were animal skins stretched over a hard framework of wood or stone. This method was employed by the Egyptians and endured through the early Renaissance, when the first cushions were produced. These cushions were loose affairs (like the trysts we've all had) that later became sewn into the actual piece of furniture. The depth of the cushion kept increasing while the padding beneath was filled with down, wool, and horsehair. (Animal lovers may be comforted to know that horses don't need to be slain in the pursuit of making a soft divan: Horsehair filling is taken from the horse's mane and tail.)

Remembrance of Springs Past

In the late Renaissance, the cushions got piled higher: if you wanted height, you put a cushion on top of a cushion on top of a cushion (with some thick padding in between for good measure). With the mid-nineteenth century came the helical, or coil spring—the same one that is used today. The advent of the coil spring meant that padding could be reduced because resilience was provided by the mighty spring. And so were born the basic principles of modern upholstery: springs, padding, and fabric. (And as upholstery became more streamlined, loose change became more plentiful: you didn't lose so many things in the crevices between all those cushions!)

By the way, some of the earliest upholsterers still survive today. You can identify these grizzled fossils of furniture history by the dozens of upholstery tacks that are clenched between their lips and by the tight grip their teeth simultaneously keep on a smoking El Producto cigar that hangs precariously from one side of their mouth.

Couch Springs Eternal

The mid–twentieth century gave us zigzag or "no sag" springs, which are flat and allow for greater freedom in design. Coil springs are stronger and more durable, but they need to be placed on a platform that allows them four to six inches of height, which seriously limits your design options. Zigzag springs allow for a greater variety of shapes in chairs or sofas. Modern upholstery also includes elastic tape and plastic lattice work under some cushions and padding in the place of flat springs; all we can say is "Feh!" (Yiddish for yechhh!) Some good furniture, however, can be found with zigzag springs. Just make sure that the originality of design really calls for them—usually because the piece has an irregularly shaped seat or back.

There's Nothing Like a Frame

Now let's shift our weight onto the frame. Originally frames were made of available wood, or, in the case of the throne chair project that follows, out of exposed, finished wood. Modern quality upholstered furniture features frames made of hardwoods such as ash, birch, and maple. Oak and other more expensive woods are usually reserved by more well-heeled folk for your tactile and viewing pleasure.

In all upholstery work, the most important concept to remember is order. The order of what goes beneath the fabric, and the way the fabric is attached, are vital to the success of an upholstery or reupholstery job. In short, the order of what goes beneath the fabric is as follows:

1. A platform upon which the coil springs will rest
2. Springs
3. Something to separate the springs from the padding
4. Resilient, sometimes hard padding
5. Soft padding
6. Something to separate the padding from the fabric
7. Fabric

Many different materials can be used in each of the layers. Older upholstery employed horsehair, down, feathers, and wool. Modern upholstery utilizes polyurethane foam, foam rubber, Dacron, and other petrochemical by-products. (If you can refine your own oil, try making your own cushions!)

Cotton batting, then and now, is used extensively in upholstery. In the upholstery projects presented in this book, we have used a variety of materials in different combinations. One thing to remember is that in upholstery, as in furniture finishing, there is no one correct way to do something. To some, a down-filled cushion on a sofa is the height of hindquarter delight. But there is a downside to down: feather-filled pillows need constant fluffing to keep their shape. (Too bad humans couldn't be fluffed back into shape, eh?) Some people don't appreciate the loose, frumpy look of down-filled furniture. On the other hand, the modern "sharp-as-a-knife-edge" look can only be achieved by using foam rubber, which isn't as comfortable to sit on as feathers. A good compromise—and the standard in good quality production furniture, especially in seat cushions—is a foam core affair wrapped with Dacron or cotton batting. This arrangement allows for a deep-down firmness, with an outer loft for added comfort. The wrap also protects the foam from airborne dirt and body oils that seem (somehow) to seep through from above and cause deterioration in the foam.

If the principle of order seems somewhat staid when it comes to upholstery, it may be comforting to know that the variety of materials used in that order can be diverse and liberating. With this in mind, if you're going to be doing a variety of upholstery projects, here is a list of some items you should have on hand, and which are available from upholstery suppliers:

Materials List

- 4-inch roll of burlap webbing for platform (available in 3-, 3½-, and 4-inch rolls)
- Heavy twine (preferably hemp) for tying springs
- Coil springs (exact number depends on the project to be done)
- Stitching twine
- ½- to 2-inch-thick foam rubber blocks
- Tack strips (cardboard, aluminum, and flexible)
- Upholstery nails (optional)

continued

- Gimp (optional)
- Double cording (optional)
- Burlap
- 2-ounce nylon thread
- A roll of cotton batting
- A roll of Dacron
- A roll of muslin
- A roll of cambric
- A roll for cold cuts and cheeses (lunch)

What Kind of Tool Am I?

Besides the appropriate materials, you'll need a range of tools. For taking apart old upholstery (which is always the most tedious part of any job) you need some form of tack or staple puller. There are as many designs of pulling tools as there are versions of Michael Jackson's nose. Speaking of noses, a pair of needle-nose pliers is ideal for removing those stubborn staples that always seem to manage to cut or scrape you. For ripping through old fabric and padding, you can purchase something called a ripping tool, which is a small serrated knife with a hardwood handle. We usually just use our mitts and pull, but for those of you who need to buy every godforsaken item on the hardware store shelf, why not splurge and get yourself one of these specialized implements?

When it comes time to stretch the webbing that supports the springs in a seat, you'll need the aptly named webbing stretcher. Don't be alarmed by the tool's metal spikes, even if it does tend to resemble something in the Marquis de Sade's arsenal or one of the more intriguing toys found in one of those S&M boutiques on the seedier side of town (you'll be going there soon to find the stuff you need for the job anyway). There are two versions of this device: the simpler of the two is hourglass-shaped and may be used effectively, but we prefer the one that looks more like a mallet and has a rubber-protected top. The rubber-covered top is used to leverage the tool against a chair's frame to pull the webbing taut (page 32).

For manipulating or stretching zigzag springs

you can use a specialized upholstery tool called a spring puller, which looks like Captain Hook's hook with a rounded end. An easier alternative to a spring puller is a pair of pliers or locking pliers (vise grips).

Tool List

- Needle-nose pliers
- Webbing stretcher
- Locking pliers (Vise Grips)
- Upholstery shears
- Electric carving knife
- Electric or pneumatic staple gun
- Air compressor (optional)
- Tack hammer
- 1/4-inch staples (with divergent points)
- Tacks (#14 size)
- Rubber mallet
- Upholstery needles
- C-clamp
- Bar clamp
- Hot glue gun
- Wood glue
- Lacquer thinner
- Denatured alcohol
- Planer chips (leftovers from smoothed boards, useful for absorbing thinners and removers)
- Lemon oil
- Quick-drying varnish
- Gong brush (a thick-bristled brush for scrubbing surfaces clean)
- Steel wool (0000 grade for finishing wood)
- Brass brush

Now Cut That Out

Do not scrimp on cutting tools! Borrowing your preschooler's blunt-edged scissors will do for cutting colored construction paper, but don't even consider them for upholstery work. Take the plunge and lay out $20 or so for a pair of upholstery shears. While we're on the subject of cutting things, you can go hog-wild and spend hundreds of bucks for a specialized foam saw to trim filling and cushions to size, but why not be more frugal and call into action the lowliest of kitchen appliances—the electric carving knife, which works just as well and is probably already lying in wait in the farthest recesses of your kitchen cabinet. Now's your chance to bring it out three times during the year: for the Thanksgiving turkey, the Easter ham, and at foam-cutting time. With an electric carving knife you'll be able to cut straight edges and bevels in foam. Just be sure to wipe any leftover meat remnants from the blades before you begin.

Guns Along the Mohair

Central to the success of any upholstery project is your choice of staple gun. A normal spring-powered staple gun (even those rated as heavy-duty) won't have enough power to fire staples into harder woods. Besides, why risk carpal tunnel syndrome squeezing the handle on a manual staple gun when you can send staples flying with just the pull of a trigger? This is the time to pretend you're Arnold Schwarzenegger.

Old-time upholsterers prefer using magnetized tack hammers and tacks to secure fabric in place because they've adopted suffering as a way of life. If you like doing things the old-fashioned way, try using a tack hammer for a project or two. Here's how: Use the magnetized end of the hammer to pick up one tack at a time, stretch and pull the fabric to be tacked taut with your free hand, bang the tack in place to secure it, then rotate the hammerhead around and bang that tack the rest of the way with the larger, non-magnetized driving hammerhead. Repeat, repeat, and repeat until your project is completed, or until merciful sleep overtakes you. You may develop your own tack-hammering rhythm, but trust us and get an electric staple gun instead. You just don't need the grief associated with attaching fabric any other way.

That said, there's one good alternative to the electric staple gun, and that is an air compressor–powered staple gun. Yes, you need a pricey and noisy (imagine the sound of a space shuttle liftoff in your workshop) air compressor to power the gun, but these types of guns are powerful enough to shoot a staple through a Buick. Other attachments that can be hooked to an air compressor include paint rollers, paint sprayers, nail drivers, and hoses—useful for directing a stream of air over fine furniture details to clean them out.

Various brands of staple guns demand various brands of staples. For projects involving lighter fabric and less padding, you can use ¼-inch staples, while heavier jobs cry out for ⅜-inch staples. We always use divergent-point staples, which are sharp-tipped staples that penetrate wood more easily than chiseled-point staples. When you go to buy staples, also pick up two or three sizes of tacks (including the larger, #14 size) to anchor the twine used in setting the seat springs. These are blue steel beauties that'll penetrate anything—including your tender flesh, if you're not careful—like ferret's teeth.

You'll need one more type of gun: for attaching trim, a hot glue gun is essential. Don't forget to buy the accompanying glue sticks designed specifically for bonding upholstery.

Mallets

Next comes mallets. Whatever mallet you choose, make sure it has a wide enough head and is suited for hammering a large surface area, but don't go overboard and purchase the kind used at carnivals to ring the gong on the Test of Strength game. The business ends of mallets are made from two basic materials: hardwood hickory or hard rubber. Choose the rubber-ended type, and get white rubber instead of black. White rubber is less apt to mark the furniture and fabrics you're working on.

Needles and Thread

In order to accomplish upholstery stitching, you need needles and thread. For blind stitching, a

> **TECHNIQUE TACTIC: TACK TACTICS**
>
> To handle upholstery tacks, spill a few from the box onto a surface. Use the magnetized head on a tack hammer to pick them up, and then use your fingers to pluck them off the tack hammer as you need them.

technique you will be able to demonstrate for friends by the time you finish this book, you use curved needles, which come in a dizzying array of sizes. Buy a few different ones for versatility. For attaching buttons to cushions, you'll need an upholstery needle, which is just like a regular needle only much bigger. They start at 6 inches and go up to 12 inches! Mammoth bolster needles are beyond the scope of this book, and the less said about bolstering the better. Besides, we're not doing any bolstering.

The thread that we use is the strongest thread that anyone can use—two-ounce nylon thread, the stuff that Hemingway caught marlin with. It comes in a variety of colors, which means very little when you're blind-stitching, or invisibly mending, for obvious reasons. You can use this kind of thread for other things, too: SWAT teams can rappel off buildings, and you can garrote your close friends, cut hard Italian cheese, and floss with it.

Tack Strips

There are a few other special items you're going to need that are unique to upholstery. The first are called tack strips, and there are three kinds: cardboard tack strips, aluminum tack strips, and flexible tack strips. Cardboard tack strips come in rolls that look like Bell and Howell movie reels; these tacks are run horizontally along the tops of outside arms and chair backs (page 95). Aluminum tack strips are always run vertically on either side of the outside chair back to define the left and right sides (pages 95–96). Finally, flexible tack strips are used around the curved outside parts of arms and backs.

There are a number of tools we haven't mentioned but you may have heard about. These include the Klintch-it tool (the button-making machine), the Baker Clip plier, fabric saws, tufting needles, and stuffing regulators. We haven't covered these because: (a) we haven't used them in this book; (b) they're too expensive; or (c) you can use something much cheaper or something you already own to get the same results.

Finding Supplies: A Walk on the Wrong Side of Town

As with every other how-to discipline, you can go a little crazy buying tools, an electric this, a pneumatic that. This is something we refer to as NS, or "Norm Syndrome" (see Abram, Norm, or *Old House, This*). We don't have every tool imaginable, and you don't need to have them, either. Our preference is to keep it simple. But where do you get the tools you need for the job in the first place? You usually can't find upholstery tools in large home centers, local hardware stores, and paint centers. Why? Because there's a conspiracy by the six or seven 93-year-old living upholsterers to keep their knowledge and tools to themselves. But seriously, upholstery is just not something that is popular with the ready-to-assemble generation, and it has remained in the domain of old-timers with more patience and skill.

With a little bit of detective work, however, you can find upholstery suppliers: Let your fingers do the walking through the business-to-business Yellow Pages, check out mail-order supply outlets, or call some of the larger woodworking supply houses for tips on where to find what you need. You can also call upholsterers and ask them where they buy their stuff, but you may get a rude response on the other end of the line.

Typically many of these places are housed in almost condemned buildings in areas boasting the highest crime rate. It's not that the planning commissions of cities say, "You have to put all that stuff in that crime-ridden area because it's dangerous." Rather, when the upholstery supply house was built ninety years ago, that area used to be a beautiful part of town: "A place where decent people could be seen," the old-timers will tell you. When you get there, you may have to hammer on the door with your fist to get someone to answer. The person who answers will try and pull a fast sales job on you, attempting to sell you what you need in bulk. He may even call you a punk. Don't despair; this is only a little crankiness that goes along with being shut inside a dusty warehouse with only tacks, coils, padding, and horsehair to talk to for years. Explain that you only want a bit of this and a bit of that for your modest job.

Choosing Fabric

Once you've found a supplier, you'll need to settle on the kind of fabric you want. For first-time upholsterers we suggest getting the sturdiest fabric you can within your price range. Remember, upholstering is all about pulling, stretching, cutting, and tacking. Sturdier fabrics will stand up to more abuse than flimsier fabrics such as silk or light cotton. Lighter fabrics will have a tendency to run anywhere they are cut and pulled, and shouldn't be the first choice for novices.

When buying fabrics, you should consider two main things:

1. Practicality. Will the fabric fit the function of the piece? Do you want a silk- or velvet-covered chair ruined by the sticky runoff from Junior's Creamsicles? Will a durable yet hard canvas afford sufficient comfort to milady's posterior as she primps at her vanity?

2. Does the fabric fit the style of the piece? Will an angular, modern boomerang pattern work on an intricately carved Gothic Revival piece? We think not. Conversely, will a fussy Victorian floral work on a Charles Eames chair of the postwar period? Again, the answer is "nay." There are many publications and books (not this one) that will transport you through different eras and will illustrate the kinds of fabrics that were widely used on furnishings in different periods.

In our projects we always try to use fabrics that are stylistically contemporary to the pieces, unless we want to make a particularly perverse point. Buying upholstery fabrics can be an adventure. Many big cities have dozens of fabric stores as well as "notions" or fabric accessory shops. Both suburban and rural landscapes are dotted with enormous fabric stores. Chain stores may often carry some fabrics durable enough for upholstery. And, of course, there are always the remnant houses, which are the source for the best buys around. Last year's fabrics, just as last year's clothing styles, are always sold at a discount. The older the fabric style, the deeper the discount. As fabrics are moved from the first-line houses' front windows to discount bins, and finally to remnant houses, $60-a-yard fabric may eventually be had for $7 a yard.

When buying remnants, make absolutely sure you can get enough to complete your project as well as correct any mistakes you might make—because once a remnant roll is used up, it may be as hard to find as the hair on *Star Trek*'s William Shatner's head.

Estimating Yardage

How much fabric do you need for a particular piece? Upholstery supply houses and fabric stores use a small mimeographed line drawing as their template for figuring this out. This template has been around for years. There are dozens of tiny pictures of various upholstered pieces of furniture on it with accompanying details about the yards of fabric needed to upholster each one. Try to lay your hands on one of these sheets to determine your needs.

If you can't locate the mimeographed sheet, or if you want to try to determine the fabric needs for a particular piece without one, here's how to measure: Get a yardstick or tape measure and measure the longest side of each existing fabric panel that you will be replacing. Next, convert feet into yards (3 feet = 1 yard). If this is your first project, round off the result to the next highest yard and then add at least a third more yards, depending on how much you seriously think you might screw up. As your confidence and skills build, you can diminish the amount of extra fabric you purchase.

Yipes! Stripes!

Stripes add an extra degree of difficulty to your project because you'll need to make them align with other stripes on different parts of a piece. Seat stripes, for instance, must visually line up with the stripes on the chair back. Otherwise, your guests might snicker and your social standing may decline.

Railroad stripes are stripes that run sideways (from one side of a piece to the other instead of from front to back). You can upholster a piece this way, but be careful, especially on seats. Seat fabric with railroad stripes may stretch after a while, and those nice, clean stripes may turn into a series of sine waves or inverted parabolas. Come bedtime, this may cause your spouse to turn to you and remark, "That fat ass of yours screwed up my upholstery job!" This in turn leads to an ugly discussion about Slim-Fast, and who really needs this sort of aggravation?

The Final Touch

The final decorative effects applied to many upholstery projects involve using gimp, which are woven lattice strips that are hot-glued over ragged fabric ends and stapled or tacked for decorative effect. Gimp is available by the inch, foot, or yard. Double cording may be used instead of gimp. Double cording is made by stitching strips of upholstery fabric around thin cardboard or plastic tubes. Double cording is easily attached

by shoving the extended nose of a staple gun in between the two cords and planting a staple into the wood. The cords are then pushed together, and no one will know your secret but you. Both cording and gimp can be adhered with glue guns.

Finally, the oldest method of hiding tacks or staples around the edges is by using decorative upholstery nails, which can be used alone or nailed along existing decorative cording and gimp. They come in two styles: the clean polished round head, and the hammered head, which are faceted so that when you hit them, your hammer won't leave a mark on them.

Upholstery tacks are used not only to set springs but in cases where no length of staple will penetrate padding, such as in corners where the padding bunches up. Upholstery nails are decorative affairs used to finish off projects. You've seen them many times—smooth roundheaded examples or the burnished faceted nailheads (commonly brass).

Project 2

VICTORIAN RENAISSANCE REVIVAL WITH A TOUCH OF GOTHIC
(and a Bit of Chippendale with Marlborough Legs)

THRONE CHAIR,
or You Sit on Me All the Time

A Little Bit of History

For every action there is a reaction. This holds true in art as well as in life. This holds especially true in the evolution of furniture design. Each succeeding school of furniture makers rejects its predecessor's work as too fussy, too sparse, too derivative, or downright ugly. Grand artistic manifestos are conceived and published to discredit predecessors and announce with fanfare and much dancing that the dawn of a new day has finally arrived. What these originators fail to

mention is that their new thing is nothing more than a rehash of a style that was made so long ago that it's assumed that the public has forgotten all about it. Sometimes this tactic backfires: The design is celebrated as a revival of a long-ago classical motif, which in turn was based on a style that came before.

This trumpeting of new styles has nothing to do with the creative talents of craftspeople, though it may have something to do with marketing. The exaltation of new styles without mentioning their rather mundane origins will always help sales. Would you buy something that said: "Partially new and somewhat improved"?

Let's take a look at the nineteenth century. Eighteen-hundred and one was a good year for most. Now let's examine 1802: it was better for some, but worse for others. Then came 1803, and nothing happened. Isn't this fascinating? Give me some real history, you say. Okay.

The nineteenth century was in large part a series of revivalist styles (styles derived from classical forms), beginning with the Federal period in the early 1800s, spurred by the passionate interest in antiquity roused by the excavation of ancient Roman cities. Neoclassic forms became all the rage. In America, classical Greek forms became especially popular because Greece was the birthplace of democracy, even though the ancient Greeks had slaves (but so did we).

Chippendale and Hepplewhite—the furniture makers, not the acrobatic act of the same name—borrowed freely from classical forms. They also adopted some Gothic and even Eastern Asian motifs, even though the general forms of their designs were much more simple, stately, even egalitarian.

Meanwhile, over in Europe, a very small man was busily conquering things, but he wasn't too busy in his travels to observe the local art and design, confiscate it, and take it all back to France with him. Once the little general unloaded his horde of wagons packed with pillaged goods upon his return to Paris, he formed a commission of artists and designers to create a new style all his own, which he called Empire. This style consisted of Egyptian, Greek, and Roman forms that were adapted to furniture and dress, and even found their way into women's hairstyles. Even though Empire-style furniture weighed a ton, it still managed to cross the Channel and set down in England, where the Brits immediately renamed the Empire style Regent. They did so because they were loath to give the grotty little man's new government a free mention in any furniture adverts.

What does all this history tell us? Simply this: Designers at that time hadn't the guts to call their styles what they were—simply styles based on already designed designs. In short, these designs were Revivalist. From 1840 onward, however, beginning with the Gothic Revivalist style, craftspeople began calling a spade a spade, or a Gothic a Gothic, and a Quatrefoil a quatrefoil (this is a circular, four-lobed abstract floral design, or button, used as an emblem decoration), and elaborately turned legs arches.

Following closely in the footsteps of the mid-eighteenth-century Gothic Revival came an even more frightening development called Rococo. At the time of its inception, it was referred to as Louis XIV, although rumor has it that this style made him as *malade* as it does us.

The Rococo style was typified by curvaceous shapes, carved fruit details, and balloon-backed, overstuffed seats with way too many pillows. In fact, in many instances you couldn't see the seats for the pillows, and sometimes if the people sitting atop these overstuffed soufflés were small, you'd have a hard time spotting them, too. In short, Rococo furniture was fit only for the palace of a fop or a frontier bordello. Still, many people go for the style, and we are not too high-fallutin' to think less of them for it. Besides, for the right price we'll consider endorsing the style because, well, our business is kind of like running a bordello.

Of Things Shakespearean

The Renaissance Revival style (1850–1890) was a reaction to the bloated, overfestooned, and fecund Rococo style. The Renaissance Revival style borrowed freely from both Renaissance and Neoclassical motifs for rectangular and linear forms.

Now it begins to get complicated. Since the Industrial Revolution in the United States had been in full swing for a few years, the number of craftspeople and factories making furniture had swelled to obscene proportions. (Such is the lot of a burgeoning capitalist society.) Thomas Chippendale's book, *The Gentleman and Cabinet-Maker's Director,* dictated styles to the vast majority of furniture makers working in the trade. But the increased global communication of the time brought a dissemination of many styles, which were then mixed together. Craftspeople borrowed from one another and added their own flourishes. This resulted in hundreds of Renaissance Revival pieces with Gothic elements, Rococo elements, and the odd cartouche, or classical frieze, that was added for reasons nobody could figure out.

Which brings us to our project.

Our Throne Chair and How We Acquired It

Our throne chair, although it is largely Renaissance, originally had quatrefoil emblems at the top of its legs, which was a Gothic Style cue and quasi-Marlborough(ey)—definitely borrowed from a Chippendale style, which Chippendale borrowed from the Chinese. Ain't that great? Let us tell you, it's enough to make your head spin. As we've noted, there was no orthodox American furniture style. Everything was a big mess, and though some may like a mess, it was all about to be swept away by a couple of guys, namely Charles Eastlake and later Gustav Stickley, who were as sick of it as you are surely sick of all this pontificating about it.

Throne chair "before"

If you want to see a real mess, check out the picture of the chair as we found it. For our show (and if you haven't seen us in motion you haven't seen us) we get our projects from a variety of sources, and mostly for free.

People either stop us on the street, write us, fax us, or shout from passing vehicles: "Have I got a project for you guys!" Sometimes they even heave furniture from the back of pick-up trucks while we stand there, mouths agape, as a massive chifferobe smashes into pieces at our feet. We have only time to hear the fading words of the driver exclaiming, "I want it back when you're done!" as a massive blue-gray cloud of carbon monoxide fumes envelops us. Later the pickup returns, speeding around the corner, with its occupants hanging out the window shouting, asking if they can get screen credit for their smashed-up contribution, or asking if they can be in the studio audience. As if we were putting together the Ibsen/Vila production of *This Old Doll's House.*

The preceding description is an overdramatization, but people do find a way of getting word to us about their furniture, and we are glad to consider interesting projects. Just don't ship anything ahead and then follow up with a note a week later asking if we got it. Send a photo instead, and we'll get back to you about whether we can feature the piece on the show.

We procured the throne chair from a friend in the furniture salvage business. It was sitting in her garage, and although she does restoration work herself, this project wasn't something she wanted to attempt. She called us and invited us for dinner, plied us with wine, and welcomed us into her nightmare, asking us gently if we could use it on the show.

We had eaten our fill and thought about withdrawing into the shadows of the cool, concealing evening, but she had cleverly confiscated the car keys at the beginning of the meal. Thus we were forced to relent.

This is also an overdramatization. What follows, however, is an accurate depiction of our earnest efforts to restore this unfortunate woman's refuse, which she presented to us without ever hoping to see it again.

To Burn or Not to Burn?

You can see that the throne chair is certainly a from-the-ground-up restoration. The joints were sound, so thankfully we didn't have to take the chair apart and reglue them. That would have meant more time and an additional show (our producers really don't like projects to last for more than two shows). There were some decorative pieces that had fallen off included with the chair—a wooden appliqué from the chair back and some crisscross latticework that went under the right padded arm. At first we thought the wood was walnut, but on closer inspection we discovered it was poplar that had been mahoganized. Mahoganized, by the way, does not denote the diminished mental capacity which may be caused by repeated viewings of the Diana Ross motion picture *Mahogany,* costarring the dapper Billy Dee Williams (not to be confused with Billy DeWolf). Mahoganizing is a finishing technique applied to poplar to alter the wood's original color and give it a more regal appearance than its otherwise grainless look. Mahoganizing makes the finish appear a deep, rich red.

Though the chair had been mahoganized, we knew instinctively that once stripped and cleaned it would be a much brighter and happier chair, since the grime and grease that it had attracted over the years would be washed away. Before we attempted any repairs, though, we had to strip away all remnants of the old, ripped fabric, spring work, nails, and tacks. Fortunately, time and tide had removed much of this already. It's a good idea to wear a dust mask when you remove old rotted and dusty fabric because you may be releasing particles into the atmosphere that haven't seen the light of day since the sixteenth century. Also, don a pair of heavy gloves when removing old tacks, because tetanus has been around for some time, too.

Exposing fabric "Triscuit"

Preparing the Chair for Refinishing

After ripping the fabric off, we found that beneath the seat and inside the back fabric was something that looked very much like a large Triscuit cracker by Nabisco.

What it really was, was a self-contained core of tightly packed horsehair, which had a burlap cover sewn around it and tacked to the frame with heavy thread. This core, which gave the original seat its height and firmness, was intact, so we wanted to reuse it. Any restoration project involves buying replacement materials, but whenever possible try and reuse original features.

Such features are usually of high quality (after all, they have lasted all these years) and it's less work to reinstall something than to re-create it. We carefully released this core from the frame and set it aside.

No other upholstery or springs were salvageable, so we began to cut the rest of the stuffing away. This included removing the old strings and twine that held the springs in place, as well as the old webbing support system. Then came the tedious and time-consuming adventure called tack removal—the bane of all upholsterers.

Removing tacks

Taking out dozens, sometimes hundreds, of tacks or staples is always the hardest part of any upholstery job because you are undoing someone else's work rather than doing your own.

The main reason upholsterers hate staples so much is that they are at least twice as difficult to remove as tacks. This is the real reason why those "ol" upholsterers prefer tacks to staples. They're not easier to put in, but they are much easier to remove because they have only one very sharp point and not two as do staples. And since tacks are tapered, they come right out after the first pry, whereas a staple has two points and you can only pry out one side at a time. Staples also frequently break in the middle, especially if they are the type that have been shot in with an air compressor. You can really start to loathe the kindly staple if you do a lot of upholstering. But we still recommend staples for fabric attachment because they can't be beat for ease of insertion—with the pull of a trigger you've attached the fabric in a jiffy.

We were not especially careful while removing this particular fabric since it was pretty much eaten away. We wanted to get the job over with quickly because it was disgusting, and the fabric removal technique that we used is not one we generally recommend. If the old fabric is cut, fitted, and attached correctly, we recommend removing it carefully to enable it to be laid out on top of the new fabric and used as a template for cutting. On the throne chair, there existed three fabric panels: The inside and outside back were simple rectangles, which were not really needed as templates since the new fabric would have to be cut oversized, tacked to the frame, and then trimmed; and the seat, which could have been used as a pattern if it had been in better shape. It was such a mess, however, that it could only have been used as a template for a tattered and torn shroud.

Regluing "ear" on chair back

Before stripping we had to reapply the loose appliqué, or "ear," on the right-hand side of the chair back as well as the latticework. It's always a good idea to do any necessary repairs

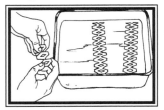

Fretwork in lacquer thinner

before stripping, because traces of remover used for refinishing could prevent the glue used to secure details in place later from adhering properly.

Take the ends of the pieces to be glued and give them a good washing with lacquer thinner, scrubbing the grain with a brass brush to remove all the glue. Remove any old hide glue on the details (you will know if it is hide glue because it will be somewhat crystalline in appearance and will flake off in bits). This glue is water-soluble—especially in hot water—so you don't have to use lacquer thinner. All you need to do is boil some water, add a little white vinegar, and use this solution to scrub the pieces clean.

Once the ends or pieces are dry, apply some yellow glue, reat-

Securing fretwork in place

tach the pieces, and clamp them in place. When clamping, remember to place a pad made of scrap wood or cardboard as a cushion between the metal jaws of the clamp and the wood of the chair. This prevents the clamp's jaws from biting into the wood and scarring it. Allow any glue job to sit overnight before you begin stripping. The same steps are almost always followed when undertaking a complex refinishing/reupholstering project like the throne chair: fabric removal, part reattachment, stripping the finish, refinishing, reupholstering, enjoying. . . .

Applying paste remover to chair back

We stripped the wood on the chair using a paste remover, applied with a cheap, throwaway brush. There was really more dirt than finish on the wood, and after allowing the remover to sit for half an hour or so, we donned heavy rubber gloves and scrubbed the chair with planer chips, which absorb the remover along with the old finish quite effectively. We then used a gong brush to scrub away excess remover and planer chip remnants.

Scrubbing chair with planer chips

Now some would say, hey! Those chips and all that dust will get stuck in the intricate carvings on the chair. This is absolutely true. And although we highly recommend using planer chips to remove old finish on flat surfaces, you may want to think twice

Using air hose to blow planer chips from detail

about using this method on pieces with intricate carvings unless you have access to, or can rent, an air compressor with a hose and air tip. You can use these to direct a jet of air over intricate details, clearing dirty, stripper-laden chips from delicate carvings and even the smallest nooks and crannies. Always wear eye protection when you do this. If one of those chips gets in your eyes it will be worse than smoke.

Buffing dried finish with steel wool

Sanding Is a No-no

We allowed the chair to dry, and then proceeded with a final wash of lacquer thinner. After it had dried completely (about 1 hour) we brushed on a spit coat of shellac (one part shellac, five parts denatured alcohol) to seal the wood and prepare it for the varnish finish coat (page 46).

Note that we never sanded during the refinishing process. With any piece that features intricate carving, there's no real way to sand without flattening the carvings. And even if you sanded only the flat parts of the piece, you might remove some of its color through abrasion, which would appear as light spots on the chair. We wanted the throne chair to be the color

of the stripped wood, which retained the color of its original stain (which may have been aniline dye). Besides, you can never get an old stain out of a soft or semihard wood such as poplar, so we worked with it.

For a final topcoat, we brushed on a quick-drying varnish, which allowed us to apply two coats in a couple of hours. After waiting overnight, we then buffed the dried finish with 0000 steel wool. This smoothed out the finish and gave it a satiny texture. We then applied some lemon oil to a large staining brush and dabbed and scrubbed the oil into the wood. We wiped the excess oil from the wood with paper towels and then did a final buffing with an old-fashioned shoe-shine brush.

This did a nice job of giving just enough shine and luster to the wood. All the wood on the chair looked beautiful, but there were a whole bunch of gaping holes where the upholstery should have been.

After the finish had dried overnight, we had to build a platform that would hold the springs in place. The platform is made using crisscrossing strips of burlap webbing. To begin the job, we turned the chair over so that the arms rested firmly on the top of our worktable, with the back hanging over the edge. Regardless of the size and configuration of your work space, ergonomics is key: No matter what operation you are undertaking, adjust the height of the piece so that you are comfortable working on it at that height. You don't want to end up walking like the Elephant Man by the end of the day, because the piece has been placed too high and has caused you to work muscles that you have never used in your life. Also realize that, depending on the operation, you may have to readjust the height of the piece each time you reposition it to carry out

a different operation. Often, it is easier to change *your* height. You can get a leg up by using interlocking milk crates as a stool, but be careful, because they can be unstable and slippery. Another method is to use the step aerobiciser that has been gathering dust in your closet. Maybe, if you dig a little deeper in the closet, you can call into action those platform shoes you saved from the 1970s to help with any height problems you may have. Your best option may be to use a step stool or a chair.

The Plot Begins to Unravel

We unraveled our lengths of vertical (back to front) webbing and cut them, leaving an excess of three inches over each end of the frame. When you begin building any platform or webbing base, always lay the center length first, followed by laying out strips to the left and right of the first strip, allowing for a gap of an inch or so between each strip. If after setting your webbing you see that there is not going to be enough room at the edge of the frame to accept a full width of webbing, adjust each piece of webbing until there is enough space, even if you must reduce or increase the space between webbing strips to make it happen. Incidentally, the reason for laying the webbing in the

Folding and stapling webbing

Webbing stretcher in action

it covers the first staples, like a taco, and staple that down in the same manner. Four staples should be plenty, underneath the fold, to give you extra strength.

A tool from de Sade's arsenal or a kinky S&M toy? Now comes your chance to use the fiendish-looking webbing stretcher that we talked about earlier. Position the rubber head of the webbing stretcher at a 45-degree angle and pull the webbing through the bottom of the stretcher's head, allowing the stretcher's spikes to grab the webbing.

Pull down on the stretcher's handle as if you were playing a One-armed Bandit in Vegas—but instead of winning the jackpot you'll be pulling the webbing taut and flush against the chair's frame. Make sure the webbing strip is straight—all the webbing strips must be parallel, gang (first timers may want to make pencil marks on the frame bottom to line up the precut webbing lengths). Once you've lined up the webbing

center first is because that is where most of the seat support is needed.

With 3 inches or so of webbing hanging over each side of the frame, use four staples or a couple of tacks to secure the center web to the chair frame's "center point."

Next, fold over that overhang of webbing so

TECHNIQUE TACTIC: STAPLING WEBBING

When stapling webbing to the underside of a chair, staple on a diagonal angle. Diagonal stapling is stronger and will bear stress better because both tines of each staple will be offset to withstand pressure more effectively. Another reason for stapling like this is that you have a better chance of missing the old staple holes because the last upholsterers didn't staple on the diagonal.

so that it is straight, while you are holding the stretcher in place, use your staple gun to shoot a staple into the taut webbing. Secure the webbing with a few more staples, release the stretcher, and snip any excess webbing off with a pair of scissors, but leave about an inch of excess webbing hanging over the chair's frame. Make another taco with the one inch or so of excess webbing by folding it over on itself and shooting another four or five staples into the webbing to secure it properly. Repeat this process, laying out each piece of webbing and working away from the center, all the while checking that each webbing length is lined up straight.

Setting perpendicular webbing

When setting the horizontal webbing (the webbing running from side to side), precut and lay out the strips the same way you did for the webbing running from back to front, and staple the center one at the edge just as you did before.

Now we get to weave. Weave under and over, over and under, in and out, just like making a pot holder at summer camp (or like the merry dolphin Flipper jumping through the waves) using fingers, hand, webbing stretcher, and staple gun as explained above. When finished, our woven platform is as tight as Billy Barty's trampoline. (For those of you who don't know, Billy Barty and the Harmonicats were a major attraction on the *Ed Sullivan* show in the 1940s, 1950s, and 1960s.)

Thank Heaven for Little Coils

When you come right down to it, it's mainly the springs that affect the degree of comfort in a chair. But in terms of installing them, they also cause the most pain. We usually come up with a series of elaborate excuses to avoid attaching springs, or even writing about springs, which brings to mind a story totally unrelated. . . . Early in his career, the late actor Richard Boone worked on a fishing scow: shrimp, haddock, mackerel, porgies, fluke, whitings . . .

For our chair, we used #2 double-cone coil springs—these are the most popular upholstery springs. You must relate the size of the spring to the size of the project. "Double-cone" means chocolate or vanilla, er, that is, it means that the coil is tight in the center of the spring and then expands in a trumpet or cone shape at both ends. Some coil springs are open-ended, meaning that where the spring ends, it just ends. Other springs are closed, meaning that the end of the spring is wrapped around the coil directly beneath it. We used open-ended springs on the throne chair.

The number of the spring denotes the number of coils above the center: a #2 coil has two coils above the center and the same number below. Standard spring sizes range from #1 through #5. The higher the number, the higher the seat will be and the more "give" it will have. Try to match the size of the springs you're replacing. If you can, bring one of the old springs with you to get the right match when you go to pick up your supplies.

Marking spring positions on webbing

Arrange the springs loosely on your bed of webbing, in straight lines horizontally and vertically. We set our springs in three rows of three. Some chair seats, however, taper inward at the back, and you may have to use one fewer spring in the back row to account for less room on the sides. Don't worry: this is standard practice, but make sure that the springs in the back row are parallel with the chair's sides, even though the springs will be offset from the first two rows. Other spring configurations may pop up as you go through life; just make sure they line up straight in at least one direction. Before sewing the new springs in place, we used a pencil to mark their positions by tracing each spring's circumference on the webbing.

After tracing, we removed all the springs except for one in the back, right-hand corner, where we began lashing the spring bottom to the burlap webbing foundation. Starting at the back, right-hand corner seems to be the orthodox way to begin, but as with the rules for serving food, nobody knows why or how this rule came to be. And speaking of orthodoxy, the right side and left side of any furniture piece refers to the piece as you face it, not as you sit on it.

When setting springs, make sure that the spring end is not at due north, south, east, or west of the chair rails. Rotate the spring so that its end sits between these compass points. The reason for this is that when it comes time to tie the springs in place, you want to avoid tying or wrapping the twine around the point where the spring ends. You will be tying twine in a criss-cross fashion across the chair and springs, exactly at the north, south, east, and west points in relation to the chair rails. If the twine bisects the points where open-ended springs end, you run the risk of the twine slipping off the springs. In the case of closed-end springs, the end of the spring is slightly rougher than the rest of the coil. In this case, not offsetting the spring could result in the twine becoming chafed or worn where it is tied in place. And when a spring becomes unsprung, look out!

Attaching spring using curved needle

Stitching twine is commonly used for attaching coil springs to webbing. Its strength and thickness fall somewhere between the 2-ounce nylon thread we will later be using for blind stitching and the heavy hemp twine used for tying the tops of the springs to the chair frame. This string is strong stuff, thick yet finished, meaning that it isn't hairy like a lot of other twines.

Back to orthodoxy: Professional upholsterers use a spring needle for spring attachment. It has a slight bend to it, and the bend is not as severe as the curved, almost semicircular, needle that we are using. But we are not orthodox. We are reconstructionists, and so we're allowed by the virtue of our status in the furniture world to use a curved needle. Besides, that's all we could lay our hands on, and the point was just as sharp as

Tying spring in place using curved needle

that of a spring needle.

After assessing the spring-tying situation, we cut off what seemed a generous amount of thread—enough to lash the bottoms of all three springs in a row with this single length, or about 4 feet. To begin the spring-attachment process, tie a knot in one end of the thread and thread the other end through the needle's eye. Then, from underneath the webbing, push the needle through the webbing close to the first spring's outside edge near the base and loop the thread over the spring's edge; push the needle back down through the webbing again. The spring should now be secured at one point.

Repeat this stitching procedure at a second, then third, point at approximately three equidistant intervals around the base of the spring. (The needle at the third point should come out across from where you should begin stitching the next spring in place.) Once the third point of the first spring bottom is lashed, pull the thread tight to secure the first spring.

Set the next spring in its place along the right, side rail. On the throne chair, this was the middle spring, but if you are working on a sofa, it will be the second of many. With the same thread, and from underneath, lash the second spring in place the same way you did for the first one. Always begin lashing from the underside of the chair.

Once the first row is finished, set the first spring of the second row, which in the case of the throne chair was in the center of the back rail. Using the same thread, lash each spring at three equidistant points until you are ready to begin working on the third and final row. (The first spring of the third row should be set in place at the left, side rail.) Let's hope that the thread you used was long enough to do the job!

When the last spring has been secured to the webbing base, pull the thread end through the bottom of the webbing, pull tight, tie a square knot, and attach the thread to the closest spot on the frame with a #14 upholstery tack. Trim off any excess thread.

Playing with Slinkies: Those Damn Coil Tops

And so begins a new day: Everybody should take a deep breath because we are about to describe the complicated process of lashing the coil springs together so they become a single, resilient unit suitable for sitting on. If you haven't lashed springs in place before, you'll have to persevere, because any reupholstery job requires that you master this process. Just keep cool.

The first thing one has to learn to do when tying springs is to visualize the final shape of the seat. Some seats are completely flat on top and squared off at the sides. These are box seat designs and require the use of a metal-edge band that defines the top edge of the box and is tied to the outside of each perimeter spring.

Other seats are domed. Typically, they are high in the center and tapered at the edges, where they become flush with the frame. The throne chair's seat shape was a cross between a box seat and a more dome-shaped seat. It was not so boxy as to require a metal edge band, but it had a definite square-shaped design with just a soupçon of a dome. There are a few things that can help you determine the appropriate seat height. When disassembling a chair, use a yardstick or a measuring tape to determine the height you think the seat should be and use the numbers you come up with to tie in new springs.

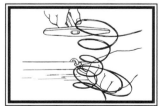
Hammering in tack

We cut two lengths of heavy hemp twine for each row of springs, making sure that they were one and a half times the distance of the frame's width, measured frame side to frame side. This gave us enough length to loop the twine around the springs as we worked to tie them down. To anchor the twine, we banged a #14 upholstery tack halfway into the chair's frame on the right-hand side where the first spring was located, and tied one end of the twine around it. We then hammered the tack in completely with the side of the hammer.

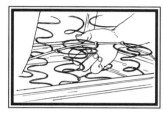
Angling springs for domed effect

We wanted a slight domed effect in the finished chair cushion, so we pushed the first spring down and angled it. We then looped the twine around the top coil on the spring closest to the back rail. If the spring is properly offset (so that its open end isn't positioned north, south, east, or west in relation to the chair's frame, as we told you earlier), the twine won't slip off or fray. (If you wanted a more boxy-looking corner, the twine could be looped around the second coil on the spring, which means that the coil would stand up straighter.) After the first loop, we pulled back toward the chair frame, simultaneously pulling down on the twine until the coil edge was at the appropriate height for the seat.

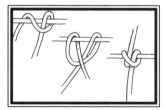
Clove hitch

After setting the height of the outside edge of the spring facing the back rail with the first loop, we looped the twine around the same edge again and made a clove hitch. Then we extended the twine across the same spring and looped the twine around the opposite side of the spring edge facing the front rail. Always maintain tension in the twine as you pull it across the top of the spring and loop it around the opposite edge of the coil. And strive to maintain it as you pull the spring down to its desired height, and tie the clove hitch. You'll find that the hardest part of tying springs has to do with keeping the twine from slipping while you tie the other side of the spring.

Once the first spring is tied (and while maintaining tension on the twine), pull the twine across to the next spring and loop the top coil on the second spring at the closest point to your last clove hitch. When the second coil is looped and adjusted for height, ensure that the twine hasn't been pulled so tight that the coils are kissing each other: this may be fun for the coils but the resulting seat will have hills and valleys. On our throne chair, the second spring in the row is the center spring, so we wanted it positioned as straight as possible when tying it at its sides. When we clove-hitched each side, we made sure that the coil was set at the desired height and was as straight and square as the head and mind of our show's executive producer. By contrast, when we tied the first spring, we adjusted the top coil to bevel slightly backward toward the chair rail, achieving the slight sloping we want in the seat (the chair's—not ours).

After the center spring was clove-hitched on both sides, we tied the third spring in place. On the throne chair, the third spring was the last spring in a row of three, and we adjusted its height and angle to achieve a similar result as the first spring by pulling down on the twine after it was hitched. Then, we banged another #14 tack halfway into the wooden frame of the seat just opposite the spring, wrapped the twine twice around the tack, and hammered the tack all the way into the chair frame, leaving about 4 or 5 inches of excess twine hanging.

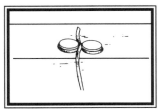

Reinforcing tack

Because there's such an incredible amount of tension on the tacks securing the twine and coils, the tacks can pull out if they are not reinforced properly (especially if jelly-bottomed Aunt Mabel sits for a spell; then all your blood, sweat, and tears may have been for naught). To stave off tack tragedy, it's important to add safety tacks. Bang another

---

#14 tack into the chair frame about an inch or so away from the first tack and wrap the tail end of twine around it. Then hammer that reinforcing tack into the chair frame.

Complete and reinforce all the horizontal rows in the way we've just described: looping and hitching, pulling, and looping.

Installing the perpendicular lengths of twine is done the same way, but with one difference: after looping the first side of every spring, you'll

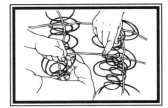

Tying perpendicular twine

encounter the horizontal lengths of twine from your earlier efforts. This situation presents an opportunity to anchor the springs one more time: loop the new twine around the existing lengths, pull tight, and then clove-hitch the back edge of the spring—a simple three-step process. You have tied the spring four ways, creating a crosshair effect. There are some upholsterers who insist on tying each spring eight ways, and we think of them as being akin to the people who alphabetize their CDs, or those who put their breakfast cereals in large glass Mason jars along with the carefully cut-out box front—as if they didn't know what a damned Cheerio looked like.

The Cover-up

The springs are sprung
The seat has riz
I wonder where the burlap is
—with apologies to Ogden Nash

The next step in fixing up our throne chair was to cover the springs with burlap. We cut a generous square from a roll, laid it over the seat springs, and then stapled the burlap to the top of

Covering springs with burlap

the perimeter of the chair. While doing this we had to pull the burlap taut, but not so tightly so as to compress the springs: we wanted to avoid changing the height of the seat. It's always a good idea to cut more burlap than you need and then trim later.

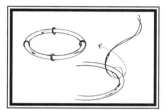

Sewing burlap to springs

Using a large curved needle, and using the same twine thread we used to attach the spring bottoms to the webbing base, we do exactly the same operation to attach the burlap cover to the spring tops, tying a knot at one end of the thread so that it will hold. Use the curve of the needle to your advantage when stitching through the burlap, around the spring, and up and out through the burlap again. Anchor the burlap at three equidistant points on each spring, until the burlap is securely attached. (Isn't it nice that you've already practiced tying springs?) Finish this off as you did the spring bottoms.

Attaching horsehair pad wrapped with burlap

Next we come to the core of the situation, er, that is, the chair cushion—something for that deepdown firmness everyone demands and desires. Luckily we saved that large, Triscuit-like pad of horsehair and burlap. It was a bit tattered in some of the corners, so we wrapped it with burlap, and used the heavy thread and curved needle to stitch the new burlap cover over the horsehair sandwich with simple, widely spaced stitches. Our goal was to achieve a fairly firm seating unit, so beauty was not para-

mount . . . or Universal, or Metro-Goldwyn-Mayer, or even RKO. . . .

Laying cotton batting over pad

We laid the pad upon the burlap-covered spring bed (isn't that poetic?) and then applied downy softness to counterpoint our core of firmness (if romance novels read like this, Fabio would be even richer). We used a generous hunk of cotton batting from our roll to cover the entire seat. (It seems like we're padding this chapter,

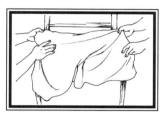

Laying muslin over cotton batting

but we're not, really.)

After trimming the cotton batting by tugging on it, we spread a sheet of white muslin over the seat to contain and secure the padding. Then we had to make release, or "Y," cuts in the muslin. Y cuts enable you to wrap fabric neatly around frame members and other obstacles. In order to make release cuts, you need to take a rough measurement of how far to cut the muslin. Once the muslin is laid out, tuck all the overhanging corners under the rest of the muslin so that they butt against the chair rails or arm posts. This is the point where the top of the Y needs to be cut. Mark this point at the first point with a pencil, and then mark the other three corners by following the same tucking method. Remove the muslin and cut up to

TECHNIQUE TACTIC: ANOTHER SPRING-TYING TIP

Sight the springs at eye level after each tie to make sure the spring heights are even. Also check to make sure that the springs taper toward the edges of the chair frame, if that is the effect you want to achieve in the appearance of the final chair seat.

Fitting and folding muslin around frame members

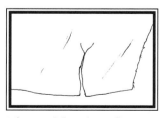

Release or "Y" cuts in muslin

Stapling muslin to frame

this point from each outer corner.

We cut our muslin so that there was a bit of excess to work with, leaving about four inches of overhang on each side of the chair. Then we stapled the white muslin to the frame the same way that we stapled the burlap, with one important difference. You may recall that we used a staple gun to secure the burlap to the top of the seat frame. This time, however, we need to staple the muslin to the channel running around the seat frame. There were intricate carvings just below this channel, and we took care not to staple into them.

Secure the muslin in place by shooting your first staple into the center of the front channel. Then do the same where the muslin hangs over at the back by pulling the muslin back at the center point, where it will be stapled. Shoot a staple in at the center of the back channel. Don't worry if there is a vertical wrinkle that runs from the attachment points on the front of the muslin to the back—we'll make it disappear. Pull on the muslin draped over one side of the chair and staple it in the channel midway along the chair rail. Then pull on the overhanging muslin midway along the other side, and drive a staple in the channel there. Make sure that you maintain the shape of the seat during the stapling process and that the muslin accurately defines the shape of the seat. Near the rails, pull down on the corner fabric and staple it in. Do this at each corner. Then continue pulling and stapling across

between the center of the chair and the corner. Keep an eye on the seat shape whenever you pull on the muslin because there's a fine line between creating a smooth, even shape and creating a series of unsightly hills and valleys, caused by uneven pulling and yanking.

Before tackling the final fabric installation, we still had to finish up the chair back. Unless you want to leave the back open and convert it into a self-service window, we suggest that you finish

TECHNIQUE TACTIC: RELEASE CUTS

Release cuts are necessary any time fabric has to be fitted around a post, frame member, or rail. With the fabric laid out on the chair, make a straight cut from the edge of the fabric to the point at which, when pulled around the post, the fabric will fit tightly without any bagging or wrinkling. At this point, make two small diagonal cuts away from the center point, so that the cut looks like the letter Y. The small triangular flap created at the top of the Y cut may be folded under muslin or fabric for a neat, finished look. Remember that when you make release cuts it's better to cut less the first time around, and have to cut a little more later once you've fitted the fabric a second time. After fitting the muslin a second time, cut the branches of the Ys again if you need to. Then fold the triangles between the Y cuts under the muslin, and fold the side flaps created by the first cut. The muslin should now be ready for attachment. Once the muslin is stapled and tacked down, your chair will have a nice, almost-finished look to it.

similar projects the way we did. Upholstering the chair back was a much simpler procedure than upholstering the seat. We made a platform out of a solid piece of burlap and tacked it to the chair back. Like the seat, we were fortunate enough to be able to use the horsehair-and-burlap sandwich that had originally been installed in the chair. With the chair lying on its back, we placed the horsehair-and-burlap sandwich on the burlap and stitched it in place with a half dozen or so stitches using a curved needle and 2-

Stapling muslin to chair back

ounce nylon thread. We added a layer of cotton batting and then tacked a square piece of muslin around the front of the chair back's perimeter to hold everything in place. The inside back was now prepared for the final layer of fabric (which we'll get to in a minute). We later covered the back of the chair facing the wall with fabric.

The last item on the agenda before covering the chair with the final fabric was to prepare the arms by wrapping them in white muslin. We

Finishing the arms—making corner folds in muslin

were able to salvage the original horsehair padding elements that formed the arm cores and used them here because, like the padding for the seat and back, they were in good condition. For each arm, we set the horsehair pads where they originally went above the latticework, added a layer of cotton batting, and then covered the horsehair-and-cotton padding with muslin. We secured the padding in place by pulling tightly on the side centerpoints of each arm, and then tacked the muslin underneath the arms just above the latticework. We attempted to make neat corner folds in the muslin at the front and back of the arms, pulled the muslin under the arms, and then stapled it in place.

Victory at Seat

Now comes the area of upholstery we've all been waiting for (and we're sure you all have been holding your breath for this one). Needless to say, it's the final fabric finishing. We based our choice of fabric on the style of the chair—it was a throne chair, and so we wanted something that echoed its regal name. We were lucky enough to find a bolt of royal blue fabric with gold fleurs-de-lys (a French name for lilies with three petals that are bound together near their bases) that were repeated in a geometric pattern. Very regal-looking indeed.

We laid a piece of fabric over the muslin and marked where we had to make release cuts where the fabric met the arms. Then we removed the fabric, cut it, and recovered the chair seat. Because of the fabric's geometric pattern, it was imperative to line up the fabric properly, both on the seat and on the chair back. Therefore, we

Stapling in fabric

TECHNIQUE TACTIC: REGULATING

"Regulating" entails adding or adjusting the padding after the muslin or cover fabric has already been attached. This can be achieved using a large straight needle, ice-pick, or stuffing regulator tool, by inserting it through the muslin and moving small amounts of padding around for a more even look. Padding can be added to fill out a sagging corner by way of the existing Y or release cut. All the corners on the throne chair were filled in using this method.

---

took great care to align the center line of *fleurs* with the centerpoint on the front rail of the chair seat. To hold this alignment we shot a staple into the fabric at the channel's center point. Next, we stapled the fabric at the centerpoint on the back, and then at centerpoints at the sides. Finally, we shot staples all along the front, back, and side edges, and folded the corners crisply and neatly, just as we did with the muslin.

Using a single-edge razor blade, we trimmed off the excess fabric hanging below the staple channel, cutting just beneath the row of staples.

Cutting the fabric for the back was child's play (and it wasn't too difficult for us, either). All we did was cut two rectangles that were an inch beyond the actual size of the area to be covered, again lining up the center line of *fleurs* with the center of the chair. We used the starburst carving at the top of the back as a guide. We also made sure that the rows of *fleurs* on the back lined up with those on the seat.

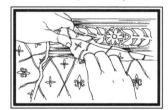

Trimming excess fabric with razor blade

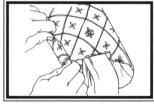

Attaching arm fabric

Once the seat and back fabric of our chair were secured, we proceeded to attach the arm fabric. We cut generous fabric strips for each arm—enough to allow the fabric to lap over itself underneath the arms. On the original chair, these lapping ends were sewn to each other, but modern times means using modern methods. We pulled each fabric strip tightly around the top of the arm padding and stapled the fabric underneath where it met. To finish off the job, we folded the front and back corners neatly inward and tucked them under the arm before stapling.

Applying glue for gimp

Attaching gimp

Gimp is similar to a frame on a picture, but is used to "frame" upholstery panels instead. It's a half-inch-wide strip of material that is hot-glued to an upholstery job to cover tacks, staples, and ragged ends of fabric (including any unsightly errors). Gimp comes in dozens of colors; we chose a gold-colored variation to complement the gold in the fabric. We cut the gimp in strips and used a glue gun to attach the gimp to the seat's perimeter, the inside back, and the outside back. This decorative trim fit neatly into the channel where the fabric was stapled. We also hot-glued gimp around the front of the arms to cover any gaps between the fabric and the wood, and continued gluing the gimp under the arms to cover the staples that were there.

Cambric or Dustcover?

We were basking in the glory of finishing the throne chair when we suddenly realized that we had forgotten the last step of any upholstery project! This is attaching the cambric, or dustcover. Cambric is a stiff, black or gray material that comes on a roll and is cut and stapled to the underside of sofas and chairs. Cut a square the size of the chair's underside and fold the cambric under itself to make a smooth seam as you staple it in place.

Despite the length of time that it has taken to walk you through this project, it was a relatively simple exercise in upholstery, yielding fabulous results (if we do say so ourselves). The only liberty we took in modifying the chair's design was removing two small wooden wheels on two of the chair's legs. We could have left the wheels on and replaced the two other missing wheels and made a wheel chair, but we felt that tiny

Throne chair "after"

wooden wheels on a substantial piece of furniture was without a doubt the stupidest design feature of the Victorian era, so we just removed the wheels and threw them away. So here we have it: a throne chair fit for a king or a queen—or maybe even a duke.

Three

STARTING TO FINISH,

Or Why Did This Brand-New Brush Dissolve When I Dipped It into That Bucket of Stuff?

Assuming you did not skip the last chapter, are you ready to put away the upholstery tools and enter the mysterious realm of finishing? Refinishing is mysterious. You may even say it's ethereal. Why do some solvents and finishes work as well together as Laurel and Hardy, while others seem to cancel each other out in the same way Bush and Quayle did? Throughout this chapter we will try to demystify refinishing as best we can. Let's get down to some terminology first.

You can "finish" a piece, or you can "refinish" it. One refinishes after stripping off an old finish, while one can finish a piece that is unfinished, or one can finish what someone else has stripped. See, it's already confusing, and this is only the second paragraph. We'll begin clarifying things by discussing solvents, stains (and coloring agents), and topcoats. Then we'll tackle a project— finishing a rolltop desk. By the end of the chapter you'll be a pro, and you'll know the difference between finishing and refinishing.

If wood didn't attract dirt and filth from the atmosphere in the first place, it wouldn't need any stinking finish at all. There are three main reasons for finishing: to preserve the wood, to magnify its beauty, and to make the wood feel as nice as it looks. You can brush on finishes or you can spray them on. But no matter how you apply finishes, let it be said that there is no one perfect finish.

In years gone by, both finisher and finishing coexisted happily. But in recent generations they have grown apart: what old-timers once accomplished by hand with brushes and hours of polishing using dyes, heated varnishes, and shellacs is now sprayed, flowed, and poured on by machines. This modern approach to finishing favors financial gain over the tender loving care that once went into treating wood. We have a great disdain for machine-finished wood, considering that it doesn't even look good in the end: a lot of furniture has so much finish on it that it looks like plastic instead of wood. Much of this has to do with what people think they want: "If the finish is thick, the wood must be protected."

Of course, this thinking is hogwash and balderdash. In fact, the more finish applied to the wood, the more susceptible the wood is to cracking. Now aren't you glad you bought this weighty tome?

You've guessed it. We're trying to convince you to do it yourself. And why? Because we're tired of people asking, "Ain't a poly better dan a varnish?" or "How many coats a dis do I put on? I didn't know you could put a varnish over shellac." Our favorite is: "Hey, you guys can finish my chair on your show and then give it back to me with a lovely fruit basket!" We can now pull out this book and say, "It's all in here. Will that be cash, check, or credit card?"

The Beginning of Finishing (So to Speak)

Finishing has a history, and some of the tips and tricks in use today have survived the test of time. The ancient Egyptians applied vivid paints to their buildings and household goods. The paint was made from berries and sacrificial animal blood and reached a relatively refined state of development. Gilding, or gold leafing, was used as a decorative effect, especially in the glorification of the Pharaohs. These techniques were adopted in other regions of the Western World. In China, the specialized art of lacquering emerged as a predominant decorating technique. The Japanese adopted lacquering and perfected it. Lacquer is made from the sap of the *Rhus vernicifera*, which grows in both China and Japan. Different lacquer grades made from the sap are colored with dyes or pigments and applied to furniture (and dinnerware such as wooden bowls). As many as sixteen coats are applied; after each coat dries, it is hand-rubbed with powdered abrasives. The final coat is laboriously polished with such exotic substances as pulverized deer horn.

Nothing much happened for a thousand years or so until the average serf emerged sitting on a plain, wooden stump. Inside the manor home, in contrast to the serf's unfinished stump, furniture was typically stained with vegetable dyes and other things such as the aforementioned berries, log wood extract, or a chemical agent, like tannic acid. A spirit varnish (a gum resin dissolved in a solvent) was applied over the coloring. These days, artists use damar varnish on their paintings, which is made from damar crystals dissolved in turpentine.

As trade with India became possible (after Marco Polo), lac bug resin dissolved in alcohol became the most popular topcoat. It is known more commonly these days as shellac.

Meanwhile, back in France, artisans seemed to have a lot of time on their hands, and apparently they spent it waiting for something big to happen, like the Reign of Terror or the next Jerry Lewis film (you figure out the difference). While they waited, they came up with an activity that they named after themselves, calling it French polishing. French polishing is quite simple but incredibly tedious (but so is Lewis's *Which Way to the Front,* with fellow funny man Jan Murray). So as not to bore you twice, we'll talk a bit more about French polishing when we discuss Moderne furniture or Art Deco (page 98).

Better Living Through Chemistry

Although the phrase "Better Living Through Chemistry" has changed the face of finishing, especially in the area of mass production of finished furniture, the old techniques and disciplines are still relevant to both professional and novice wood finishers.

Our specialty on our TV show is hand-finishing, which is different from the high-tech finishes found on most modern production furniture available today. Hand-finishing isn't that difficult, but it's important to know about solvents, what they are, and what they get mixed with. Also, it's important to understand what stains are and how to make them, as well as how to select the best topcoat (final finish) for the job.

Solvents

The following are the most commonly used solvents for finishing and painting. But what the heck is a solvent? A solvent is a substance that dissolves another substance such as an old finish. A solvent is also a substance that can dissolve into another substance, resulting in the making of a new substance, known as a finish. Don Herbert, eat your heart out!

Denatured Alcohol

Denatured alcohol can be bought in quarts or gallons. *Denatured* means that the nature of the alcohol has been changed so that it's not suitable for consumption. Denatured alcohol is an excellent remover of old shellac finishes. It may also be used to thin shellac when applying a new finish, and it can be combined with powdered aniline dyes as a liquid base. Denatured alcohol is good for cleaning many different surfaces, including glass and mirrored surfaces, but refrain from using denatured alcohol to clean surfaces coated with shellac because, as we said before, it acts as a remover in this instance.

Lacquer Thinner

Lacquer thinner will dissolve just about anything. It is used mainly as, well, a lacquer thinner, and to remove old finishes. Whenever wood is stripped, eliminate any excess remover left on the wood by washing it down a couple of times with a 1:1 mix of lacquer thinner and denatured alcohol. Do this also to remove any traces of the old finish still left on wood after it's been stripped. Lacquer thinner may also be used to clean stiff brushes, providing they are not nylon or hair-bristle brushes coated with old latex paint. Always wear eye protection and rubber gloves when using lacquer thinner. Open windows and set up exhaust fans if you're working indoors—the fumes given off by lacquer thinner are noxious.

Paint Thinner

Paint thinner, or mineral spirits, is a petroleum-based solvent used for thinning varnishes and enamel paints and for cleaning brushes as well as dirty furniture surfaces. It is the solvent of choice for finishers and painters. Gum turpentine may also be used as a paint thinner. Turpentine gives off an offensive odor and can cause headaches. Mineral spirits are, therefore, more widely used in furniture work these days.

Naphtha

Naphtha is another petroleum-based solvent that is used mainly for thinning paints, enamels, and varnishes. When mixed with these substances, naphtha speeds up drying times. It can be used as a degreaser and for cleaning waxy buildups on tabletops and kitchen cabinets (make sure you extinguish all pilot lights in appliances, water heaters, and furnaces before using it). Wear gloves and eye protection when using naphtha.

Other Solvents

There are several other commercially available solvents, including xylene (used for thinning some synthetic varnishes and paints) and acetone (the base for nail polishes and removers).

Stains

There are a lot of stains out there, and the first thing you should know about stains is that they aren't finishes or protective coatings. Stains are coloring agents used to enhance the existing wood color, highlight the grain pattern and, in the case of lesser-quality woods, change them for the better. Stains can be used selectively on blemishes in the wood—such as sap streaks—to improve their looks. By staining sap streaks before the rest of the piece is stained, allowing the stain to dry, and then staining the rest of the piece, a more uniform look can be achieved.

Many less desirable or cheaper woods are often stained to make them look like finer woods. Take birch or maple, for instance: these woods are strong and durable, and the grain is not very pronounced. Their imperfections are often disguised with a cherry or mahogany stain. This process of making a cheaper wood look like mahogany is known as mahoganizing.

The main thing to remember when using stain is to be comfortable using it. Don't feel that if you make a mistake when applying a stain the result is irreversible, even though speed is a virtue when staining. Use long strokes when applying stains to wood. Apply oil-based stains with a brush, or use a lint-free rag dipped in stain to apply the stain to the wood (paper towels are lint-free and also good for staining). Wipe off any excess stain on the wood with even strokes, and use a brush to dab up puddled spots of stain in hard-to-reach corners. You want your job to dry evenly for a smooth, professional-looking finish.

As far as speed is concerned (let's say you're staining a large desk or wardrobe), you know that you are working too slowly if the stain where you started is dry by the time you finish staining the whole piece. If this happens, simply go over the dry surface with a paper towel soaked with the stain to reactivate it. If you're applying an alcohol-based stain (containing aniline dye) and the same thing happens, wet a towel with some alcohol to remedy the situation. Unfortunately, some bloopers can't be eradicated: drops of dark stain on pine may leave blots that cannot be removed. If you screw up tremendously, wash everything with lacquer thinner, get out the sanding paper, and plan on a hard few days of sanding to expose bare wood again.

The Order of Things

The best trick for successful staining is knowing what order to do things in. Let's say you're about to stain a section of raised walnut panel wainscoting. With your bucket and brush in hand, you have two choices: to go from one end to the other, working left to right, or to go across the top first and work your way down. In this case it doesn't matter which way you do it, just so long as you stick to the same sequence with each successive step. With the wainscot, we'd begin by going left to right, staining all the raised panels first. Once the panels were finished we'd go back and stain all the rails (horizontals) and stiles (verticals) along the edges of the paneling. After the stain had been applied, and with crumpled paper towels at the ready, we'd begin wiping the stain from the raised panels, working left to right again. And then we'd wipe the rails and stiles. This particular method isn't carved in stone. There is no manual that says that this is the absolute right way of staining, but it does follow an order, and it's the way we'd do it.

Safety Precautions When Using Stains

The safety precautions that go along with applying stains depend on the type of stain being used. You should wear gloves when using oil-based stains or aniline-dye-and-alcohol mixtures. The latter type of stain will dye the skin, and if you are using a blue dye your hands will look like they belong to a Smurf. On our show we always wear gloves—they protect our manicures. At one time, we had filthy, manly, grime-encrusted hands, but things have changed. We now have ink-stained hands as a result of signing autographs, writing books, and counting filthy lucre.

Keep dirty towels or rags saturated with oil-based stains in a bucket of water. Don't let them sit on the floor—they may spontaneously ignite. And of course, common sense tells you (along with the label on all finishing products) to make sure there is adequate ventilation when working with stains, which may cause nausea and headaches if their fumes are inhaled over a period of time.

Oil Stains

Oil-based stains are the most widely used and readily available stains on the market. They are made from oil-soluble dyes dissolved in a mineral spirits base. When you work with these stains, try to avoid stirring or agitating them because if this happens the stain will dry more opaque. Oil stains come in a variety of colors and can be intermixed—even if they are different brands! Just read the can label to be sure that the stain has a spirit base. Oil stains may also be darkened using oil pigments that have been ground in oil, such as japan colors (page 45). Oil-based stains don't penetrate the wood as nicely as aniline-dye-and-alcohol stains, but they are quick and easy to use and they won't raise the grain of the wood—that is, the fibers of the wood won't absorb water and swell.

Homemade Oil Stains

If you're the kind of person who wants to save money and make your own oil stains, all you need are two basic ingredients: oil paint and paint thinner. Pour some paint thinner into a can or bucket and add some color paint. You can add oil-based white paint to paint thinner and create a whitewash stain for oak. Thin the solution with thinner until you achieve the consistency and color you want. Apply the stain with a brush or lint-free cloth and wipe off the excess stain with a cloth, going against the wood grain. If you want a brown stain, mix oil-based brown paint with thinner. Mail-order outlets and woodworking supply houses also carry a wide selection of oil paint colors.

Oil Colors

These are pure pigments that are ground and added to linseed oil. They are used for making stains of varying colors, and may be used to tint oil-based paint.

Aniline Dyes

Aniline dyes are powder dyes that penetrate deeply into the wood and are available in alcohol-soluble, water-soluble, and oil-soluble versions. The alcohol-soluble variety dissolves in wood alcohol or methanol and will not raise the grain of the wood, but alcohol-based dyes have a poor lightfastness, which means they will fade. The water-soluble type are light fast, which means that they will not fade. The disadvantage of the water-soluble variety is that you will have to sand lightly after staining because the water in the stain will raise the grain of the wood. The oil-soluble type is not used much because of its tendency to bleed into varnish topcoats applied over it.

Japan Colors

We have used japan colors on our TV show many times because of their quick-drying characteristics—they dry in about 1 to 2 hours. (Time is money, especially when shooting tape.) They are finely ground pigments mixed in a varnish vehicle. Their color concentrations are exceptional, making them great for creating stains and for touch-ups. They also dry to a flat luster and can be varnished over.

Oil Finishes

Oil finishes are also known as tung oils and Danish oils. These types of finishes can be hand-rubbed over wood surfaces that have been sanded smooth, usually with 600-grit silicon carbide finishing paper or higher. By virtue of its name, Danish oil suggests that it is used by Scandinavians. In truth, Danish oils simply consist of substantial amounts of oil diluted with varnish. They can be applied with a brush, rubbed on with a cloth, or sanded in. They penetrate wood well and enhance its natural look without adding any reflective quality. Oil finishes afford little, if any, protection and wood finished this way must be reoiled periodically. For this reason the Danes, Swedes, and Finns are very attentive about using coasters when they drink. And if a small, open-faced sandwich laden with oily herring lands facedown on a table, all the better—it's just rubbed into the wood. Skoal!

Bleaches

While they are not truly stains, bleaches change the color of wood. Regular laundry bleach is effective on oak and mahogany, but make sure the wood is absolutely clean before applying it—especially if the wood has been stripped. Sanding and washing wood with a water-and-vinegar solution is imperative for good results with bleach; if the piece is oak, we would even suggest that it be scrubbed with wire brushes, washed again after sanding, and then washed some more, because this very porous and very tough wood can take the abrasive qualities of the steel bristles. Dirt blocks penetration of the bleach into the wood. One telltale sign that the wood hasn't been cleaned enough is the bleach beading up on the wood like water on a windshield. If this happens, it's time to go back to sanding and washing the wood.

Once the wood has been bleached, wash it clean with a water-and-vinegar solution. When dry, the wood will be slightly rough to the touch because the grain will have been "raised." It will then need to be sanded lightly with fine sandpaper. If you sand too much, or if you sand with coarse or medium sandpaper, you will scratch off the bleached surface, permitting spots of the underlying unbleached wood to show through. The effect is positively horrible.

Besides laundry bleach, hydrogen peroxide may be used to lighten the color of wood. Hydrogen peroxide may be purchased at hardware stores and home centers. Hydrogen peroxide for finishing (as opposed to coloring hair) is sold by the box. Inside the box you will find an A bottle and a B bottle. The contents of these bottles are mixed together in an earthenware or glass container and then applied to the wood with a nylon brush. Always wear eye protection, gloves, and old clothes when working with any type of bleaching agent.

Once again, if the peroxide bleach beads up on the wood surface, the wood needs to be cleaned. It is possible to stain a piece after it has been bleached, but you can never bleach something after it has been stained. So bleach well, for you may never bleach again.

Fillers

While fillers aren't stains, they lend color to the wood nonetheless. A filler is used to fill the pores of open-grained woods such as oak, mahogany, and walnut after the wood has been colored, usually with aniline dyes. You need to fill the pores for decorative effect—and so you don't need to use as much finish. If you don't want a sleek look in the finish, you don't need to fill the wood. An alcohol-based aniline dye should be used on such woods because if you use an oil stain and apply an oil-based filler, you may wind up removing the stain. Why? Because oil cancels oil. The oil filler, however, will not affect the alcohol-based dye.

Fillers come in neutral colors and wood colors, such as brown mahogany and dark oak. They are made from ground-up pigments floating in a naphtha base. They are thinned using paint thinner or naphtha and are brushed across the grain and left to dry. Excess filler is rubbed off, again across the grain, with a piece of burlap or a bunch of old horsehair saved from the upholstery project in Chapter Two. When the excess filler is removed you'll notice that the residue from the filler will have left another color on the already stained wood. Seal the filler with a spit coat of shellac, allow it to dry, and apply some varnish.

Topcoats

Now that you have an idea of how solvents and stains work, let's consider topcoats, or clear finishes. There are two main varieties: solvent-release finishes and reactive finishes. Shellac is a solvent-release finish: Once it's applied, the solvent is released into the air, leaving behind a dry, glossy finish, or topcoat, that may be redissolved in its alcohol solvent. Lacquers are also solvent-release finishes which are resoluble with lacquer thinner.

Reactive finishes are oil-based varnishes and polyurethanes. Once the varnish or "poly" is applied and left to dry, it reacts with the air (oxygen) and leaves behind a strong protective film on the wood that cannot be redissolved in its solvent base, usually paint thinner or turpentine. Paint thinners and naphtha are good solvents for removing wax and grease buildup on finished surfaces. These solvents won't harm shellac, varnish, poly, or lacquer finishes. Still with us?

Shellac

From our earlier history lesson you should be already aware that shellac has been around for quite some time. Furniture made in the nineteenth and early twentieth centuries is often coated with a shellac finish. You can purchase ready-made shellac in quart and gallon containers at hardware stores and home centers. Shellac is an easily applied, lovely finish, but it has one fatal flaw: As we've mentioned, it is soluble in alcohol, and with the advent of the cocktail hour (which you'll remember was invented by William Powell in the *Thin Man* movies), life became problematic when drinks got spilled on shellac-finished furniture. Shellac is available ready-made in amber or clear in a 3-pound cut, which means that 3 pounds of shellac flakes have been dissolved in 1 gallon of denatured alcohol. If you want to make your own shellac, you can buy shellac flakes from a woodworking supply house and dissolve them in alcohol yourself. Place the flakes in a glass jar and pour alcohol over them to create your own brand of liquid shellac; the ratio of alcohol to flakes is about 5:1 (page 16).

You can mix amber and clear shellacs to get a more blond look in the final finish. Remember that shellac *is* indeed coloring the wood ever so subtly with each application. A brownish wood coated four or five times with amber shellac will result in the brown wood becoming softer in color with every shellac coat. However, if you have applied a wash of thinned white paint as a stain over an oak mantel, you may want to apply only clear shellac. If you use amber you're going to get a dirty yellow effect when the yellow coat dries over the white stain. This is important to know if you are trying to match a finish that already has a dirty yellow look. Generally, for dark woods or darkly stained woods, use amber shellac; for light or naturally colored woods, use clear shellac.

Shellac straight from the can is very thick and messy to use, and you are more apt to get runs and streaks using it this way. That's why it is better to cut it with denatured alcohol and make a wash coat or, as we like to refer to it, a spit coat.

In the early days of finishing when things were done by hand, shellac was used not only as a sealer for wood but also between coats of oil stains. Once the furniture was stained and allowed to dry completely it was shellacked with a spit coat of shellac and allowed to dry. Once dry, it was sanded very lightly with fine sandpaper and stained again, until three coats of stain (sometimes of varying colors) and three coats of shellac had been sandwiched together. The idea was to build layers of color with various stains and enhance those colors with amber shellac. Up to three coats of varnish were then sometimes applied. You could call this the *pousse café* of finishes. If you want to try doing this yourself, attempt it only on deeply grained woods such as oak. Oak is rough and has a deep-pitted grain that allows all the coats of shellac to stick to the wood. Never apply polyurethanes over shellac (page 48). Shellac is great stuff to use on paneling, chairs, newel posts, and banisters. But it shouldn't be used alone on areas subject to heavy use such as dresser tops, dining-table tops, and bar tops.

The simplest way to achieve a shellac finish is to apply a spit coat to wood, allow it to dry, and then sand lightly with 320-grit silicon carbide finishing paper. Then apply another spit coat, allow it to dry, and wax the resulting finish (page 58). You've sealed the wood and the result is an attractive natural finish, which will be dull-looking but definitely not boring.

If a glossier effect is desired, follow the Old World method of shellac application. In this case the amount of alcohol is decreased in each subsequent shellac coat, thereby increasing the amount of shellac resin and ultimately resulting in a more reflective surface. Always start with a spit coat (five parts denatured alcohol to one part of 3-pound-cut shellac), and apply it to a stained surface. Apply the next shellac coat (a 4:2 mix of alcohol and shellac), the next coat (a 3:3 mix), and a final coat (a 2:2 mix), allowing each coat to dry in between. You should allow the shellac to dry between coats for about 2 hours or until dry to the touch; sand between coats with successively finer silicon carbide finishing papers, beginning with a 280 grit and moving to a 320 grit. This method will allow you to build up nice, even coats.

When brushing shellac, it is best to use natural hair bristle brushes, or if you want to get fancy, go to an art supply store and get yourself a good badger hair brush. Do not use foam brushes or nylon brushes because the chemical solvents in shellac will dissolve them.

> **TECHNIQUE TACTIC: SPIT COAT RECIPE**
>
> One part 3-pound cut shellac (clear or amber) to five parts denatured alcohol

Lacquer

Another solvent-release finish is lacquer. (We're concentrating on clear lacquers, as opposed to colored lacquers.) Lacquers consist of nitrocellulose dissolved in solvents with plasticizing ingredients that help promote flexibility and reduce brittleness. Lacquers are available in various sheens: gloss, semigloss, and flat. Spraying and brushing lacquers are basically the same, with one difference: the solvent content of brushed lacquers evaporates more slowly, allowing any brush marks to even out (or flow out) before hardening. Spray-on lacquers are always thinned with lacquer thinner. And although they impart a lovely even sheen, a spray booth with exhaust fans needs to be used to achieve suitable results.

Most furniture on the market today has been finished with sprayed-on gloss lacquer. The reason for this is largely economic. Lacquer dries much more quickly than varnish, so many more coats can be applied in a shorter amount of time. Lacquer also has excellent flow-out quality, which means it dries smooth and virtually dust-free—provided that the specialized spray booth where the lacquering takes place is dust-free. Most nonprofessionals will use brushing lacquers, which are much easier to use than spray-on lacquers. Brushing lacquers also dry very quickly, which gives you the ability to apply up to three coats in a short period of time, depending on weather conditions (brushing lacquers usually dry within half an hour but take longer to dry in high humidity).

Both spraying lacquers and brushing lacquers have excellent durability, color retention, and reflective qualities. But they also have their downsides. (This comes from two guys who have both done hundreds—maybe thousands—of touch-ups on gloss lacquer tabletops.) Gloss lacquer is the most maddening to spot-repair. But possibly the worst drawback of all is the smell of lacquer: Its seductive odor often encourages one to inhale the fumes, resulting in blurred images of dancing sugar plums in your head that become more vivid when set to the sounds of Pink Floyd. If you're going to use lacquer, wear a respirator equipped with appropriate filters and provide adequate ventilation.

The best brushes to use for lacquers are Chinese bristle brushes made from natural fibers. Clean them in lacquer thinner, and don't use foam brushes or nylon brushes.

Varnish

Most varnishes are oil-based (we'll discuss water-based varnishes in Chapter Six, Project Eight). "Oil-based" means that the solvent used is mineral spirits in an alkyd-resin base. The word "alkyd" is derived from the component structure of alcohol and acid which, when cooked in soya oil, becomes the flexible base material we call varnish. On the back of the can of most varnishes you will find listed:

- Soya alkyd
- Mineral spirits
- Linseed alkyd

The above ingredients tell you that the varnish is oil-based. If silicates and/or silica are listed, then you are dealing with a satin varnish. Silicates and silica are flattening agents that will dull an otherwise glossy finish. When you want a finish that has reflective qualities but that isn't too glossy, you should use a satin varnish. Alkyd varnishes have good weathering properties, are light in color, and are fast-drying. Varnishes can also be easily rubbed out to a highly reflective glossiness. They provide a high degree of protection, and though they dry much more slowly than lacquer, they are much more flexible. This means that they will expand and contract with the natural movement of the wood when the weather changes. Lacquers, on the other hand, tend to become brittle and are more prone to cracking over an extended period of time. Heavy blows or dropped objects may crack or chip a lacquered surface.

Polyurethanes

Polyurethane has been around since the mid-1800s, but it didn't become popular until the 1950s. Why? The improvement of the alkyds in the varnish industry had made varnish easier to produce and more durable; the popularity of varnish as a finish surpassed even that of shellac. And what explains polyurethane's rise in popularity? First off, polyurethane is a plastic and because plastics are petrochemical by-products (the garbage left over after gasoline has been refined), it is to the advantage of the mega oil companies of the world to enthusiastically advocate using this "garbage" in any way possible. This may also explain why plastic is used extensively for a myriad of questionable applications, some of which border on the ludicrous. Have you ever seen a coconut wrapped in clear plastic on the supermarket shelf? To protect it from what? A bruise? You'd need a ball-peen hammer to do any harm to these babies! The chemical companies that make polyurethanes seem often to be owned by the big gas companies. And this coincides with our oil cartel conspiracy theory, which is solely the opinion of the Furniture Guys and other thinking individuals. Of course, we will readily endorse any plastic device, chemical or otherwise, if a sizable valise filled with doubloons is delivered to us at the following address: Third House on the Left, Dead of Night.

This is not to say that polyurethanes are totally bad news. They do have their strong points, the foremost being their strength and resistance to wear and tear. Polyurethane applied to floors protects wood from water, inks, and nail polish remover, which would eat through any lacquer finish in a second. While polyurethane is wonderful on floors, there are drawbacks to applying poly to furniture—especially outdoor furniture. For one thing, polys have the worst adhesion properties of any finish. The same quality that repels stains prevents any subsequent coat of poly from adhering to the coat under it. That's why you must read the label instructions on the can to determine the window of opportunity, or "sensitive time," for applying subsequent coats of polyurethane. If you don't follow the instructions to the letter, there is a very high likelihood that the second coat will flake and peel off. If this occurs, you'll need to remove the remaining dried poly with chemical removers or suffer the sheer anguish of sanding the poly off and starting all over again.

Over the past ten years pigmented polyurethanes have emerged on the scene. These are mixtures of a stain and a polyurethane that may be applied with a brush or sprayed on. As with most time-saving products, however, there is a disadvantage: If these products peel or become lightly scratched, the dried coating comes off and reveals the unstained wood underneath. This wouldn't occur on a piece that was stained a couple of times and then topcoated separately with polyurethane. In this instance, a small scratch or minor peeling would of course remove the clear finish, but the stain would remain intact and permit an easier touch-up.

Sprays

All of the above topcoats are available in spray form. Lacquers are available as clear finishes (gloss and satin finishes) and in colors. Toner sprays, which are clear lacquers with a color base or tint, are available as well and come in many wood colors including maple, mahogany, light walnut, extra-dark walnut, golden oak, dark oak, and so on. While they are not economical for use on large pieces of furniture, toner sprays are good for spot repairs or for coating small items. Make sure you wear a respirator when you use any kind of lacquer, spray-on or otherwise.

Since you're now an expert on shellacs, oils, and varnishes, let's tackle our third project: finishing an unfinished rolltop desk.

Project 3:

UNFINISHED ROLLTOP DESK

As Gypsy Rose Lee once said, "Let's take a break from stripping." So let's do just that.

The first two projects in this book involved stripping, sanding, pulling, tugging, and lots of sweating to get them to the point where new finishes and fabric could be applied to the pieces.

These activities are the worst and dirtiest parts of furniture repair because you are undoing work that has already been done. An appealing alternative is to work on unfinished furniture—the do-it-yourselfer's tabula rasa.

If you are a fledgling finisher, a piece of unfinished furniture is an ideal project to start you on your way. And for the more experienced it is a way to experiment with more complex finishes for the first time. Furniture stores specializing in unfinished furniture can be found in most locales, and many manufacturers sell directly through mail-order catalogues. These stores often carry finishing supplies as well, so you can purchase all the ingredients for the job, from stains and varnishes to lacquers and brushes.

A few years back, unfinished furniture evoked two images: slapped-together pine bookcases, and assorted early American Colonial bric-a-brac (pie chests, butter churns, country cupboards with heart-shaped valance work, and lots of flying wooden eagles). One only had to hang up an inexpensive print of Grant Wood's *American Gothic* to complete the picture.

These days (cue the jazz music) unfinished furniture styles are as numerous as the variety of meat cuts that the struggling young actor Richard Boone had to deal with daily as an assistant butcher while waiting for his first big break (sirloin, rib eye, eye of round, brisket, rump roast, shoulder, London broil, flank steak, and delmonico all yielded easily under his stainless steel knife blade). The variety of unfinished furniture styles are many, and so are the woods they are made from. Some manufacturers offer the same piece in different woods—pine, oak, ash, and poplar—the choice is yours. Add to this the incredible savings associated with purchasing unfinished furniture, and it's definitely an option to explore.

One caveat about choosing unfinished furniture: Make sure that the piece you buy is pulled from virgin stock in the storeroom. Also avoid the "tchotchke lane" in unfinished furniture outlets. You'll only find tacky wooden knickknacks such as candle holders, paper towel racks, and stupid placards with sayings like "Who's in the doghouse now?" waiting to deplete your bank account. Don't buy anything off the showroom

Rolltop desk "before"

floor even if it appears free of stains, because the grease and oil left by people touching and handling unfinished furniture will give you nothing but deep suffering when it later comes to staining and finishing. Visible marks are often impossible to remove. The job of the finish, of course, is to keep the grease and grime associated with everyday living off the wood, as well as beautifying the wood in the process.

We have often seen finished versions of unfinished pieces sell for more than double what an unfinished version would cost. Our rolltop is an example. We purchased it for about $900. It is constructed of good quality white and red oak, has solid drawers, a hanging file drawer, brass hardware, a keyed lock on the tambour, and a keyed lock on the top middle drawer. The same finished desk on sale in a downtown department store cost a walloping, wallet-busting $2,000! If you're willing to put in six hours of staining and varnishing (drying times not included) spread out over a few weeks, you will awaken one morning to discover that you have created a desk just as beautiful and with a finish just as attractive as (if not better than) the finished one that cost much more.

Materials List

- Can of 3-pound cut shellac (or shellac flakes to make your own finish)
- Denatured alcohol
- 220-, 320-grit garnet sandpaper, 400-grit silicon carbide finishing paper (600-grit is optimal)
- Selection of stains (dark walnut, red mahogany, golden oak)
- Paper towels
- Crystal varnish
- 0000-grade steel wool
- Liquid wax
- Soft cloth

Tool List

- Screwdrivers (for removing hardware)
- Plastic bucket
- Chinese bristle paintbrush
- Rubber work gloves
- Foam paintbrush
- Tack rag
- Eye protection, to be worn during stripping and sanding (if you're sensitive to dust—or you just want to look like Atom Ant)
- Exhaust fans, for use during stripping (if you're working in a padded cell or other enclosed space)

Sanding drawer slot edge

flats, leaving all the edges sharp and knifelike, prone to splintering and able to draw blood if a probing thumb or finger happens to rub against them. By sanding at a 45-degree angle or so, you can turn the edges and soften them so they won't cut.

Removing drawer hardware

Beginning the Job

Begin by removing all the hardware, and place screws, knobs, and other items in a container such as a cup for later reattachment. Next, pull out all the drawers—for the rolltop that amounted to fifteen, ranging from the small drawers in the upper section to a larger hanging-file drawer on the bottom right. It's a good practice to number the drawer bottoms with a felt-tip pen to correspond to the slots (from left to right) from which they were pulled. Some drawers may look uniform in size but slight variations in fit may make replacing them a maddening exercise, roughly like trying to get a square peg to fit into a round hole. You might also want to mark the numbers in pencil on the rail of the slot where each drawer belongs.

Once all the hardware is removed, lightly sand all edges with 220-grit garnet sandpaper. Machine sanding at the factory only surfaces the

Removing nameplate with pliers

Removing nameplate with screwdriver

Sanding drawer edge

Painting spit coat on inside of drawer

Because the rolltop was made of solid wood with plywood panels, and because plywood tends to absorb more stain than solid wood, we applied a spit coat of shellac (one part 3-pound cut shellac to five parts denatured alcohol) with a Chinese bristle brush to all the wood surfaces, including the insides of the drawers, to seal them. Allow the spit coat to dry for about 15 minutes and then sand again with 220-grit garnet sandpaper. The shellac will seal the pores of the wood, especially those in the plywood, permitting a more even coloring overall when the stain is later applied. The idea behind the sanding is to remove the shellac from the high parts of the wood while leaving the wood pores filled. Omitting this spit coat step would allow the plywood panels to absorb more stain than the surrounding surfaces made from denser wood. The plywood would end up looking much darker than the surrounding surfaces.

Oil stains for compound finish

Staining and Shellacking

Since the rolltop's styling imitated furniture from the late Victorian era, we decided to treat the desk with an Old World compound finish. For the color and look that we wanted, we used a mixture of three oil stains: a special dark walnut, red mahogany, and golden oak. When attempting a job of this size, make sure you mix up enough stain to get you through to the end of the job. If you run out it will be hard to remix the stain in the same proportions to get the same color. We went through about a gallon of mixed stain, which consisted of one part special walnut, one part red mahogany, and one part golden oak. We used a quart of each, mixed together in a plastic bucket (don't use the paper buckets from the paint store because their seams are sealed with wax and oil stains will eat right through them). For the last coat of stain we used a quart of golden oak.

Make sure to wear gloves when using stains. Stains work best when applied with bristle brushes made from hair rather than synthetics. You're always going to use more stain on the first coat because the insides of all the drawers and the shelf bottoms have to be coated. With the rolltop it was a real pain having to work all that stain into the smaller drawer slots of the upper sections. The good thing was we only had to stain them once because once drawers go back in place you wouldn't be able to see that we hadn't followed up with subsequent coats. Why work

TECHNIQUE TACTIC:
THE PROPER CLEANING OF BRUSHES

Most brushes should be cleaned well after using. Chinese bristle or "real hair" brushes should be cleaned with the appropriate solvent. Oil paint should be cleaned with paint thinner, while lacquers should be cleaned with lacquer thinner. Fill a container with just enough solvent to submerge the brush. Bend the bristles against the bottom of the container, forcing the solvent into them. You should repeat this process several times using fresh solvent each time, so use only the amount of solvent you need for the size brush you have; otherwise you'll be going through a lot of solvent.

Once the bristles look clean, it's a good practice to rub the brush under water and on a bar of regular hand soap. Work up a good lather and then rinse it well. Now you see why we always use throwaways for the show. Throwaways are very good to have around, but it's best to have a handful of good brushes for top coating and finish painting.

Good brushes also come wrapped in a convenient "tie-around" piece of cardboard, which captures and holds the shape of the bristles until the next time you want to use the brush.

Shellac brushes can be cleaned with denatured alcohol. Nylon brushes can be cleaned with soapy water. You may want to invest in a "paintbrush spinner." This is a nifty device for spinning the excess solvent from the bristles of the brush. The brush clips into the front jaw and the handle is worked almost like an old-fashioned insect sprayer—you pump into an empty bucket; the centrifugal force ejects the solvent from the bristles.

Applying first stain coat

hard on something you won't see?

Rub off excess stain with paper towels. They don't leave any lint behind, and this helps contribute to a smoother final finish. If you find that the stain where you started has dried, reactivate it by wiping the area with a paper towel soaked in some fresh stain: Dip a brush into the stain and dab it onto the paper towel.

Oil stains need at least twenty-four hours in which to dry; longer if the weather is humid. Stains will feel sticky if they haven't dried. If the stain has dried normally, it will appear dull and flat and will be dry to the touch. Some may want to call it quits at this point and simply apply a topcoat of varnish. If we had done this, the show on which we had featured finishing the rolltop would have been cut short by about twelve minutes, and contractually we would have had to refund some money. Since we had

Applying first stain coat

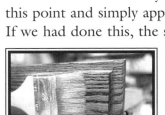

Applying spit coat to drawer

spent every cent advanced to us, this was not an option (besides, you would have been made to endure a forty-five-minute-long Martha Stewart special on toasting the breads of our immigrant ancestors). We applied three coats of stain to add depth and richness to the color of the rolltop, and then we applied several final finish coats that

Applying spit coat to tambour

were of a different color. You may run into problems applying stain on top of stain because there is a possibility that each application will pull up the stain coat under it, due to the fact that they are all oil-based (see page 44). This may result in light areas and a lesser concentration of color overall.

So what needs to be done to prevent this? Simply this: apply a spit coat of shellac between each coat of stain. This will seal the first oil stain while still allowing the next coat of stain to penetrate the wood grain. Oak is grainy and porous enough to permit multiple layering like this, but other denser woods such as maple and birch may not be.

Sanding desk

We waited for the shellac to dry for about 15 minutes and then sanded lightly again with 320-grit silicon carbide sandpaper. Sanding at this point is critical, and you have to endeavor to do it properly. Sanding too hard will abrade the edges, pulling off shellac along with the stain. Be careful around any rounded edges such as the ones on the rolltop. Rounded edges should be sanded smooth before any staining work begins in the first place. If the sandpaper cuts into the rounded edges at this point in the process wear lines will appear. Any time sandpaper cuts through a stain and fin-

ish it is referred to as "breaking the edges." If this happens you'll have to restain or touch up these areas later with touch-up markers (page 119). Use very little pressure when sanding. Allow the sandpaper to glide across the wood lightly as if it were a skater waltzing up the ice to the strains of Émile Waldteufel's immortal "Les Patineurs." The sandpaper should just scuff the surface, creating a fine, powdery dust.

Removing excess stain with paper towel

Apply the second coat of stain over the shellac sealer coat. Paint the stain over the entire desk, working from the top down, inside and outside, and then wipe off any excess stain with paper towels.

Allow the stain to dry overnight—or longer, just to make sure. Remember, if the stain is tacky to the touch (aren't we all sometimes?) let it dry thoroughly. When the stain is dry to the touch, apply another coat of the shellac sealer, let it dry for 15 minutes or so, and sand again with 320-grit silicon carbide sandpaper. Remember to sand gently and pay attention when working around edges. (All this drying sounds tedious, but it really isn't, if you throw in a few amusements. While the piece is drying, try playing outdoor games, developing relationships, and eating fine food.)

We applied a third coat of stain, wiped it off, allowed it to dry, and then sealed it with another spit coat of shellac. When the third coat had dried, we sanded lightly again, and draped a coat of plain old golden oak over the entire desk. This gave the desk a supremely rich color. We then removed the excess stain by wiping with paper towels. There are a helluva lot of paper towels being used here, and you know why—since they're lint-free, they're excellent for finishing furniture. Some time ago when we first started appearing on TV, one woman wrote us and informed us that she wasn't watching our show anymore because we were very wasteful. The best reply we can come up with is that at least we're recycling old furniture when we refinish it.

Once the excess golden oak stain had been soaked up and dried, we applied *le dernier expectoration jacquett,* or the last spit jacket (er, coat) over the stain.

So let's review what we've done so far. We stained and shellacked, sanded, stained again, and shellacked again, then sanded (yawn), stained and shellacked, sanded, and then applied a plain golden oak stain, and shellacked. Yes, it's repetitive, but so are John Grisham's books. We're counting on those same fans to love this project, too.

Topcoating with Varnish

When the shellac had dried on the final golden oak stain, we sanded with 400-grit silicon carbide sandpaper to prepare the wood for a varnish topcoat. Then we applied three successive topcoats of a furniture-grade crystal varnish, available where you buy your furniture supplies and paint. Crystal varnish is less likely to add color to the finish than amber or spar varnishes. Steer clear of spar varnishes even if the clerk at the paint store tries to convince you they're the best. Spars are good for boats and outdoor furniture. They are

I had just finished applying the last spit coat to the tambour when she came into my office. I couldn't help looking at her legs—they reminded me of something, something I couldn't quite put into words. They were something along the lines of a Chippendale, right down to the ball and claw foot. She came toward me, her hips moving as if they were attached to butt hinges. As she came into the light I noticed that she had brought her Bombay chest along for my appraisal. It was enormous. She leaned forward and whispered, "I need your help." It didn't take me long to recognize the fragrance of dark lemon oil. She stood there shaking, her lips trembling. I could tell by her looks and the way she carried herself that she had gone through life taking one shellacking after another. She was cold. She told me so and then revealed that she had left her drawers somewhere—somewhere she couldn't remember.

I stood over her, feeling protective: "How about a topcoat?" I asked, lighting a smoke, knowing full well that later she'd be rubbed out.

—From I, the Refinisher
by Mickey Spilledstain

resilient and remain pliable, enabling them to expand and contract with each changing season. For this reason they never dry to a complete hardness. Use a crystal varnish instead.

Always be wary of what salespeople tell you (though that does not include us if we're trying to sell this book somewhere and you need copies to give away to friends and relatives over the holidays).

When applying varnish, always use a new brush for each new job. And whatever you do, do not use brushes that have been used to apply oil stain, no matter how wonderfully you've cleaned them. It's also a good idea to beat the bristles of the brush against your (or a friend's) hand to remove any loose brush bristles so these don't drop onto your freshly shellacked or varnished surface. Of course, more expensive brushes won't shed their bristles, and this is a good reason to use a more expensive brush for varnishing in the first place. You'll have to dig those rogue hairs out of the finish with a fingernail or pin when you notice them later. If you want to avoid this ugly scene altogether use a foam brush, which doesn't have any bristles at all. They're inexpensive, come in sizes ranging from 1 to 4 inches, and can be thrown out when the job is done.

Dip into the varnish with your brush, inserting the bristles into the varnish so they are no more than three-quarters

Dipping into varnish

immersed. Do not scrape the bristles against the rim of the can to rid the brush of excess varnish; this creates bubbles that will flow back down into the varnish inside the can and will be picked up when you dip your brush into the can again, resulting in a bubbly finish. Instead, lightly tap the hard part of the brush against the edge of the container while laying the brush horizontally over the container's opening to encourage excess varnish on the bristles to drop back into the con-

Applying varnish topcoat to desk sides

tainer. Pull the varnish-loaded brush across the wood surface and work in long strokes until the area is covered.

We varnished the sides of the rolltop first, applying the varnish to the inside plywood panels (or flats), and then we moved outward toward the edges. The important thing to remember when varnishing is to make sure you are covering all surfaces with an equal amount of varnish. (You only need to shellac, sand, and varnish the interior surfaces once if you are so inclined.) If you are not paying attention to how much you are loading the brush, you'll wind up either with unsightly drips or with bare spots where too little varnish was applied. Work under good lighting conditions, where the light source can bounce off the finish as you work. This way you can see if you've missed various spots as you go

> **TECHNIQUE TACTIC: PREPARING TO VARNISH**
>
> When applying the varnish topcoat, pour some of the varnish from the can it comes in into another container. Don't draw from the can of varnish because dirt and dust attached to the brush may contaminate the contents of the can and result in dirty varnish. Before varnishing dust the wood off with a tack rag (page 17).

flats were coated. In furniture parlance the horizontal sections are called rails and the vertical sections are called stiles. Use the same long, even brush strokes to achieve a smooth finish.

Once the panels, rails, and stiles are varnished,

Applying varnish topcoat to rails and stiles

Applying varnish topcoat to small drawer panel

apply varnish to the individual drawers—flat parts first, then edges—and brush varnish over the tambour. Watch that no varnish puddles in corners or between the ridges of the tambour. If you miss any, puddling drips will appear as gravity does its work.

Once the varnishing is completed, stand back and eyeball the whole job. Check for drips and other imperfections. If you find any drips, use a brush to smooth them out.

We allowed the varnish to dry for two days, then sanded lightly with 400-grit silicon carbide finishing paper. The desk was then brushed clean and tack-ragged to prepare it for a second varnish coat. Applying the second varnish coat is no different from

along. Ideally, you'd have a soundstage like the one where we shoot our TV show. It's warm and the lighting is terrific.

After applying the varnish topcoat to the panels on the desk, the horizontal and vertical sections surrounding the

applying the first. Use the same brush (make sure it's clean or use a new foam brush) and remember to transfer the varnish used for the job into another container. And no sweaters, please.

Applying varnish topcoat to small drawer edges

Applying varnish topcoat to tambour

paper in preparation for the third, and final, varnish coat. Because there were already two coats of varnish on the desk, we were able to be a bit more aggressive when it came to sanding the third coat. The more varnish layers are applied, the more sanding the layers can take. The goal is always to evenly sand the surface while still being careful around all the edges (they are still more susceptible to the abrasive quality even of smoother sandpapers such as the 400-grit one used here).

Rubbing Out

What is rubbing out? Simply, it is the process that removes dust bumps in the final coat of finish. In rubbing out, the varnished surface is simultaneously polished. Here's why rubbing out is needed: Once varnish is applied,

If by chance you are varnishing a piece of furniture in the winter and have to wear a sweater because it's cold, take note: First, you shouldn't be varnishing in the cold because varnish won't dry properly in colder temperatures (anything below 60° F). Second, it's very likely that the varnish will attract dust and fibers from the sweater you're wearing. In other words, get a heater, take your sweater off, or wait until spring to varnish.

The drying time for the second coat, however, was longer and we let our rolltop dry completely for about a week before sanding again with 400-grit silicon carbide finishing

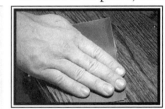

Folding finishing paper

TECHNIQUE TACTIC: TIP FOR A SMOOTHER FINISH

In the eighteenth and nineteenth centuries, finishers or (as they were called then) varnishers used a varnish pan. This was a vessel made of tin that held sand. The vessel was placed over a fire to heat up the sand. Another vessel containing varnish was placed atop the sand. Heating varnish in this way encouraged the varnish to flow out when it was applied over the wood, resulting in a spectacularly smooth finish. We can't recommend that you do this yourself because varnish is highly flammable, but you can get similar results—especially if your work area is cool—by immersing a pan filled with varnish in another filled with boiling water to heat up the varnish. Don't, under any circumstances, do this over an open flame! Once the varnish has heated up it will flow nicely over the wood when applied with a brush.

its setup time may be one to two hours, as outlined on the product label. The setup time is the time it takes the varnish to feel dry to the touch. But with the amount of dust floating in the air, some dust always settles on the varnish before it has dried completely. An hour or two can be a long time when it comes to migrating dust mites. In order to rid a freshly finished surface of these pests it needs to be rubbed with fine sandpaper in combination with steel wool and wax.

Prepare a piece of 400- or 600-grit silicon carbide finishing paper by cutting a sheet in half width-wise, and fold the sheet in thirds. Place the fingers of your closed hand over the paper and apply pressure with your thumb to hold it in place, and

Sanding wood

begin sanding with even strokes across the wood surface. Sand the wood until it appears gray (still paying attention to the edges). The gray coloration is caused by the act of abrading the varnish and will vanish once some wax is applied.

Sanding is pretty straightforward on flat surfaces. It is more tricky

Folding finishing paper

Sanding edges

Folding finishing paper
for wider edges

Sanding flats

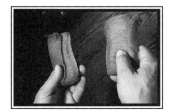

Separating steel wool pads

when it comes to sanding the drawers and the raised panel edges. To sand these surfaces, adjust the sandpaper so it fits into the edges: fold the paper and work it into channels along the raised elements.

The wider parts of the drawer edges can be sanded by applying pressure with your thumb. The flats of the drawers can then be sanded using the same method as you used to sand the flats on the larger surface expanses—by applying pressure with your fingers.

Once the sanding had been completed, we went to work on the desk with steel wool to make the surface ultra-smooth. There are many grades of steel wool that can be bought at hardware stores and home centers, but not all steel wool is the same. Cheaper brands are spun loosely and will fall apart when they are handled. Better brands are spun tightly and are more firm. We can't recommend one brand over another but we can offer a bit of advice: Squeeze the bag the steel wool comes in. Good steel wool will feel firm and tight.

Use 0000-grade steel wool for rubbing out a finish. This grade is preferred by professionals and novices alike. A typical bag will contain twelve pads or so.

Unraveling steel wool pad

Laying one pad atop another   Rolling up pads

Rolling up pads

Rolled-up pads   Pulling pad apart

Pad in thirds

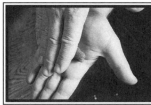

Rolling third between hands
to make padette

Separate the pads from the bunch. Take one pad, peel it open, and unravel it so that it is about 14 or 15 inches long. Lay two of these peeled-out pads one on top of the other, and roll them up to make a larger, more durable pad that is stronger and better suited for rubbing out wide, flat surfaces on large pieces of furniture.

To make smaller pads to aid in rubbing out molded edges and to get into corners, pull a single pad apart to make three "padettes." These

Four padettes

Using padette on drawer molding

can be made by simply taking a steel wool pad and pulling it apart in thirds. With one-third of the pad separated from the rest (which at this point can also be used as a tiny beard) roll it between the palms of your hands until the steel wool is compressed.

Use the padettes to rub out the areas around the molded edges and flats of drawers. Remember to be careful around the edges!

The bigger areas on the rolltop should be worked the same way, but using the larger, rolled pads. Apply even pressure on the steel wool; you should be able to feel the wool cutting into the finish and polishing it.

When using steel wool, work on the piece in the same order you used to stain and shellac the rolltop desk, just to keep the operation of things straight: top, sides, insides, drawer bottoms, and drawer fronts. As we noted earlier, it's not absolutely necessary to follow this particular order, but it's a lot easier if you have a working order.

Waxing

Remove all the dust created by the steel wool by vacuuming it up or wiping the desk down with a lint-free cloth. You're now ready to apply wax to the rolltop. You can use any type of wax for the job, but stay away from white cream polishes, especially if you're working on an oak finish. Oak

is very porous and, even though there's finish on the wood, you'll find that after applying a cream polish and wiping it off you'll be left with white-colored pores. Cream polishes contain opaque solids that fill in the wood's pores and can't be wiped away.

Dipping cloth into wax

Applying wax

Use a dark paste wax or a dark liquid wax. Note that waxes are different from cream polishes—waxes are emulsified in petroleum distillate solvents. Apply wax with a small cotton cloth dipped in the wax. A piece of an old T-shirt run through the wash several hundred times is best. Do not use an official Furniture Guys T-shirt (available from us) to apply the wax, though it is ideal to wear while waxing.

Buffing away excess wax

Allow a half hour for the solvent in the wax to evaporate. The resulting smeared, dull residue on the wood is dried wax. Use a clean cloth or soft paper towels to buff the dull finish and remove most of the excess wax. Then finish off the job with a good, intense buffing using a soft cloth to bring out the maximum shine, or Shinus Maximus, the Roman inventor of the wax job.

Reinstall all the hardware you removed at the beginning of the project and insert all the drawers in their appropriate slots.

By looking at our "after" picture you can see the richness of tone and grain of our rolltop and almost hear the hum of the shine. This is a true Old World look, and there are no real shortcuts that can be used to achieve it. A lot of steps?

Maybe. And though each individual step is not that time-consuming, there are a lot of them. We advise that anyone attempting a finishing job take lots of breaks between steps, steps between breaks, and cocktails in between all that stepping and breaking.

Rolltop desk "after"

Four

HOW TO BUY FURNITURE,
or Foraging for Furniture

Aunt Rose is dead.

The solemn mourners gather in the parlor of her large Victorian home on the hill. The grandchildren, nieces, and nephews sit on overstuffed velvet easy chairs and chintz settees. The caterers unwrap trays of cold cuts and lay them out on the walnut table and matching sideboard.

Fond childhood memories are recalled—the table that became a fort, the spindled two-floor staircase that became a castle, and the cakes that were lovingly prepared and set out to cool on the porcelain-topped hoosier in the kitchen. As the memories drift upward, curling around the elegant brass-and-cut-glass chandelier like spiraling smoke, one question arises in the minds of the assembled mourners: Who gets the furniture?

Eyes dart around the room as the various family members fixate on the pieces they most desire (or rather, are "owed").

"I listened to her prattle on about her dead husband all these years, and for that I need that armoire," harps one hopeful mourner.

"But I have no closet space, and I was the one who fed her like a child after the stroke. That bed is mine, you hear," asserts another.

"You fools can't appreciate this furniture, and I was her favorite. She would have wanted me to have it all, God rest her soul," someone else interjects.

Sound familiar? While aunts like Rose drop like petals from a flower all the time, have you ever stopped to wonder what happens to the furniture of the deceased? The usual scenario is this: An estate sale is announced, furniture dealers are contacted, and the entire contents of the deceased's home are hauled away to auction houses, antique shops, and flea markets. Sometimes the contents are just ignobly piled on the sidewalk and wait for the garbagemen to arrive, whether they are sent by the municipality or are professional scavengers equipped with cell phones and late-model pickups.

But what about the average person? How do you go about finding these treasures, and what do you look for? And what about bargaining and bidding for furniture when it ends up being sold at auction? But why would you want to buy old furniture in the first place? Why not just toss out the old junk and get something new? The last two questions can be answered by asking yet another question: Do you know what new furniture costs and what it's typically made of?

Furniture is pretty pricey and it is often made from inferior materials, namely sawdust and wood chips (our names before we changed them to The Furniture Guys). This mix of glue, sawdust, and wood chips is known as flakeboard or particleboard, which we call the Potato Buds of furniture because it can be ground up, pressed, dipped, and shaped into any form a craven manufacturer of this stuff desires. Once it dries, flakeboard can be veneered with a wood veneer or vinyl. And though it can also be painted to look like real wood (and may even be as heavy) it is never as strong or as durable. That's why in fifty (or even ten) years from now your grandmother's flakeboard furniture won't be sought after or fought over. It will simply be an ugly, sullen mass of tangled, broken things hauled away in a garbage truck for use as landfill—a testament to our charmless throwaway culture.

Although bona fide antiques (pre-1880) are still quite expensive, there are fine examples of mass-produced furniture from the late 1800s through the 1950s that can be found in second-hand stores. If you know what to look for, you'll be able to find quality furniture that is vastly superior to most furniture made today. The "old" stuff you're seeking is made from solid woods or features high-quality veneers laid over solid wood substructures. Wood veneers today may be a mere 1/16 of an inch in thickness. Compare that to the typical thickness of prewar veneers, which measured from 3/16 to 1/8 of an inch in thickness. Our experience has been that many people tell us that they don't make things like they used to.

We agree that the quality of furniture construction in the last thirty years has dropped off dramatically. Not only are veneers thinner, but tried-and-true methods of joinery used for hundreds of years in furniture-making have been completely abandoned by many manufacturers of middle- and low-end (read "affordable") furniture. What used to be doweled, pegged, or dovetailed is now stapled with pneumatic air guns being operated by preoccupied workers shooting one staple into a piece of furniture in between rapid-fire staple wars with one another. (We know whereof we speak, because we've had these jobs ourselves.) Of course, there are many fine craftspeople out there and there are high-end manufacturers still using old methods and solid woods. Unfortunately, their stuff is quite expensive to buy because of the time and care they put into their work. A lot of custom cabinetry costs money, too, for these same reasons.

The Sales Pitch

Let us now move from the factory to the sales floor to witness the great bait-and-switch finish pitch. This happens when consumers are lured into furniture stores via ads in newspapers or tags on store-window demo pieces that make claims that the dining set offered for $3,000 to $4,000 is made of cherry, or has a "cherry finish." Often the salesperson will support these claims, standing next to the deals being offered and repeating with mock enthusiasm that, "Yeah, the set is made from solid cherry and it's beautiful." What's often being sold, however, is a combination of birch and maple, some of which is solid and some of which is plywood, as well as some flakeboard. Birch and maple have similar grain patterns and can be neatly disguised to resemble a cherry finish by being colored with a cherry stain after sanding. This same alcohol/lacquer thinner–based stain is then added to clear lacquer to make a toner, which is then sprayed on the wood, masking the characteristics of the counterfeit wood. After repeated coatings of a clear gloss lacquer, the illusion is complete.

Are there any solid cherry furniture sets out there in this world of deception and lies? Yes, but expect to pay a lot more for them than $3,000 or $4,000. Anyone who works with wood—especially cherry—knows that the beauty of wood lies in its natural color and its gradual darkening over time. When cherry is finished so as to enhance its natural color, the result is a luxuriously deep and rusty appearance—a far cry from the bogus dark red that less truthful furniture dealers call cherry. So beware: He who sells shoes on Tuesday can sell furniture on Thursday.

The Big Decision

This brings us to the big decision: How do you decide whether to restore the old stuff you have or to buy new? First, look at things from a dollars-and-cents point of view. How much did the old piece cost? Was it perhaps a castoff from an old, wilted Rose? Then figure out how much an older piece in bad condition would cost to have professionally refinished (make sure you get several quotes) compared to the cost of doing it yourself. Don't forget to include the cost of materials. And don't forget to add the sense of accomplishment that goes along with doing the job yourself. Imagine regaling your friends with the details of every aspect of the project while they politely pretend to care about your recent dabblings in woodwork. If the cost of doing it yourself isn't considerably less than the price of a comparable new piece, you screwed up the addition somewhere.

Aunt Rose Isn't Dead

There is another scenario to consider, of course. Let's say Aunt Rose is being kept alive on a respirator and that there isn't any inheritance on the horizon. You'll have to go shopping for furniture but you don't like the prospect of dealing with the peddlers selling faux cherry. The answer to this conundrum is to seek out old furniture. But where do you start looking? Used furniture stores are one option. We've taped many segments of our show on location at such establishments, and many of these places are filled from floor to ceiling with every type of furniture imaginable—from camelback sofas to statuary, from entire dining sets to tiny knickknacks. You can sometimes find pieces worthy of restoration among the detritus.

There's also the countryside. On any temperate weekend there are numerous outdoor flea markets to poke around in. To find flea markets, visit large, local antique stores, where you'll often find flyers and newsletters listing dates and places fanned out on tables near the entrance. Or simply ask the proprietors of these big antique stores if they know of any flea markets in the area. They may be reluctant to tell you at first, but they'll often cave in.

Outdoor flea markets, often covering many acres, are becoming a growth industry. Folks rent tables and display their wares. You can find everything from soup bowls to nut trays. Some flea markets feature a specific type of item or embrace a certain style.

Flea markets are for-profit endeavors run by professionals. You won't be cheating an unsuspecting vendor out of a Chippendale because you'll be matching wits with furniture dealers who have been trading for profit, not people who have cleaned out their basements and spread the contents on a card table on their front lawn. In other words, bring cash.

Tag Sales

Tag sales may also be run by professionals. Think of them as a yard sale administered by a huge conglomerate such as Gulf and Western. In a tag sale, the entire contents of a house are displayed, everything is tagged, and a specific time for purchase has been predetermined. The regimented nature of these sales, however, doesn't mean that the prices aren't negotiable. Break the rules and offer to remove an item before 9 A.M. for a certain sum of money. Your chances of success increase when there is a low turnout at the sale.

To find good tag sales, check classifieds in newspapers catering to upscale neighborhoods. Rich people have nice furniture, because they can afford it. Their kids buy nice furniture, because they can afford it, too. When the old people die in this elite community, no one knows what to do with all the accumulated stuff. This problem is expressed quite nicely by the following equation:

$$D\,(RP) + RCWGF = MFFU$$
(Death times Rich People plus Rich Children with Good Furniture [of their own] equals More Furniture for Us)

Furniture Auctions

A furniture auction is best defined as a legal capitalistic feeding frenzy. You don't have to go to Sotheby's or Christies to participate in the frenzy, either: popularly priced auction houses dot the nation in downtown buildings and suburban warehouses everywhere. County auctions draw hordes of people—sometimes filling areas the size of a football field. There is a furniture auction in Crumpton, Maryland, that is so huge the auctioneer circulates in a golf cart among buyers and sells single pieces, lots, and entire rows of furniture at one time, barking: "All right, I'm selling from here to there . . . What am I bid?"

No kidding.

Many of these auctions are civilian-friendly, meaning that you can go to them and easily master the bargaining process. Others move at a breakneck pace and you're liable to buy things you don't even want. Don't wave to a friend or blow your nose: The auctioneer may take this to mean that you've made a bid. Watch a couple of these more advanced auctions a few times before participating, just to see what it's like before you take the plunge.

Many dealers at auctions have traveled hundreds and even thousands of miles to snatch up a good deal. They drive their trucks from auction to auction before returning to their home base store. You can always tell who these dealers are by their bleary eyes and wired-with-caffeine pallor. Often they can be seen taking catnaps on the sofas they hope to buy. Remarkably, they seem lucid when bidding on the pieces they have their eyes on.

High-end auctions are at the other end of the furniture-foraging spectrum and are held in most midsize to large cities. Some of these operate on a weekly basis and are open to the public. Others are more exclusive, by-invitation-only affairs. All auctions offer a preview time, when potential bidders have the chance to look over the goods being sold. Preview times may last up to two full days before the auction or may occur only an hour or two before the bidding begins. During the preview, home in on the items you'd like to bid on and check the values in reference materials you've brought along. (There are many good furniture reference books on the market that will give you a ballpark figure for what something's worth.) Set yourself a limit, or just go nuts outbidding everyone else for that perfect piece you spotted during the preview period.

Yard Sales

Sunday is the sacred American yard sale day, when countless families empty the contents of their humdrum lives onto their pesticide-treated lawns and sit on folding chairs (also for sale) with their open cigar box tills waiting for customers to drive up and take their junk away. To find yard sales, follow the paper signs tacked to telephone poles or look in the classifieds for dates and addresses. (If you find a mint-condition game called Mousetrap, give us a call.)

Hitting Rock Bottom

Modern-day trash picking is hip. We're not talking about the guy wearing a big wool hat in August pushing a shopping cart—he's got his own style. We're talking about doing a little research to find what you're looking for. A call to your municipality's sanitation department to determine when bulk trash is picked up is a good first step toward finding the furniture of your dreams. Bulk trash is often picked up every few months throughout the year. This is the time when people can have anything, regardless of size, picked up for disposal. To avoid funny looks from passersby, make trash picking a night caper or do the dirty deed at dawn. Be prepared for competition from amateurs and professionals alike. With a little experience you'll discover the best scavenging spots—the places where people truly don't know what they're throwing out.

Happy foraging! Keep your eyes open, and don't forget to write or visit Aunt Rose. You never know when a well-worded suck-up will yield an heirloom. Here are some ideas: "Oh Aunt Rose, this mahogany armoire reminds me so much of you: elegant yet strong," or, "How I'll always remember your sponge cake cooling on the mahogany sideboard, and by the way, how's that pain behind the left eye?" See, isn't that easy? Try making up some of your own lines to use on the old girl.

The above methods of procuring furniture may develop into a fun hobby or evolve into a career of sorts for some people. But many people don't have the time or inclination to go searching for restorable old furniture. The chase can be fun, but it demands a lot of time—especially if you're searching for a matching set of just about anything.

How to Buy New Furniture If You Have To

More people buy furniture during the holiday shopping season than at any other time of the year. Is this because it's too cold to trash-pick?

Perhaps. We think the reason grows out of the fact that a recliner goes well with a bottle of aftershave lotion, and as long as you're buying that $6 tie for Uncle Abe, you might as well spend an extra $2,799 on a twelve-piece living-room sectional, complete with massage unit, wet bar, egg timer, and a Pitney-Bowes stamp machine. After all, you're already in the store—right?

There's a tremendous selection of furniture out there to choose from. Unfortunately, most of it is only fit to join the holiday Yule log burning in the fireplace. Beware: particleboard (those imitation "woods" made of formaldehyde glue, wood chips, and sawdust) may look nice when it gives off a dazzling array of colors as it burns, but it also creates poisonous gas in the process. This makes a great headline for the tabloids: FIVE EXPIRE FROM FLAKEBOARD FIRE!

So let's talk about buying furniture to keep instead of furniture to burn. First off, there are what we like to call the "bottom feeders." These are the sofa, love seat, cocktail table, and two end table combinations that cost $799. You've seen ads for this stuff on the back of the Sunday newspaper's TV magazine. The furniture industry calls this stuff "promotional furniture" because it's too embarrassed to call it crap (and because it could never be sold without a full-page ad on the back of a low-end TV mag).

People buy this stuff thinking it's a great deal. Almost half the furniture bought in America is promotional furniture. Imagine that 50 percent of the cars on the highway were Yugos. Well, the promotional stuff has the same life expectancy— but with no removable ashtrays! The major ingredients used in the manufacture of this low-end furniture are pine frames—complete with knots—assembled with staples, covered with rice-paper-thin fabric, and filled with one main ingredient: air. This kind of furniture would have a more useful life if it were used as freight pallets. Our advice: Stay clear of this stuff.

One rung up on the furniture food chain is ready-to-assemble Nordic furniture. This stuff is designed to travel in flat cardboard boxes from Third World countries where it's produced cheaply, delivered to the store, purchased cheap, and set up in college dorm rooms. Why dorm rooms? Because if you think it's going to last longer than four years, your combined SAT scores were under 700. In general, be wary of furniture that needs to be assembled with a 3-inch hex tool that looks like the letter L (an Allen wrench) and has to be tightened periodically.

A somewhat recent marketing device for moving new furniture into homes across the nation is custom-ordered upholstered pieces. The scenario is this: you sit in the customer service area of a store and select your favorite style of sofa, chair, or love seat. Then you choose a fabric from a wide selection of swatches, with the assistance of the store yenta. The problem with this approach (aside from recurring nightmares of swirling fabric patterns set to a Bernard Hermann score of slashing strings) is that you can never know how a specific fabric will really look on the frame you've chosen until you've taken delivery. And then it's too late: returning the item is difficult because, "It was made especially for you, darling . . . "

At the high end of furniture buying comes what we like to call the decorators' scam. We must differentiate between interior designers and interior decorators. Designers attend schools, train, and graduate with degrees. They have the credentials to effectively design interiors for industry and for individuals. Often they are employed by design firms and work hand-in-hand with architects and engineers. The only credentials you need to become a decorator are business cards, a wide scarf, the ability to arrange things, and a so-called eye for color selection. These people are often unschooled, untrained individuals who, with the kids out of the house and time on their hands, bought a stack of *Beautiful Wonderful Houses* and proceeded to collect customer fees (as well as pocketing kickbacks from the furniture showrooms they steer people to). The actual labor involved on their part consists of having coffee, positioning bric-a-brac on the étagère (shelves with a huge markup), and arranging an assortment of dried flowers in a three-foot-high jade vase. Why not buy your own stack of decorating magazines?

This said, is there any way to buy new furniture without being fleeced? There is hope, but it means stepping out of your world and into our world. And hope costs money. Good furniture is not cheap, because the bulk of it is handmade by real craftspeople who care about what they're making. Real furniture is made from solid woods, real wood veneers, coil springs, and natural-fiber fabrics. This furniture can be purchased at high-end furniture galleries, which are sometimes located in larger furniture stores. Remember, some large furniture conglomerates sell many levels of quality, which is directly related to price. A good-quality large piece of furniture like a sofa, dining table, or armoire will cost more than $1,000. Smaller pieces such as end tables and nightstands start at $300.

Checking It Out

Buy what you can see and feel on the showroom floor, but never purchase the floor model itself. Try grabbing the top parts of the furniture and moving them. Do they move? Can you hear joints cracking? If an armoire is leaning to one side, it is quite evident that its joints are weak. If there is any give in the wood or if any parts seem loose, the piece could be missing the interior corner blocks that in quality construction hold the piece together tightly.

Also, open everything that can be opened; remove drawers and inspect them for dovetail joints where the drawer sides meet the drawer fronts. Drawer facings (fronts) that are not dovetailed but that are instead joined with staples point to inferior construction: in a year or two you'll open a drawer and be left holding the drawer front—handle and all. Look for real wood with legitimate grain. Examine the backs of wooden dressers for clues about the piece's construction. Check the wood edges of the top and sides in the back—they're often unfinished and you'll be able to tell if the wood is made from solid planks, veneered plywood, or flakeboard.

Telltale Clues for Determining Construction Materials

Real wood will look like real wood, with real wood grain markings.

Plywood has layered striations that show up as layers or laminations.

Particleboard looks like Rice Krispies Treats, with a concomitant shelf life.

Eye the length of dresser tops and look for warping and irregularities in the finish. Are all drawer fronts the same color or are there slight variations?

Notice that we haven't advised that you ask salespeople questions. This is not to say that the average salesperson wouldn't know the difference between veneer, flakeboard, or real wood if it bit them in the ass. But we think that an informed consumer is best informed when self-informed.

Inspecting Upholstered Pieces

Unless a uniquely designed piece of furniture used only for special occasions calls for zig-zag springs for its wafer-thin seat, stick with coil springs (page 33). The acid test with chairs is to sit on them. Plant it hard, then get up and check for fabric puckering (we're not talking about ass kissing here). If the fabric looks puckered after you've gotten up, either it wasn't attached tightly enough or the springs may be cheap. With sofas, lift a front corner about four inches off the floor. Walk away if the back corner stays on the floor. You're testing the solidity of the frame construction, and what this test result just told you was bad.

Beware of spindly screw-in legs on upholstered pieces. These are typically screwed into small pieces of hardware known as T-nuts that are harbored inside the frame. Legs secured this way will eventually loosen and will need to be constantly retightened. Better construction features legs attached through built-in corner blocks at the corners. Test legs by turning them: if they turn, it means they're screwed—which is what will happen to you if you buy something with these legs on it.

Making Lifestyle Choices

Let's belabor the obvious for a moment. You should choose your furniture to match your lifestyle. Highly polished lacquered tops are lovely to look at, but they have no place in children's rooms and in fact don't belong anywhere near children unless you're prepared to go around with spray polish constantly getting rid of little fingerprints. We know many people have living rooms that weren't meant for living (we've even been in homes where rope barriers are strung across the door to the living room). For those rooms that do see a lot of living (especially kids' rooms) consider natural finishes such as oak, maple, or pine. A lot of kid-functional stuff can be sanded down, primed, and painted as the child grows to match whatever disgusting color scheme is officially endorsed by MTV in the coming decades, be it black or paisley. As babies crawl and then learn to stand they'll have plenty of opportunity to salivate and beat on the furniture with their toys and spoons. Years of this abuse will result in a wonderfully warm, distressed look that is prized in the homes of the bourgeoisie.

Also consider your lifestyle when choosing furniture fabric. Silks and cottons belong behind the off-limits sign attached to the rope barrier across your living room doorway. Gawking friends can view the nice stuff from afar while relaxing on the loosely woven polyester blends in the rooms where Nintendo games run night and day.

Ask the salesperson for a demonstration of how tough and durable the loosely woven miracle fabric you've chosen is. In a polite way ask, "Is this fabric sturdy?" As if rehearsed, the salesperson will pull a ballpoint pen from a pocket and then thrust it (D'Artagnan-like) into the fabric as if it were a foil being used to fend off one of Richelieu's thugs.

"See," the salesperson will say, "nothing can harm it."

The pen swordplay routine came from the directions in the factory service bulletin explaining that any small cylindrical object jabbed into the fabric will not cause damage. But we'll bet that if you took out a penknife and sliced the fabric and asked, "What about a cut like this?" the sound of his jaw hitting the floor would be followed by: "Will that be cash, check, or charge? Do you want the fabric Scotchgarded?"

Well, do you? Of all the scams in the retail furniture racket, this question covers numbers 1 through 3 and is comparable to the extra $300 you pay for having pinstriping applied to the sides of a new car. Scotchgard and other brands of fabric coatings offer excellent protection against stains and soiling. But stores charge $50 to $100 for this extra protection, which essentially involves thirty seconds of spraying $2 worth of chemicals over the fabric with an exterminator's pump sprayer. Is this a great country or what?

After the salesperson gives you his best price and while the sales slip is being filled out, insist that the fabric protection be included for free. Trust us: They're making money off the sale. We can almost guarantee that you'll get the treatment for free—and if they refuse, go purchase a $9 can of Scotchgard at the hardware store and do it yourself. Follow the label directions for the correct way to apply it.

While we're on the subject of fabric protection, bear in mind that these products are not miracle workers. They are really designed to give you time to quickly blot up a spill that has beaded on the fabric rather than soaked into it: a spill from Tuesday can't wait until Friday, and dry dirt will end up ground into the fabric if it isn't brushed away in relatively short order.

This is some load of mendacities, huh? So let's talk again about unfinished furniture where you don't have to worry about any defects in the finish (at least, not until you've applied it yourself). One of the biggest advantages of unfinished furniture is the freedom you have in experimenting with a variety of techniques you can apply to a single piece such as the hallrack we tackle in the following project.

PINE HALLRACK

Pine is a very versatile wood. It can be stained, varnished, and painted. In its natural state pine is considered representative of much country furniture and it is popular because it is plentiful and cheap. Because pine is soft, pine furniture often features carvings and detailing. The door fronts, sides, and valances on many pine country hutches feature carvings and cutouts. Today, pine tends to equate with "cheapness" in the minds of many. But pine is often a misunderstood wood, and those under the impression that pine doesn't stand up to more expensive woods are often thinking of knotty pine, which is a cheap and rough-hewn wood used for underlayments and shimming (filling gaps between planks of wood to make them level).

Pine hallrack "before"

To dispel pine's bad reputation, we turned an inexpensive pine hallrack with a mirror into a sumptuous, eye-catching accent piece. (The most famous example of an accent piece, in our opinion, is Charo, but we digress . . .) An accent piece is a piece of furniture that is distinguished by its design, color, or style and that complements the other furniture and decor in a home.

Our hallrack was meant to be placed in an entrance hall near a door. It features a couple of hooks for hats and jackets, a drawer for stowing keys, gloves, and glasses, and a mirror that allows visitors to check on the status of their skin blemishes as they enter.

Materials List

- Aniline dye
- Hide glue
- Paper towels
- Earthenware, enamel, or glass container (for mixing dye)
- Denatured alcohol
- Black oil paint (1 pint)
- Spray-on shellac
- Soya alkyd resin varnish (quick-drying)
- Liquid wax (or see p. 72 for alternatives)

Tool List

- Screwdrivers (for removing and replacing hardware)
- Sponge
- Plastic bucket
- 220-grit garnet sandpaper
- Tack rag
- Medium-size (2-inch) Chinese bristle paintbrush
- Rubber gloves
- Respirator with appropriate filters
- 1/2-inch flat sable paintbrush
- 320- and 600-grit silicon carbide sandpaper
- 0000-grade steel wool
- Fine mesh paint strainer

It's a Dirty Job, but Someone's Got to Do It

To prepare the hallrack for its makeover we first removed the drawer handles and coat hooks and put them in an easy-to-remember place for reattachment later. Then we wet the wood. Whenever you're working on pine, it's a good idea to wet the wood. Use a wet sponge or a rag wrung out in a bucket of water to rub all the wood surfaces. Avoid overwetting—don't soak the wood. Then wait for the wood to dry. Doing this will raise the grain of the wood, which promotes a better final finish after sanding. Pine is very absorbent, and the wood fibers will expand nicely.

Once the wood is dry, use 220-grit garnet sandpaper to sand the wood free of any sharp edges introduced in the manufacturing process. Sand the flat surfaces until they feel absolutely smooth to the touch. Wipe off sand dust with a lint-free cloth or tack rag. Do a good sanding job at this point in the project. You want to avoid having to sand irregularities out of the wood later, particularly if you've gone to the trouble of staining the piece, which is our next step.

We used a water-based aniline dye (page 45) to stain the wood. Water-soluble dyes provide the best lightfastness, or color retention. They also won't smear or look muddy when they dry if you fail to wipe off the excess dye—a problem with some oil stains. Aniline dyes are dissolved in alcohol and then diluted with water, and can be applied with a brush or wiped on with paper towels.

Dr. Jekyll and Mr. Hide: Tips for Successful Staining

In some circumstances you may need to limit the degree to which stains and dyes penetrate certain woods. Furniture that is made with a combination of solid woods and plywoods (such as the

Mixing aniline dye—spooning dye powder

rolltop desk on page 49) absorb stains and dyes differently depending on where they're applied. Similarly, deep sap markings in pine will not absorb stain or dye identically to the

Mixing aniline dye—adding denatured alcohol and water

surrounding wood, resulting in uneven finish coloring. To limit the penetration of an oil-based stain into a soft wood such as pine, a spit coat (page 47) of shellac is first applied as a sealer, the wood is sanded, and then it is stained. When using alcohol-soluble aniline dyes, such as we do here, hide glue should be used to seal the wood before the staining process begins.

Hide glue can be purchased at an art supply store and through woodworkers' supply catalogues. Hide glue is first heated in a double boiler (or a similar glue-pot) and then brushed onto the wood with a paintbrush. Once the glue has dried overnight, it should be sanded down with 220-grit garnet sandpaper and dusted off with a tack rag before the dye is applied to the wood with a medium-size Chinese bristle brush. Had we applied a shellac sealer as a spit coat before the dye was brushed on, we'd have had a big mess on our hands, because the alcohol in the dye would have made friends with the alcohol in the shellac sealer and together they would have become one—one big mess, that is.

For best results, mix aniline dyes in earthenware, glass, or enameled containers. We used the following recipe for our hallrack: 1 ounce of aniline powder, 1 cup of denatured alcohol to dissolve the powder, and 1½ cups of water to dilute the entire mixture. The alcohol in the recipe minimizes the degree to which the wood grain will rise.

Anilines are available in wood colors and are generally described in terms of wood varieties, including mahogany, walnut, oak, maple, and cherry. They are also available in primary and secondary colors including blue, red, yellow, and green. All are intermixable.

Always wear gloves when working with and applying dyes. If you don't wear gloves, your hands will get stained and will remain that way for quite some time. And because dyes are dyes they will color clothing fabric as surely as they will your skin, fingernails, and hair. We once dyed a couple of desks with a methylene blue aniline dye and forgot to wear gloves. We paid dearly for our folly: we ended up looking like a couple of Smurfs for a month or so.

Brushing on dye—but please wear gloves!

Wiping off excess dye with paper towels

We applied the dye using a regular 2-inch Chinese bristle paintbrush, and followed up by wiping off the excess dye with paper towels. To lighten the color of the dye job somewhat, we then wiped the treated wood with another paper towel soaked in alcohol. The alcohol acts on the dye by "pulling" it out of the wood a little without resulting in a dramatic color change.

The dye was allowed to dry for an hour. Then, because the dye had been mixed with water, the wood grain had risen a bit, and we had to do some light sanding with 320-grit silicon-carbide sandpaper. Wipe off any dust with a lint-free cloth or a tack rag. (Light sanding won't affect the wood color.)

Preparing to Paint

Our intention with the hallrack was to create a two-toned effect by highlighting the flaring crown molding, leg posts, and the bevel molding on the raised panels beneath the drawer with a muted black paint, complementing the blazing red stain applied to the rest of the piece.

To mute the black paint, we added an ocher-colored oil paint to some black oil paint, then some white paint, and a bit of rose-colored paint and mixed the concoction up in a tall glass jar. We used these colors to soften the starkness of the black and because we happened to have these particular paint colors on hand. You can try other colors to lighten or soften the black. Sometimes stark black as an accent color is too overpowering. For instance, the right amount of umber oil color or japan color (available from Mohawk Finishing Products or Constantine's; see page 145), which is an earth tone, added to black oil paint will create a licorice color. But licorice is black, you say? Well, when you bite it and look at the bitten end, it's kind of a brown color, right? That's the color you will eventually get by adding umber. There is no recipe. Just keep adding the umber to the black and stirring and checking it until it seems right. If it becomes too thick, you can thin it with paint thinner.

Before applying the paint, we sealed the crown, posts, and raised panels (everything that would be covered with the paint) with a spit coat of shellac. But rather than using our standard spit-coat formula—a mixture of denatured alcohol and shellac (page 16)—we used a spray-on shellac from an aerosol can. If we had used an alcohol-based solution and brushed the spit coat onto the wood, we would have created a mess because the dye we applied is alcohol-soluble. By spraying the shellac onto the wood, only the spray mist of shellac comes in contact with the wood and there is no risk of ruining the dye job. One rule to remember is that alcohol-soluble

Applying black paint to crown

Applying black paint to post

Applying black paint to inside beveled edges

products should *never* be mixed together, particularly if they are brushed on. Twelve-ounce cans of aerosol shellac are available at hardware stores.

Once the spray shellac had dried for about 30 minutes, we sanded the wood with a piece of 320-grit silicon carbide sandpaper until the wood was smooth. We dusted off, tack-ragged, and then applied the muted black paint to the posts, crown, and raised panels.

With the hallrack laid flat on the floor (or tilted and held by a helper) the black paint was applied to the beveled edges on the hallrack's lower door panel using long, single strokes from a ½-inch flat sable paintbrush purchased at an art supply store.

Painting appliqué

With the same flat sable brush used for the beveled drawer details, we painted the appliqué below the crown. We decided to paint the appliqué rather than leave it a natural wood color for two reasons: appliqués are usually stamped out of harder woods, like birch or maple, and they absorb stain differently from the surrounding wood (making the appliqué lighter), and our particular piece would have looked unbalanced if the appliqué hadn't been painted.

Away We Go—Varnishing and Sanding

Once the black highlighting had been completed, we let the paint dry overnight. Then, to prepare the painted parts for a varnish, we sprayed them with a light coat of shellac from a spray can as

TECHNIQUE TACTIC: GETTING THE RED OUT

Many people ask us what to do about removing the stain from dark red mahogany furniture that they have purchased and stripped, only to find that it's next to impossible to remove the red from the wood. The stubborn red coloring is an old aniline dye—the red won't come out of the wood no matter how many times the wood is washed with lacquer thinner: the lacquer thinner itself simply turns red and the piece never lightens.

There is only one way to remove old aniline dye. Sadly, the process is quite involved and is not always successful—but once again, if you are serious, dedicated, or just a plain ordinary "nut," you can try this remedy. Do not attempt the following bleaching process on veneered furniture, because the bleach will penetrate the veneer, loosen the underlying glue, and cause the veneer to lift away from the surface. Be sure to wear eye protection, a respirator to protect yourself from the fumes that lye produces, and work gloves.

Add a 12-ounce can of lye to a gallon of hot tap water. Lye is available in hardware stores and supermarkets. Stir about a cup of wallpaper paste (first make a creamy mixture by adding cold water to approximately 8 ounces of the powder) into the hot water-and-lye solution. Then apply the solution over the wood with a natural medium-size paintbrush, keeping the solution wet for 10 to 15 minutes by misting it with a spray bottle if necessary. You may need more than one brush, as the lye mixture tends to destroy bristles. You can also use a rag tied to a stick as a kind of swab. Avoid undertaking this operation in direct sunlight, as the paste may dry out. Then, using household scrub brushes, and plenty of water from a hose or a bucket, wash the paste off the wood. If you are treating oak, scrub with a wire or brass brush to remove the bleaching solution from this open-grained wood. Allow the wood to dry and then use a sponge to scrub some laundry bleach into the wood surface. Once the surface has been adequately bleached and cleaned, apply white vinegar to the surface with a clean sponge or cloth to neutralize the bleach and to prepare the surface for a new finish. When the wood is dry, sand, stain, and finish the surface as desired.

Applying varnish with brush

Applying varnish over beveled molding

Applying varnish to rail

we did after dyeing. Since the varnish we planned to apply over the entire piece was oil-based and the paint we used for some of the hallrack's parts was oil-based, we wanted to avoid a situation where the varnish was pulling the freshly applied black paint off the hallrack.

Once the shellac had dried on the painted black parts, we sanded them lightly with 600-grit silicon carbide sandpaper, and used a tack rag (page 17) to remove the dust. The next step was to coat the entire hallrack with varnish. We used two coats of a newer variety of soya alkyd resin

Various brushes useful for refinishing

TOOL TIP

If you're serious about refinishing, you should purchase several different styles of artists' brushes. A couple of flats, some ovals, small rounds, and some lettering or liner brushes will make a good basic assortment. These brushes come in handy for edges, bevels, appliqués, and other places where regular paintbrushes can't reach.

varnish—known as quick-drying varnishes because they set up in half an hour or so and can be recoated within three hours (see sidebar for instructions). They aren't as fast-drying as lacquers, but they are good for novices, home-owners, and hobbyists for precisely that reason.

While the first coat of varnish dried, we took a lunch break. The cafeteria where we ate featured a macaroni dish made with five kinds of cheese, which we christened "Cheese Valdez" because the amount of oil on the bottom of the dish's cooking pan looked like a miniature re-creation of the famous Alaskan oil spill. The dinner rolls accompanying the dish, however, were quite appetizing.

After the varnish dried, we sanded the treated areas with 320-grit silicon-carbide sandpaper, again being careful not to damage the dyed-wood

After leaving the tedium of the meat life, Boone headed west to seek his fortune in Hollywood. The pickings were slim in the entertainment business at that time. He found himself swimming upstream against the tide of matinée "pretty boys" that the industry had become enamored with. Needing to work, he took the only job that was open to him—a daytime counterman at Schwab's: eggs over easy, scrambled, poached, soft-boiled, hard-boiled, omelettes, the odd soufflé on weekends, flannel cakes, waffles, and creamed chipped beef on toast. And then there were the meats: sausage (both link and patty), bacon, pork roll, ham steak, and scrapple. The breads included wheat, white, and rye, toasted corn muffins. During his rare free moments he thought whimsically to himself: Aside from the eggs, I've done this work . . .

edges (you remember about breaking edges [page 53], right?). A smooth final finish can never be achieved without sanding between varnish coats. We then dusted off the piece and applied a second coat of varnish the same way as the first.

Once the second coat of varnish had dried, we used 320-grit silicon-carbide sandpaper to lightly sand the varnish coat and then buffed with 0000-grade steel wool. Then we applied a light-colored liquid wax with a clean cloth (page 58) and allowed the wax to dry.

The "after" picture of the hallrack reveals the hallrack's beauty as an accent piece—but without a foreign accent. If the hallrack did have an accent, it would be more like an eastern twang. With a hallrack like this you'll get comments along these lines: "Is that an air-loom?" "You did that yourself?" "We saw the Furniture Guys do it, so we bought one just like it." But our favorite is, "I didn't come to look at furniture—where's the food?"

Pine hallrack "after"

TECHNIQUE TACTIC: APPLYING VARNISHES

Quick-drying varnishes are used the same way as regular varnishes. If you are using a gloss type, as we did, remember that gloss varnishes should not be stirred. Stirring or agitating the can in any way can create air bubbles that will later show up in the final finish. Don't even dip your brush into the varnish can; pour the varnish to be worked with into a clean tin can or jar and dip into this supply. Discard any excess.

Many people seem to believe that the more coats of varnish applied to a piece of furniture, the better protected it is. In fact, the more coats of finish applied, the more susceptible the finish is to cracking if something hard is dropped on it. The trick is to sand well before finishing, apply a "cut" coat of varnish that has been thinned with paint thinner (one part varnish to one part paint thinner), and allow it to dry. After sanding and tack-ragging, an unthinned coating of the same finish should be applied and allowed to dry. These coats should provide more than enough surface protection. Use a couple of different-size Chinese bristle brushes to apply the varnish. Use a wider brush for larger, flat surfaces and a smaller brush for moldings and the like.

TECHNIQUE TACTIC: DON'T RECYCLE VARNISHES AND PAINTS

When pouring varnish from the can into another receptacle pour just enough to coat the piece you are working on. Never pour unused varnish back into the original can. This goes for all lacquers, polys, shellacs, and paints (unless you want a dirty-looking effect).

TECHNIQUE TACTIC: FISHEYE FIX-IT

Small craters, or "fisheyes," may develop in a varnish, lacquer, or polyurethane finish on a freshly stripped piece of furniture. Fisheyes are caused by residual silicones in many easy wipe-on spray polishes. Even though the wood was stripped and the polishes should have been dissolved and removed in the process, they remain embedded here and there in the wood and prevent the new finish from adhering properly.

One antidote is to clean off the area that has puckered. If the new finish has dried, however, you'll have to strip all the finish off and start from the beginning, because you can't spot-strip something like this. If the varnish is still wet, remove it by wiping the wood with clean paper towels. Next, wet the wood with paint thinner or naphtha and sand the wet thinner into the wood. Then wipe the wood clean with paper towels and allow the surfaces to dry.

Apply stain (if desired), allow it to dry, and apply a spit coat of shellac. This barrier coat will seal in the residual silicone and your finish should dry flat and smooth.

You can add fisheye flowout, a commercial additive, following the directions on the label (usually 10 drops to the quart). This should be done after the piece has been washed well and many times with paint thinner or naphtha. Happy fishing!

TECHNIQUE TACTIC: ALTERNATIVES TO LIQUID WAX

If only paste wax is available where you purchase your hardware supplies you can liquefy it for easier application. Liquid wax is more convenient to use, especially when applied to corners and turnings. To make liquid wax from paste wax, pour three or four tablespoons of paint thinner (paint thinner won't harm existing wood finishes) on top of a surface where paste wax has been applied with a cloth. Swoosh the thinner-and-wax around using a clean rag, then squeeze out the rag, and continue polishing the surface with the cloth.

You can also make liquid wax another way: Dig out the paste wax from its can, put it in another container, cover it with paint thinner, and mix the paste and thinner together. Use this method or the one above. It's your choice.

Making your own liquid wax can be laborious, especially if you want to make it from a block of beeswax. Purchase a block of beeswax from a major hardware store or plumbers' supply outlet along with a block of paraffin wax (the same wax used by Grandma to seal her preserves before she moved into a condo where she now gets everything delivered). Use a knife or chisel to whittle shavings from the beeswax and paraffin blocks and place them in a big enough sealable container to hold them. Cover the shavings with paint thinner, which will dissolve the wax and make it appropriate for application with a brush or rag. Once applied to the wood surface, allow the solvent to evaporate and use a soft cloth to buff the finish to a nice bright shine.

OAK CONSOLE TABLE

If you think we're finished with unfinished furniture, think again—the next unfinished project we took on was an oak console table or sofa table that we purchased from the same outlet where we got the rolltop desk (page 49) and the hallrack. The legs on the table are a modified Queen Anne style and their height makes the table ideal for placement behind a sofa—hence the name sofa table.

A table like this gives you even more tabletop area to fill up once the coffee table and end tables are spilling over with *TV Guides,* ashtrays, knickknacks, Chinese food cartons, G.I. Joe action figures, and the odd dead bird dragged in by the cat.

We decided to color this lovely piece with a natural finish while accentuating the grain using a decorative process known as pore-filling. The top and sides of the table are made of white oak, which is a bit more expensive and less abundant than red oak. Largely due to cost, therefore, red oak is used to make most unfinished and finished furniture. If a piece is made of white oak, a tag or label attached to it will boast of this fact.

The finish we wanted to apply to our oak top was one we had originally presented on one of our older TV shows (the ones with Imogene Coca). We applied the following concoction to finish a couple of Adirondack chairs on the show, and it's the same one we're going to apply to the console table. Here's the recipe:

1 quart of water
1 quart of white vinegar
All the rusty metal and iron you can find

Place all of the above ingredients into an earthenware crock, cover the opening, and allow it to sit for a week or so. This recipe originally appeared in the first edition of the *Finishers Manual,* published in 1827 and now reprinted as *The First American Furniture Finishers Manual, A Reprint of the Cabinet Maker's Guide of 1827* (New York: Dover Publications, 1987), edited by Robert D. Massey, Jr. If we had invented this recipe we would surely be selling you a couple of quarts of the stuff along with each copy of this book. The old recipe recommended throwing in, among other things, hoops ("O, Priscilla, art thou finished with thy skirt?" and the reply: "Art thou finishing again, Jacob? Would that we had a couple of gents to pen a book on the subject . . . ").

Once our concoction had steeped for a week or so, we removed the iron scraps and metal bits

Oak console table "before"

Materials List

- White vinegar
- Rusty metal scraps
- Naphtha
- 80-, 150-, and 220-grit garnet sandpaper
- 320- and 400-grit silicon carbide sandpaper
- Denatured alcohol (1-gallon container)
- 3-pound cut white shellac
- Plaster of Paris (5-pound box)
- Artists' dried pigments
- Yellow oil paint
- Flat white oil paint
- Brush-on lacquer

Tool List

- Earthenware container for mixing stain
- Fine-mesh paint filter
- Wire brush
- Tack rag
- Latex, medical examination gloves
- Clean rags
- 2-inch Chinese bristle or badger paintbrush

(nails, chisels, old hinges, machine parts, etc.) and strained the liquid through a paint filter (available where paint is purchased) into a smaller plastic container. The strained liquid was a muddy brown-green color (the Snapple company phoned to say it was interested in marketing the stuff, but wasn't sure what to name the new flavor—Swamp Scum or Pond Scum Supreme).

Applying the strained liquid as it came from the crock to oak will color the wood a deep black. By diluting the liquid with different amounts of water, varying gray and silver hues may be achieved. The Adirondack chair that we mentioned presented us with an interesting challenge: we discovered that a board of ash had been substituted for an oak board in one place. We weren't aware of this when we made our purchase because the way the chair was packed with others prevented us from seeing this board. The iron-rich solution that we made in the crock doesn't react well with ash because ash does not have the same tannin content as oak. Tannin is a chemical present in the wood already. Some woods have heavier concentrations, some have no tannin at all. Tannin in conjunction with the vinegar/rust solution creates a chemical change and turns the wood a different color. Tannin, or tannic acid, is also used in the tanning industry to color leather. We remedied the problem by painting a thin wash of black paint onto the wood surfaces, wiping it away as if it were a stain (page 43), and allowing it to dry. We then applied a spit coat (page 16) of shellac over the

coat of paint/stain to seal it and allowed the spit coat to dry. We were then able to proceed with varnishing.

A similar challenge arose with the console table that we're working on here: Its top was made of white oak but its legs were made of ash. Ash has similar grain markings to oak and you'd have to have trained eyes like ours to know the difference.

If we had applied a brown oil stain to the table the oak parts would have looked brown and the ash legs would have taken on a sickly yellow color. The difference in stain effects is due to differences between the two woods' natural colors: ash is pale yellow to white in color and white oak is more straw-colored. Some may not be able to tell the difference at all in the finished product, but those with a discerning eye for color will most definitely exclaim: "That ain't right!"

And so we repeat, the only way this homemade stain will work is if there is enough tannin in the wood for a proper chemical reaction to occur. Ash does not have enough tannin in it and therefore will not turn black when the Pond Scum (the name we settled on) is applied.

You get the picture, right?

We have a table with a white oak top we can color black, and four legs that won't turn black because they're ash and have little tannin. Oh, what to do . . . what to do?

Preliminary Sanding and Wire Brushing

There is one way to deal with this oak/ash predicament. First, as with any unfinished wood project, you should always sand, not only to remove imperfections, but to remove fingerprints and slight indentations in the wood. It's also a good idea to wash the wood down after sanding with some naphtha (page 43) to remove any grease.

We sanded the table with 220-grit garnet sandpaper to flatten out sharp edges that result from the manufacturing process and might have cut us as we proceeded with the project. We also removed the legs by unscrewing the nuts from the threaded bolts under the table.

Project 1
Pine Hoosier

Project 2
Throne Chair

Project 3
Rolltop Desk

Project 4
Pine Hallrack

Project 5
Oak Console Table

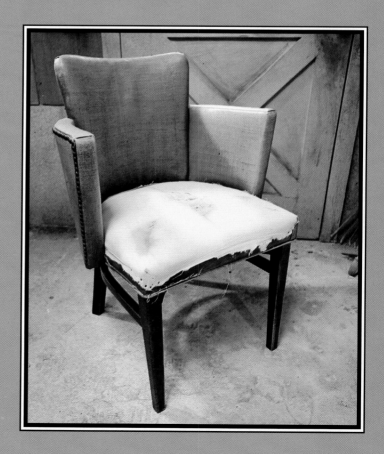

Project 6
Moderne Chair

Project 7
Art Deco Table

Project 8
Walnut Table

Project 9
Mid-century Modern Chair

Project 10
Mid-century Modern Table

Once the top and sides had been sanded smooth, we scrubbed the surfaces with a wire brush to open the pores in the wood, which would allow the stain to penetrate more easily and enable us to do our fabulous decorative pore filling later on. We left the legs for later.

Be careful when scrubbing wood with wire or brass brushes. Brush lengthwise, with the grain—try not to brush against the grain; you run the risk of scratching the wood. A lot of people furrow their eyebrows when we tell them that you can use wire brushes on wood, but using them on oak is safest because oak is tough (like us, in some respects).

If you were able to see a cross section of oak, what you would see is this.

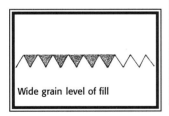

Wide grain level of fill

Magnified cross section of oak

Scrubbing with wire brush—
"tumbler action" going with grain

The wood grain on our tabletop was very deep, so when the wood was sanded, the sawdust was pushed into the pores, clogging them. When we refinished the rolltop desk in Chapter 3, we wanted to close

Straining pond scum from crock

Scrubbing with wire brush

the wood pores, so we left the dust in them and stained and finished over the filled pores. Here we did the opposite—we used a steel brush to scrub the wood, so that the steel bristles of the brush would dig down and pull the dust out. Use a tack rag or clean cloth to wipe off excess dust. Our intention in clearing out the pores was to enable the pond scum finish to penetrate the wood more deeply.

Next we strained the liquid through a paint filter into another container (have a helper hold the filter). Paint filters come in a lot of different mesh grades—choose the finest mesh for filtering this concoction. Straining the pond scum through a paint filter rids the finish of dirt and paint shards that could scratch the wood when the finish is rubbed in.

With the wood sanded, cleaned, and wire-brushed

Applying pond scum

we painted the pond scum all over the table's top and sides—commonly referred to as the table's apron. If you watched the TV show where we did this you saw the instantaneous change in the color of the wood. And if you didn't watch, let us re-create it for you now:

JOE: And we paint on the pond scum, and you can see . . .

ED: Look, an instantaneous change!

BOTH: *Wow!*

Applying our homemade finish yields an effect roughly similar to that of the elements on exposed wood in the outdoors. When new spruce or oak fences and park benches are exposed to the weather, they turn from warm, natural wood brown tones to grays in a very short period of time. This is caused by rain and snow and by the elements that this precipitation contains (iron being one of them). When the precipitation enters unprotected wood, the elements in the rain or snow transform the color. The solution we made and applied speeds the weathering process, and the solution's greater concentration dramatically deepens the weathered color effect.

Because this wood-coloring treatment is nat-

TECHNIQUE TACTIC: STEAMING DENTS AWAY

Let's say you're at an unfinished furniture outlet and you see a piece that you absolutely adore, but (there's always a but) it's the last one in the store, and it's been discontinued. You have your heart set on it, and the store will sell it to you for peanuts, but (again) it's got a couple of dents from something that's been dropped on it or from the sharp elbow of a sleeping salesman who used it as a leaning post during the month of June. (Because there's no finish on the piece you should already be determining what needs to be done to fix it.) Here's what to do: Purchase the piece and take it home or have it delivered. Plug in a steam iron and lay a damp cloth over the dents. Place the iron on the cloth until the wood fibers swell enough to hide the dent. Lift the cloth occasionally to check. In most cases (unless a hatchet or cinder block has fallen on the surface) the unsightly indentation will disappear as the wood fibers swell. A steam iron can also be used to remove dents on finished pieces, but with finished furniture the process is a bit more complex. The steamed finish is likely to look clouded when the steam iron is removed and the finish will need to be restored using padding lacquer (page 75).

ural there is no need to apply any type of neutralizer. Some sediment may have settled in the strained liquid, and as a result, you may find a green or brown dust peppering the wood. This can be wiped away with a damp cloth after the wood dries.

Wetting and sanding the wood repeatedly will encourage the wood grain to rise to its maximum point—a point where the grain will no longer expand. This process ensures a smooth overall finish. It will also ensure that rough spots on the wood won't show up once stain or dye has been applied. (Layers of varnish and lacquer will only magnify blemishes in the wood.)

One lesson to learn from badly finished furniture is how not to use electric orbital sanders and air-powered circular sanders on wood. On poorly finished furniture squiggles and circular abrasions are telltale signs that such machines have been used improperly. Expending a little bit of effort to hand-sand furniture is preferable to machine sanding, we feel. If you do use a power sander, do your final sanding by hand, using a piece of sandpaper wrapped around a wood block that fits in the palm of your hand.

Painting on finish

Decorative Fill

Our pond scum solution turned the white oak a deep charcoal black, except for two light lines that ran the length of the top. Because there was less tannin and more sap in those bands, the chemical change that turned the wood color to black did not take place. This difference in coloration added to the natural color range of the finish and improved the look of the table, in our view.

Mixing fill

Sanding tabletop

Once the finish solution was completely dry (a few hours) the tabletop had turned a dull, slate gray color. The water in the solution had raised the wood grain slightly, and it was therefore necessary once again to sand the surface lightly with 320-grit silicon-carbide finishing paper. The object this time was to sand down the "hairy" wood fibers by sanding at a slight angle to the grain, thereby cutting off the fibers. Instead of sanding straight with the grain, you sand at an angle like this: /. The back-and-forth motion cuts the fibers of the wood off instead of pushing them back into the pores. Sand just lightly enough to smooth out the wood: sand with one hand and feel the results with the other. If you sanded correctly at the beginning it shouldn't take much work.

After sanding, to ensure that the wood pores were adequately cleaned out, we scrubbed the stained surface one more time with a wire brush, going with the grain. Then we dusted off the tabletop using a tack rag and applied a sealer coat of white shellac—a spit coat of five parts denatured alcohol to one part 3-pound cut shellac (page 46). We brushed this all over the top, sides, and legs, and allowed them to dry.

We then proceeded to mix a fill—a paste for filling pores in wood—to apply over the table using regular plaster of Paris and artists' dried

**TECHNIQUE TACTIC:
TIPS FOR SUCCESSFUL SANDING**

To achieve a smooth final finish, preliminary sanding is very important. Follow these directions to achieve a good finish:

- Always sand wood before any coloring agents or topcoats are applied.
- Begin by wetting the raw wood and allowing it to dry.
- When it is dry, sand the wood with the appropriate grit of sandpaper: open-pored woods such as oak may be sanded with 80-grit garnet or aluminum oxide sandpaper.
- Then wet the wood again and allow it to dry.
- Sand the wood with a higher-grit sandpaper (150 grit for oak).
- Repeat the wet/sand process two or three times as needed.

paint pigments for the filler—available at any art supply store. To make the mix, first combine the artists' dried pigment and dry plaster. Make more than enough to cover the entire surface to guarantee a consistency in color. Mix the dry powders thoroughly (wet a small amount in another container to check if the color is the one you want). When the fill is satisfactorily mixed, place a convenient amount in a small container (an old, discardable yogurt or ice cream container works well) and add enough water to make a pastelike slurry. Mix up only small amounts with a gloved finger as you go along because plaster sets up quickly—if you mix too much and you work too slowly, a large batch may dry out, leaving you with a lump of hard stuff resembling dried mayonnaise. Each working batch should have the consistency of a paste thick enough that if it is applied on a vertical surface it won't drip off (roughly the consistency of the world's most perfect food, Marshmallow Fluff).

Applying paste (fill)

Apply the paste with your fingers (wear medical examination gloves if you're squeamish). Rub the fill firmly into the wood, moving your fingers in a circular motion to force it into the pores of the table's surface.

Once the paste is spread over the entire surface, remove the excess by rubbing across the grain, first with your fingers, and then using a slightly dampened cloth. *Be sure to rub across the*

Removing excess paste with dampened cloth

grain. If you rub with the grain you may wipe the fill out of the wood pores.

When all of the excess paste had been removed, the tabletop took on a chalky look the color of the artists' pigment—vaguely resembling the complexion of Rolling Stones guitarist extraordinaire Keith Richards after two weeks on St. Barts. To rid the surface of this chalkiness we wet a rag, wrung it out well, and pulled it across the grain to reveal a glorious black-and-ochre color in the wood.

PERSONALITY PROFILE: GEORGE FRANK

In the 1920s, a Hungarian man named George Frank revolutionized the finishing industry in France by introducing a technique whereby the open grain of wood was filled with contrasting colors.

Frank had come from Hungary with a work permit specifying that he had completed an apprenticeship as a cabinetmaker and a diploma that certified him as a Master of Stains and Wood Coloring (which he attained by studying hard at night school). After working his way through several menial jobs, he was able to land a woodworking job where the salary and working conditions were good.

Furniture finishing wasn't the respected skill then that it is today. Wood-carvers were respected the most, followed by gilders. Frank did a lot of work on his own in his spare time. He experimented late at night with different finishing materials and methods, and singed a few nose hairs while trying out a few of the more radical ones.

Frank created a host of wood samples—all were dyed and had the pores filled with contrasting colors. The samples were finished using a technique called French polishing (page 98), a labor-intensive process that is really more of an art than a simple technique. These samples took more than five years to complete.

The place to work at the time was a company called Jansen, Inc., which was the most prestigious design firm, located in the very heart of Paris (where else would you want to be if you were Numero Uno?) on the Rue Royale. After three different cabinetmaking jobs between 1924 and 1928, Frank finally landed a job at Jansen after his samples had been presented to the big shots. Although Frank admits in both of his books, *Adventures in Wood Finishing* and *Wood Finishing with George Frank,* that he did not invent French polishing, he did invent the finishing technique of wood-pore filling: "By allowing this technique to become part of the public domain, I have helped pave the way for a monumental breakthrough in wood finishing."

So you see, it's important that we recognize this great man for what he has done for the finishing industry.

Thank You, Mr. Frank.

Sanding after paste removal

When the wood had dried from this final wiping we sanded lightly with 400-grit silicon cabide finishing paper to remove extraneous clumps of paste. Sand very lightly—you want to avoid cutting into the wood.

Now take a brief but deserved respite from pore filling before going on to the legs because, after all, we are leg men.

Painting the Legs

Remember that the legs on the table are ash and consequently cannot be blackened with the pond scum as the table surface was. We decided to deal with this situation by painting the legs a different color. We mixed some yellow oil paint with some flat white oil paint to approximate the color of the fill. This ultimately gave the legs a mustard color, which in turn evoked a craving for an Oscar Meyer wiener every time a certain Mr. Feldman of Philadelphia cast his eyes on the table.

Using a 2-inch Chinese bristle paintbrush, we applied the paint to the detached table legs, which had been sanded and shellacked earlier. When the paint dried (overnight) we sanded lightly with 320-grit silicon carbide finishing paper and applied a second coat of paint, wiping any excess dust off with a tack rag after each sanding. Because the white base paint was flat, not glossy, the paint dried to a flat luster. If we had wanted a shinier finish, we would have applied a varnish on the painted legs for a more lustrous effect. Had we had the time (the show is only 21 minutes long), we'd have varnished and sanded and varnished and sanded and varnished and sanded and then rubbed the final finish out to a full bright shine using steel wool and wax (page 56). The resulting table would have taken on a higher-class "Grey Pouponesque" look, though as the legs exist now, they have a more utilitarian or, shall we say, Gulden's hue.

Lacquering top

Lacquering the Top

We coated the top with lacquer because it is a durable and good-looking finish. We knew that this would ultimately become a well-used table placed behind a sofa and that lacquer would protect the table. We also wanted to reveal how easy brushing on lacquer is—most people are under the impression that it can only be applied by spraying it on. You can apply three coats of lacquer in one day; if you used varnish you'd have to wait a day between each coat. The crowning glory, of course, is that lacquer is the clearest of finishes, showing off to best

advantage the effects of the fill we applied earlier, along with the grain and the black stain.

Proceed with the lacquer as with varnish, pouring the lacquer to be applied from the can into another container. Be sure to use a clean "hair" bristle brush for brushing lacquer. You can use China bristle, which is hair from a Chinese pig—see, there's another fabulous fact you've learned!—or a badger brush, which costs a lot more but is a better applicator by far, though sadly a bad thing for our tiny badger friends. But, you ask, why is it a bad thing for the badger and not for the weighty hog? You ask too many questions. Read on. Load the brush with lacquer by dipping the bristles three quarters of the way into the lacquer. Avoid getting the ferrule—the shiny crimped metal band that wraps around the brush to hold the bristles in place—wet. Then drop the loaded brush gently onto the surface, but don't let go of the handle!

Pull the lacquer-loaded brush along the surface in a line about a foot long, and then dip the brush into the lacquer again (pulling the brush toward you will make the job easier). Brush on another coat beside the first one, pulling the brush along, matching the length of the first stroke. Continue dipping and pulling the brush along in 1-foot-long lengths until the surface is covered. Use full, wide strokes and pull the brush across the surface to even out the coats, starting at one edge and pulling the brush toward you.

Brushed-on lacquers dry more slowly than those that are sprayed, because they contain added drying retarders. The retarders slow drying time and allow brush marks to flow out as the surface levels. Don't rush, you have plenty of time—but don't get half done and go off for lunch.

We brushed on one coat and let it dry for a couple of hours, then sanded with 400-grit silicon carbide finishing paper, tack-ragged the top to remove the sanding dust, and applied a second lacquer coat. Once that had dried, we screwed the legs to the table and stood back, admiring our handiwork.

We could have worked on the finish a little

more by rubbing out the finish on the console table. Instead, we left that for our next project, where we will demonstrate how to create an

Oak console table "after"

even more wonderful-looking finish. But first we're off to France, where we'll talk about a style of furniture called Moderne.

Five

ART DECO,
or Fred and Ginger and Nick and Nora

To understand the antecedents, emergence, and ramifications of Art Deco furniture we must first examine and understand the Industrial Revolution and its bastard children: advertising and pop culture. "Whoa!" you say. You don't have time for all that nonsense? Well, to be honest, neither do we.

We will, however, present for you a quick overview of the last 100 years in furniture design. This will segue into what we really like to do (cough)—explaining how to hold a staple gun and paintbrush, tie a spring, and wipe on a stain, while simultaneously telling jokes and wearing dresses.

When last we left our furniture time line, Victorian furniture makers were running out of old styles to revive. If you recall, we covered Gothic Revival, Rococo Revival, and Renaissance Revival earlier in this book (pages 26–27). Furniture design subsequently evolved into a style that could be termed Reactionary/Synthesis, in which designers and artists developed new designs in reaction to previous, outmoded (or awful) designs essentially by copying them and reworking them into something "brand-new." Or more simply put: "This is mine and it's nice . . . that over there stinks."

At least the Revivalist designers had the guts and honesty to admit they were copying from past masters. And it's not as though furniture designs of the last century aren't exciting and original—rather, we believe, it is the rise of that multiheaded monster, hype, that forces designers onto soapboxes where even slight admissions of derivative influence in furniture design are a sign of weakness. The exceptions to these admissions are cited influences so obscure they succeed in furthering the reputation of the designer, as well as clouding the obvious, less obscure influence, William Morris—master furniture maker.

Allow us to explain (and it's about time, isn't it?). A major movement in the latter part of the nineteenth century was the Arts and Crafts movement. England's William Morris, furniture designer, maker, and taste purveyor to the Victorian masses, opened his own firm and banned Revivalist styles from his shop. He advocated a return to simplicity in design using more rectilinear shapes while maintaining a high degree of craftsmanship. The Arts and Crafts movement was the first design movement to be tied to political ideas (Napoleon's Empire style [page 27] notwithstanding). The mid-1800s saw the works of socialists and utopians being cited as the raison d'être for returning to basic honesty in the culture of the working people. And what better way to revolt against the bloated bourgeois lines of the Rococo (*et al.*) style than with the simple, well-made furniture designed by William Morris and his pals?

The truth of the matter, however, was that simple, well-made furniture was already being made by working-class people—and had been for hundreds of years in villages and towns all over the world. William Morris wasn't really as revolutionary as he thought he was. Some, such as the Shakers, have gotten credit for their designs, but other folks such as the Swedes, the Pennsylvanian Germans, and hundreds of other primitives—craftsmen and women who had been building furniture for themselves and others in their villages since the Dark Ages—watched as their designs were appropriated by others. Common Old World craftsmen before William Morris's time were denied entrance to the salons of high society but went merrily ahead making the same sturdy furniture they had always made. And because they hadn't been exposed to mainstream design changes it was impossible for them to rebel. Simple as that. Today, examples of simple country furniture that is now called "primitive" can be found at many country auctions.

The real development in the mid-nineteenth century that gave rise to political consciousness *cum* pontificating (boy are we two to talk) was the rise of the middle class. While the nobility had always had their own craftspeople working for them, their numbers were small. The rise of the middle class and their sheer numbers created a need for mass-produced furniture. The rise of the middle class in turn gave rise to large Victorian houses with parlors, sitting rooms, studies, and nurseries that needed to be filled with furniture. The easiest way for these new consumers to get hip to the tastes of the time was to buy a book like the one that you're holding in your hands. Back in the 1870s Charles Eastlake's *Hints on Household Taste* became a sort of classic (much like what we're hoping will happen with this book). Eastlake preached simplicity and spoke in terms that appealed to the Victorian middle class. He later achieved great success in America. Could this man have been the Martha Stewart of the nineteenth century?

Eastlake's book created a craze in interior decoration all over England and America. Magazines on the subject multiplied along with the amount of furniture and bric-a-brac filling the Victorian homes of the day. As you can see, yuppies weren't Ronald Reagan's invention (though the parallels to the Ulysses S. Grant Administration are eerie).

While not generally grouped in with the Arts and Crafts movement, Eastlake designs have certain similar characteristics: simplicity of shape, a lack of Revivalist excess, and the first "high-style" relationship of form to function.

Let us retreat a little by saying that most Arts and Crafts furniture was truly original, even inspired. It reveals what can be accomplished when talented craftsmen combine simple design and use fine wood in building their furniture.

Now, here's a heavy dose of design irony: The proponents of the Arts and Crafts movement in England who largely rejected modern industrial society (read mass-produced furniture) were now designing furniture with exposed hinges and joints with an absence of any hand-carved elements. Here was a design that was made for mass production if there ever was one.

But did these toffee-nosed back-to-nature snobs set up such an operation?

Noooooooooo.

It was beneath them. It took an American son of a stonemason by the name of Gustav Stickley to see and exploit the absolute beauty of the design. In 1898, Stickley, already successful in the furniture business, took a trip to Europe. On his return he exhibited his work at the Grand Rapids Furniture Exhibition, showing simple oak furniture made with plain oak boards, made to highlight the beauty of the wood. The design and features of the furniture had an Arts and Crafts influence but with a character that was totally American. The style became known as Mission. It features design details that include exposed mortise-and-tenon construction, where horizontal wood elements are joined to vertical ones with the joints exposed and not covered with decorative elements with upholstered caps, and simple flat iron hardware. The wood used is always quarter-sawn white oak, finished by fuming. The process involved erecting several tents made of heavy canvas inside of which several pieces of furniture were placed. Vats of ammonia were then wheeled in and uncovered. The tents were sealed tightly and the ammonia gas reacted with the tannin in the wood (and wooden you?), changing the wood's color from a pale yellow to a beautiful warm brown, which was then shellacked and polished.

Stickley did not like the title Mission and preferred calling it Craftsman Furniture. Some believe this moniker to be an homage to the Arts and Crafts Movement, but we suspect it has something more to do with his trying to wrangle an early endorsement deal from the then fledgling tool company Sears and Roebuck, which makes Craftsman brand tools. But the real reason is much more interesting and clever: Stickley was a businessman and his businessman sense told him to place the Craftsman name on his own line of manufactured furniture and home furnishings. He even went so far as to affix the Craftsman name to houses! All of these could then be purchased through ads he placed in his own magazine called (guess what?) *The Craftsman.*

The magazine's articles extolled the virtues of Stickley's designs and were flanked by numerous pictures and ads for furniture, knickknacks, and housewares all made by . . . you guessed it, Stickley and others of the same ilk. This was probably the first appearance of the advertorial. Though the magazine discussed and examined other designs it's pretty obvious it was an advertising vehicle promoting Stickley's designs and products.

The upshot of all this is that the most important design concept shaping twentieth-century furniture styles had its intellectual roots in the Arts and Crafts movement, where form follows function. Countless country craftspeople and cooperative groups such as the Shakers had always followed this principle and incorporated this philosophy into their own designs.

More Artsy-Fartsy Stuff

Another furniture design that had its roots in a deeply intellectual movement was Art Furniture. This aesthetic movement was a forerunner to the 1960s, when flower children with middle-class roots rejected tired middle-class values for something new. Those embracing the aesthetic values of Art Furniture were also middle-class rebels who rejected the accepted truths of the day that were tied to strict Victorian morals and designs. This even included rejecting Queen Victoria herself. The movement's chief spokesman was Oscar Wilde (who we like to think of as the Michael Jackson of his time, but with a very bad barrister).

Wilde very much favored the design of Art Furniture, which drew on motifs based on Japanese and Gothic styles: sinuous carvings, floral elements, and spindles which were usually painted black. Interior spaces boasted pale painted walls rather than the decorative patterned papers popular at the time. In short, Art Furniture had nothing in common with overbearing Victorian design. Although Art Furniture rejected the histrionics of the Victorian Revival styles, it unfortunately rejected much of its comfort as well. Wilde's love of sparsely decorated rooms apparently did not prepare him for his sparsely decorated jail cell after his set-to with the Marquis of Queensbury, a lover, no doubt, of the aesthete's archenemy, Rococo. . . .

> *Speaking of Wilde brings to mind a story concerning the young Richard Boone, who we find working behind the counter at Schwab's, where he got his first big break. The porcelain-skinned Hurd Hatfield had already signed for the title role in* The Picture of Dorian Gray *and was ordering his usual breakfast of two poached eggs atop a mound of corned beef hash with black rye toast. Boone turned to look at the waitress when she yelled, "Adam and Eve on Blarney and burn the wood!"*
>
> *Hatfield saw him and swallowed hard. Hatfield was reported to have exclaimed, "That face . . . that's the face we need in the picture!"*
>
> *Boone grimaced. . . .*

Art Nouveau

A combination of the Arts and Crafts movement and the Aesthetic movement created the Art Nouveau style, which blossomed in the early twentieth century. Art Nouveau derived its elements from nature and appealed to those who rejected the more aggressive Victorian revivalist styles with their intricate, ornate carvings copying Gothic and Rococo themes replete with claws, heads, and the occasional full dragon. Art Nouveau satisfied those with a craving for a more naturalistic and organic ambiance. Although Nouveau spread in the furniture world, it became more popular when incorporated into the decorative arts such as lamps, glassware, and jewelry. Its most prominent theme became the plant, with sinewy fronds, gently curving leaves, and vines that created a latticework. These elements were displayed most prominently on the backs of chairs and cabinets. While Art Nouveau copied nature, Art Deco combined nature with a machine-age angularity influenced by a combination of Cubist art and the burgeoning discipline of industrial design. Art Deco became the first furniture style to glorify the industrial age in the very theme of its designs—streamlined trains, cars, and ships depicted in carvings and etched mirrors.

Mackintosh—Not the Apple

Every school of design is easily enough described by its basic elements, historical antecedents, and famous adherents (yeah, sure). While designers who worked within these styles certainly have their individual charms, it takes a true artist to create and synthesize their own style into something that has such individualistic elements that it rises above the constricting labels that we have been laying on you. Such a man was Charles Rennie Mackintosh. Mackintosh was an architect of the Glasgow School of Art. He is to furniture design what the great Thelonious Monk is to jazz (without the collection of fanciful hats). In other words, his work defies categorization because he works outside the mainstream.

No Sauerkraut in This Apple Basket

Mackintosh's impact can be felt throughout the history of twentieth-century design in both the Bauhaus and Moderne schools. Often referred to as an Art Nouveau designer, Mackintosh's shapes are more rectilinear than typical Nouveau and borrow from the Arts and Crafts movement—incorporating various Celtic designs, the most predominant being interlocking wood gridwork on chairbacks that echo the tartan plaid from his Highland home. Upon visiting the Highlands and viewing the Mackintosh archives we discovered that one of his particularly clever marketing ploys was to present buyers of his dining sets with free coupons for a pound of haggis. This offer wasn't popular beyond Scotland's borders, and in other parts of the world a tam-o'-shanter was substituted for the haggis.

While Mackintosh was peddling his designs in Scotland, over in Vienna, Josef Hoffmann was taking cues from Mackintosh. Hoffmann was the founder of the Wiener Werkstätte—not a hot dog stand but the Viennese version of the popular Arts and Crafts movement. That is to say, the Wiener Werkstätte advocated a return to the handmade furniture made by happy workers laboring together in harmony, munching on a sandwich, sauerkraut, and sipping a cool drink at lunch.

Meanwhile, across the Atlantic, architect and designer Frank Lloyd Wright, based in Wisconsin and New Mexico, began integrating the designs of Hoffmann and Mackintosh into the designs of the homes he himself was building. The motto "Buy the home, buy the furniture" could never be more true than in the case of Frank Lloyd Wright's designs.

Much of the furniture designed by these visionaries in the early part of the twentieth century was meticulously made and beautiful to look at it, but the truth of the matter was that it was totally impractical as furniture because it didn't function well; it was designed solely for its thematic unity with their house designs (which nobody had to sit on). Sitting on a Frank Lloyd Wright dining chair is like sitting on a low, hard stool with an ironing board at your back. But do you think Wright cared? Of course not; his clients had all paid in advance, the house was built, the roof was already leaking, and he was in New Mexico aggravating his maid.

To politely debunk another influence theory, Wright often preached that the low, boxy design of his houses, which in turn influenced his furniture, was the result of his having grown up in the flat prairie country of the Midwest, though any fool can plainly see that he was deriving his inspiration from Japanese design. Here again we advise all designers not to be ashamed of their real influences. Then, when it comes time for us to write about designers and their influences we won't have to expose them as the thieves—er, synthesizers—they were.

Waiting for Art Deco

This trend toward the modern, sometimes radical (and often unsittable) creations we've just described would have continued had it not been disrupted by a short yet nasty interlude called World War I, or the Great War (or *WWI*, starring Marlene Dietrich and Richard Barthlemess, with music by George M. Cohan . . .).

This four-year escapade was a rather rude awakening for those with naïve notions pertaining to furniture craft cooperatives, a return to simplicity, and other loosey-goosey ideas. Postwar design therefore became more influenced by industry than by pastoral country crafts. The world was now seen as a cruel, spinning top in which the upper classes demanded and got their luxuries while the working masses received the leftovers, as well as the corned beef hash from three nights before.

But luckily for the masses (especially those in America) the rapidly growing furniture industry was able to provide, for the first time, reasonably priced, mass-produced versions of the latest furniture styles. This dynamic is seen most clearly in the development and dissemination of the Moderne or Art Deco style. (Whew! You never thought we'd get there, huh?)

Art Deco, also known as Moderne, takes its name from a Parisian exhibition that was held in 1925 called L'Exposition Internationale des Arts Decoratifs et Industriels Modernes, which translated meant, ahh—for the true translation you'll have to send 25 cents to: Furniture Guys, Very Heavy Industries, Third House on the Left, Behind the Abandoned Furniture Shop, U.S.A.

Just kidding. Translated, it reads: The International Exposition of Decorative Arts and Modern Industry. Many Art Deco designers had been turning out examples of their work for some years before this gathering in 1925, but the Exposition revealed to the world that something new was afoot. And what a foot it was!

The Exhibition's name defined a brand-new synthesis of design styles that were influenced by the mechanized world, not only in how they were manufactured, but also in the ideas behind their actual creation.

As with Empire furniture a century before, this new French design drew on many international influences. These influences ran the gamut from the Far East—with Chinese lacquer work becoming very popular—to Egyptian and Aztec designs. So-called Jazz Modern, which drew on the hard-cut angular patterns pioneered by Georges Braque and Pablo Picasso in their cubist paintings, also exerted an influence on Art Deco.

Cubism, in fact, was the overriding artistic movement at this time. The influence of the mechanized world on art became recognizable first in the works of the Cubists before World War I, and these aspects were now being incorporated into furniture design. French Deco is especially fascinating because of the diversity of influences it drew on, from the exotic emblems of tribal antiquities to the futuristic patterns derived from the most recent creations of the industrial world. All were covered in veneers of the rarest type. Add about 50 hours of French polishing (page 98) and you have the rare beauty of Art Deco. But is Deco for the masses? Think again, François; this was luxury Deco, strictly meant for the upper crust.

All Hail Old Glory

It took manufacturers in the United States to translate and make this style accessible to the working class. While high-class Deco swept into our collective consciousness through the images of Fred Astaire tap-dancing away in Continental locales and on the Deco-inspired ocean liner *Normandie,* designers in the States had already begun to adapt Deco in their own way. In American Deco, the design influences of the French were still apparent, but the use of materials changed radically. As a substitute for exotic veneers, manufacturers turned to early plastics such as Bakelite and catalin. Chrome, steel, aluminum, and other metals that were already being used by the German Bauhaus school were employed decoratively, as well as structurally. In this way, American Deco was more stylistically aligned with the Modernity theory behind Deco than with the use of industrial and synthetic materials for their own sake.

The signature features of American Deco were frosted, etched glass and black lacquer. Although veneers were used extensively, they were never as sumptuous as those created by the French, which were made from Brazilian and Indian rosewoods, Macassar Ebony, Burl Amboyna (AM-BOY-NYA), Burl Thuya (TO-YA), Burl Ives (Frosty the Snowman), and Palm (which was very costly and hard to work with because the high quantity of silica in the wood's resin dulled saw blades). These veneers were always French-polished.

Ironically, just as Deco began to get popular in the United States, so did airborne stockbrokers, bread lines, and apple carts. The most exposure the average Joe had to the Deco style during the Great Depression was through a barrage of advertising and through the designs of public buildings, where gargoyles, balustrades, and voluptuous naked Greek people were replaced with sunbursts, lightning bolts made of chrome, amorphous shapes, and more naked Greek people (though they appeared much skinnier and more angular this time around). Let this be a cue to all fledgling designers, as well as those yet to be born: Styles may come and styles may go, but naked people are always good.

Art Deco was also highly visible in the popular magazines of the day, which showed various Hollywood starlets recumbent on chaise longues spraying their swanlike necks with Shalimar from Cubist cut-glass atomizers. In darkened theaters across America and around the world, everyone was watching the swirling dances of Fred and Ginger, listening to the sophisticated patter of Nick and Nora, and becoming enraptured by the lush elegance of Marlene Dietrich. They all danced, chatted, and sashayed through frosted-glass-and-black-lacquered salons dispensing gibsons from shiny chrome cocktail shakers. Ahhh . . . all this while most of America sat on milk crates eating potatoes off a stick.

On the other hand, maybe this highly decorative and sumptuous style was just what America needed in its time of austerity, even if it was only being viewed on a flickering silver screen from the balcony of a movie theater. Of course, anyone could have come into contact with Art Deco if they wanted to by simply walking through the Chrysler Building in New York City and touching the various Deco elements that line the building's hallways. And did you know that the cocktail table was a by-product of the era itself? Lowered chair heights resulted in lower tables. With the rise of the post–WWI bourgeoisie in Europe, the cocktail was a welcome friend who would not talk back.

We would like to postulate that Art Deco was the last form of decorative representationalism; that is, art (or design) that attempts to depict an object that exists—the opposite of abstract in furniture design. The same could be said of Cubism, from which Art Deco borrowed many of its design cues. Cubist art was a prismatic explosion of what the artist's eye beheld. Talk all you want about the lady with the pointy nose where her ear should have been and both her eyes all cockeyed and crazy; but she was a lady—a crazy lady, but a lady nonetheless.

It was the same with Art Deco design: there were crazy and wild etchings of angular figures, some drawn from nature, some from science, but there was ornamentation nonetheless. The ornamentation didn't add to the functionality of the piece nor to its tensile strength, but the decorative elements were pretty to look at. In contrast, the next great movement, or design school—which happens to overlap with the Deco school in the great time line of furniture history—did away with any and all traces of bourgeois sentimentality and design in favor of pure function (it will be sardonically commented upon by us in a later chapter). This style has come to be known as Mid-century Modern, because no one can figure out what else to call it.

Our next two projects are fine representations from the Art Deco or Moderne period. They combine simplicity of design with modular construction. These elements of design made it quite easy for us (thank goodness) to refinish and reupholster them.

We wanted to be faithful to the luxurious aspect of the Moderne style by choosing a plush mohair fabric for the chair, and though the table was not French-polished (mainly because we didn't have the time) we will present the instructions for creating a French polish.

Project 6:

MODERNE CHAIR

So where do you go when you need a Moderne chair?

You go to a place that might be called Art Deco Palace, or if you're in Hollywood you can go to Bruce Dern's brother's place: Mo Dern's Emporium. We live in Philadelphia, so once we had wiped the cheese steak grease from our hands, we decided to go to a store called Moderne, which houses some of the finest examples of Deco furniture in the city. The owner, Bob, is a friend of ours, though he would prefer you to believe otherwise. The most important reason we chose this establishment, however, was that it is right down the street from Joe's place.

Now's a good time to tell you how masterfully we come by the projects you see us toiling over on the show. In the first shows, see, it was kind of easy. We had a lot of crappy old furniture stored in our homes that needed fixing, so we used what we had. When we had finished with these pieces and had completed taping our TV shows, they went back into our homes for more abuse.

After a while, the furniture in our houses looked quite nice. Before we knew it our homes became showplaces that we would often rent out for large weddings or movie-set wrap parties. You may have caught a glimpse of Ed's rec room in Scorsese's *Age of Innocence* or Joe's king-size walnut Victorian bed, which was used in Coppola's *Bram Stoker's Dracula*.

Nowadays, we usually have ongoing struggles finding ideal pieces to fix on the show. When we do find them, they must meet certain criteria. First, they must not resemble any of the furniture we have already fixed on the show—it's enough that people have to put up with the same us day in and day out! Second, the actual repair or process of finish or upholstery must be interesting. Even though Ed expresses a desire to do a button segment every show, I have saved you all from seeing that by giving him doughnuts.

Another way we acquire projects for the show is through our friends in the furniture business. In our city there are hundreds of antique shops, thrift stores, auction houses, and vintage furniture stores with inventories for every taste and every style. There are outlets specializing in Mission style furniture and others that specialize only in Deco. Some of these outlets have been featured on our show—we're seen going through the places sharing the expertise and wit of the personnel working there. We get a lot of furniture by promising never to go back to the store. Sometimes this strategy works well, but at other times the furniture stores have a restraining order issued immediately.

Which brings us back full circle to Bob Aibel, the owner and proprietor of Moderne, otherwise known as the Dean of Deco or the Maven of Moderne. We taped a TV segment with him in his showroom, which houses many exquisite examples of Moderne cabinetry and various chairs covered with sumptuous, solid geometric fabrics. The pieces displayed in his main showroom were all ready for examination and sale to those with equally sumptuous bank accounts. Bob goes to France periodically (without us, we might add) and purchases vast amounts of native furniture, which he then ships back to his store. Some of it is ready for placement on the showroom floor immediately, while some pieces need attention. When Bob tires of Mickey Rourke film festivals and the Jerry Lewis pay-per-view channel (that's 1-800-L*A*D*Y), he makes his way back home to supervise the restoration of the work.

Furniture awaiting restoration is housed on the store's second floor, along with the appropriate facilities for spray shellacking and spray painting furniture. We looked around the second floor and found two suitable projects: a small mahogany cocktail table that would need full stripping and refinishing and our *projet du jour*— a small French chair or, as we like to call it, "*la chaise de Lautrec.*" (As an interesting side note, in his portrayal of Henri de Toulouse-Lautrec in the John Huston film *Moulin Rouge,* the distinguished actor José Ferrer worked at his actual full

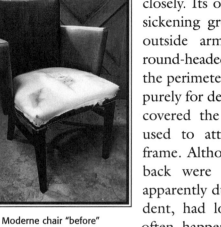

Moderne chair "before"

height of four feet six inches for the only time in his career. In all his other roles, he was perched atop prosthetic legs that gave viewers the illusion that he was the height of an average man.)

Let us examine the chair more closely. Its original upholstery was a sickening green vinyl. Its back and outside arms were studded with round-headed upholstery tacks along the perimeters. These tacks were not purely for decorative purposes—they covered the staples that had been used to attach the fabric to the frame. Although the chair arms and back were upholstered, the seat, apparently due to some French accident, had lost its upholstery. This often happens when you have the deadly combination of vinyl, a hot summer day, and a fat lady in culottes (another French creation). The damage occurs when the bonding of perspiring flesh and vinyl creates a mighty vacuum that literally sucks and tears the seat vinyl loose from its moorings. Bob informed us that the *derriere* in question had in fact belonged to Madame de Gaulle.

Materials List

- Mohair fabric (1½ square yards)
- Naphtha
- Lint-free cloth or paper tools
- Methanol (alcohol) dye
- Spray-on lacquer
- 0000-grade steel wool
- Tack rag
- Burlap
- 2-inch-thick foam-rubber padding
- Dacron padding or cotton batting
- White muslin
- Aluminum and cardboard tack strips
- Cambric

Tool List

- Tack puller
- Locking pliers (for loosening chair panel bolts)
- Rubber gloves
- Spray booth
- Respirator
- Electric carving knife for cutting foam rubber
- Staple gun
- Rubber or hickory mallet

Removing decorative tacks with tack puller

We began by removing each decorative tack with tack pullers. We took care not to bend the nail shafts as we removed them and sealed them in a jar for later use. (Remember, intending to recycle something is almost as noble an act as actually recycling.)

Once the tacks had been removed, we then proceeded to remove the staples holding the vinyl in place. We were also careful in removing the staples because we wanted to keep the vinyl intact to use as a template for cutting the new fabric we planned to use in reupholstering the chair. The outside back and arms were covered by a single piece of fabric that, when laid out, resembled the cowl of the French crime fighter Mike Armoire. Because the original designers of the chair had covered it with this full-piece back and arm panel, they had had to use decorative tacks to hide the staples that ran around the chair's perimeters. For reasons we will explain, we chose to create separate outside arm and back panels.

We decided to cover the chair with mohair. Yes, you read it right, mohair. This cream-colored fabric is attractive, luxurious-looking, and representative of fabrics used in the Moderne era. But it had one feature which made it less than ideal for this particular project: The nap of mohair is considerably high. We used the mohair because Bob, the chair's owner, wanted us to use it; he said it was in keeping with the era and style of the piece, though we think it was because he had it lying around and wanted to use it up. Nap refers to the tiny fibers that stand up perpendicular to the woven cloth. The nap of the mohair fabric, if magnified, would reveal a bristly prominence like the burr cut sported by the late Frank Sutton—known to millions as the irascible Sgt. Vince Carter on the show *Gomer Pyle U.S.M.C.*

Because of the chair's diminutive size and its streamlined design, the mohair needed to be tightly folded at the corners where the edges of the fabric ended. The fabric in many cases would have to be folded over itself to accommodate the corners, creating a double thickness of fabric along the edges. Due to its thick nap, folding the mohair in this manner would create bunching and noticeable bulges that would inevitably detract from the clean lines of the chair. It would also expose the base fabric beneath the nap when folded sharply at the edges of the arm and back.

With all the vinyl stripped away, we discovered that the chair had been modularly constructed in four discrete sections. Each section was connected to a neighboring section with a series of threaded bolts and nuts. The back unit included the seat back and rear legs; the seat unit was made up of the seat and front legs. The arms were able to be removed by using a set of locking pliers (Vise-Grips) to loosen threaded bolts hidden in the recessed areas of the chair.

Modularity was an important feature of the Moderne style. It allowed for high-speed assembly because individual workers could produce individual parts that would later be bolted together by a guy named Lucky Pierre—so named because he was the only one lucky enough to see the whole chair put together. We appreciated the modularity of the chair because it allowed us to upholster each part separately before reassembly. This is why we decided not to use a single piece of fabric to cover the outside arms and back as the original designers had done; we cut three separate panels instead.

We reused three separate cardboard panels defining the curved shape of the chair's inside back and arms beneath the padding. There was also a cardboard panel defining the curve on the outside that we decided not to reuse because the mohair was so thick that it didn't need stiffening.

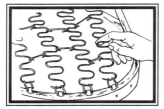

Seat with padding removed, showing zigzag springs

With the seat padding removed we discovered that the underlying zigzag springs were in tip-top condition. Zigzag, or "no-sag," springs look like the wavy metal bands that reside beneath your buttocks in most furniture made today. What makes these springs different from the coil springs? The answer must be indelibly embedded in your mind after the Rites of Springs section of Project 2 (page 33). Zigzag springs are cheaper to manufacture and much easier to install, and that pretty much explains their popularity among the venal furniture manufactures of today. This wasn't always the case: zigzags came into use because designs—particularly in the case of Moderne—demanded them. Coil springs, though more resilient than zigzags, require a little headroom in seats and chairbacks. Zigzags, because they are stretched across an area and do not take up precious vertical space, allow for greater freedom when designing furniture. Seats and backs made with zigzag springs can be made stylishly thin and adjusted to take on almost any shape, making them ideal in Moderne, Bauhaus, and other twentieth-century design schools eschewing the deep, boxy designs made by their furniture forefathers.

Applying dye

With the chair disassembled and stripped down to the springs, we proceeded to refinish the exposed wood surrounding the seat's base and extending to the legs. Every upholstery project demands that you make repairs and do any finishing before attaching any kind of expensive fabric to a piece. (Have you ever seen a chair where the finishing was done after the upholstery was applied? We have. It isn't pretty.)

The wood on the legs was poplar that had been mahoganized (page 29). We didn't want to strip the finish off because it was still in good shape, and who needed the extra aggravation anyway? In some spots the legs showed scratches, but these were minor defects that could later be hidden cosmetically (page 119).

The first thing that had to be done was to clean the legs using a naphtha-saturated cloth or paper towels (page 43). We then stained the legs with a dark-red mahogany dye, which is the same dye we use for the table in our next project (this is known as a sneak preview). These dyes are called ultra-penetrating and are methanol- (alcohol-) based. They dry quickly and have deep wood-penetrating qualities—be sure to wear gloves when working with dyes. Use paper towels to wipe the dye onto the wood speedily but gently. The methanol in the dye's base could potentially soften and destroy a lacquered surface if the dye is allowed to sit on it for any length of time, making it important that the dye be applied sparingly and lightly.

Using spray gun in spray booth

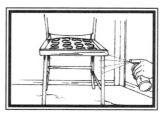

Using spray can in spray booth

Once the legs had been dyed they were allowed to dry for an hour, readying them for a new spray coat of lacquer. We used a professional-grade spray gun hooked to an air compressor to carry out this process. We even went to the extent of constructing a small spray booth out of wood and plastic. The plans came from a book we had purchased, and though this contraption had a small fan attached to it, it was not really designed to suck large quantities of noxious fumes from the surrounding area but made to fit conveniently on a tabletop. The sides, back, and top shielded the object being sprayed from dust, while the small fan would expel excess lacquer, called "overspray," away from the piece (Overspray can settle on and mar a newly lacquered surface). **Warning:** We do not recommend that anyone use spray guns or build spray booths in their basements. First of all, you run the risk of flooding your neighborhoods with swirling clouds of noxious fumes, re-creating the scene from an old *Outer Limits* episode called "A Feasibility Study" where a city block is picked up and transported to another planet and all that's left behind is a giant smoking crater. So, if you start playing around with spraying nitrocellulose lacquers in the confines of your tiny basement, the pilot light of your furnace may erupt and send you out beyond the Magellanic Clouds.

Lacquer that comes in aerosol cans is much thinner in consistency than brushing lacquer. It needs to be thin in order to get through the little pin hole of the push button at the top of the can. Because the lacquer is so thin, more coats usually have to be applied. It is suggested that two or three thin coats are better than one thick coat.

Spray-can lacquers can also be used on small projects like the one here because the areas to be covered are relatively small. Covering the legs and arms of a chair is not as extensive as covering a five-foot-long tabletop. Be sure the can is full. Canned sprays have a tendency to spit as they become less full, so it's best to use two or three full cans until each can is half full.

On the show, we placed the chair inside the spray booth after loading the gun with clear gloss lacquer that was diluted with lacquer thinner. We donned respirators equipped with the appropriate filters (if you're spraying lacquer, use a full face mask to protect your eyes) and pulled the trigger on the gun to coat the legs and adjoining wood parts. The new lacquer immediately brightened the otherwise dingy wood. We allowed the lacquer to dry for about an hour and did a light buffing with some 0000-grade steel wool and tack-ragged the chair. We then sprayed on a second coat. All lacquer coats that are

sanded should be tack-ragged before applying another coat of finish.

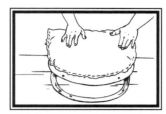

Placing burlap over springs

Placing foam core and cotton batting over burlap

And Now for the Upholstery

With the wood finished, we could begin upholstering the chair. The first element that we had to deal with was the seat, since it is the first part your body comes in contact with when you sit down (unless you are getting on in years and need to first place your gnarled and wrinkled fingers on the arms in order to aim your posterior, after which you utter the great "ummmpht"—the "taking the load off" sigh).

The zigzag springs were sturdy, tight, and not rusted, so we left them as is. There are two basic ways to pad a seat: One way is to add many layers of thin padding, such as when thin foam is followed by thin Dacron or cotton batting, building up a seat to nice, soft loft for an overstuffed look and feel. Although this is a common procedure, it would be impractical for a small chair such as ours. The second way to pad a seat—and the one more suited for a small, tight-seated chair such as ours—is to create a firmer, self-contained pad that would provide additional support on top of the zigzag springs. Zigzag springs are not as sturdy as coil springs and work best in a rigidly padded, tight seat. A sturdy pad also prevents the zigzag springs from leaving wavy indentations on your buttocks after you've been sitting for a while.

Before laying in any padding, we stretched a solid piece of burlap (not webbing) over the top of the springs, and tacked it to the perimeter of the seat frame. On this bed of burlap, we laid the beveled foam core. For additional comfort and loft we added two inches of cotton batting atop the foam.

The original padding used in the chair seat was a sandwichlike affair consisting of horsehair (a very sturdy material) surrounded or sandwiched by cotton batting. We could have reused the sandwich padding in the same way we reused the padding in our Throne Chair project in Chapter 2, but since we had already done it on that project, we dared to be different this time. We used a hunk of 2-inch dense foam trimmed to the seat's shape with an electric carving knife. Using the electric carving knife enabled us to bevel the edge down and away from the top so as to conform to the angle at which we would be pulling the seat fabric over the pad.

At the foam store (look in the Yellow Pages under "Foam Rubber"), you will find many densities of foam available. Foam comes in many grades or densities, the same as people's skulls. The softest grades of foam are usually used for pillows while the hardest are used for seats.

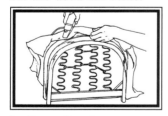

Stapling muslin to frame

None of the padding could be attached to the chair seat. Rather, it had to be secured by a sheet of white muslin cut to overhang the chair sides when laid over the padding. We pulled, stretched, and tacked the muslin to the bottom of the frame, first tacking the muslin in place at the center of the front rail. Next, we pulled the muslin to the back rail and tacked it to the underside and center of the back rail, and then stapled in the centers at the sides. This process may be better conceptualized in terms of a clock face: first sta-

---

TECHNIQUE TACTIC: SOLVING PLEAT PROBLEMS

Pulling the fabric tightly at the centerpoints will create deep pleats in the muslin. To ensure an even, smooth surface, make sure that you pull the fabric tightly over the edge of the frame as you continue stapling the muslin to the frame. As the fabric is stretched, the tension will eliminate unsightly creases. Attaching muslin is good practice for later fabric attachment.

TECHNIQUE TACTIC: DEMERITS FOR DIMPLING

When upholstering, avoid stapling padding to the frame. If padding is stapled in place you run the risk of creating depressions created by the staples, which will show up as little craters or dimples and will be visible even after the fabric is attached. Padding should always be held in place by wrapping it with muslin and then attaching the muslin to the frame.

---

ple in at 12, then staple at 6, then 9, and finally 3. Each time you staple, remember to pull the muslin tightly outward from the center. Then staple between the center anchor staples, always remembering to pull tightly before pulling the trigger. Fill in all spaces between the staples until you have a tight and smooth surface.

We proceeded to upholster the chair's inside back. The upholstery process was greatly simplified because of the chair's modular construction: on a normal, nonmodular chair the fabric would have to be pulled through the cracks in between the seat and back before stapling.

With the chair lying before us in sections, each of the willing supplicants (the seat, back, and arms) awaited our attention and could be attended to individually, in any order. The inside panels needed to be upholstered and the chair reassembled before proceeding on to the outside panels, which could be done when the chair was reassembled.

We upholstered the inside back by tearing a generous amount of cotton batting from the roll and shaped it into a trapezoid, mimicking the shape of the back itself, and placed it atop the existing cardboard panel. We did not remove this panel because it was in good shape and its curvature defined the inside surface. If you ever work on a chair like this, you want to encourage the cotton batting to wrap over the frame by pushing it between the fabric and the frame, which will create rounded edges when the fabric is attached over the top. Using the same stapling procedure as on the seat, we next stretched muslin over the padding of the inside back and tacked it to the frame on the outside back. The arms are handled in the same way (very little brain surgery involved here) by applying cotton batting over the cardboard panels and securing the cotton in place by covering it with a sheet of muslin pulled around the frame and stapled into the outside perimeter of the frame. We did not staple the muslin to the top of the frame but to the edge that faced away from the chair. We repeated the same process on the other arm.

With all the inside panels covered with muslin, the chair components were ready to be covered with mohair.

Laying mohair over seat

To begin upholstering with our mohair, we had to think long and hard about how to wrap the thick-napped mohair fabric around the small, tight corners on the chair. Cutting the seat fabric was easy enough: we simply traced the outline of the seat and added about 6 inches on each side. Then we spread the fabric over the top of the seat. We began stapling the mohair in place by firing a staple through the fabric and into the underside of the seat frame at the centerpoint on the back. Pulling the mohair over the front of the seat, we anchored the mohair on the underside of the front of the chair frame with a staple in the center.

Then, we did the same thing as we did with the muslin—we pulled the sides tight and fired staples into the fabric and underside of the chair frame at 3 and 9 o' clock positions.

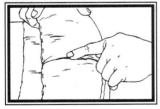
Pleats in back of chair seat

Because the back of this chair seat is semicircular in shape and the mohair fabric was quite thick there was no way, no matter how hard we pulled, to upholster the back of the chair seat without creating pleats.

We made two pleats at the back of the chair equidistant from the centerpiece where we had first stapled—points where the rear chair legs would hide the pleats once the back had been re-

attached. Aren't we clever? You'll be clever too; just keep reading. We continued stapling the material, all the while pulling it tight and attaching it to the underside of the seat frame toward the front legs. Once we reached the front legs, we made a cut in the fabric up from the bottom to enable us to fold it flush with the back of the front legs.

Stapling fabric near legs

Stapling at vertical fold

Stapling along underside near vertical fold

Then we pulled the fabric tightly to one side between the front and back legs, stapling as close as possible to the legs on the underside of the chair seat frame. (We would later cut the excess fabric and trim it flush with chair legs.) On the front of the seat we finished stapling the fabric to the underside of the frame on each side of the center, anchoring staples right up to the front legs.

At each seat corner, we made a crisp vertical fold that visually continued (and aligned with) the vertical line of the front chair leg. Again, because the fabric was thick, we had to make this fold tight and had to trim any and all excess fabric beneath the fold before so it did not look as if a small animal had burrowed in and was hiding in there waiting to attack. At the bottom of the folded corner, we stapled in flush to the very top of each chair leg. We repeated this process with the other corner and finished our work on the seat.

Making release cuts

Upholstering the inside back of the chair was our next task. This was easy to do, because the chair was completely disassembled. The curved cardboard sheet that defined the inside back was still intact, so after writing some smutty French phrases on it in magic marker, we proceeded to cover it with cotton batting and then tacked a sheet of white muslin over the top.

We then moved on to covering the inside back with fabric. Since the back of the chair included the back legs, release cuts had to be made at the bottom of the fabric piece precisely at the point where the legs attached at the bottom of the back. Release cuts are made to enable the fabric to be pulled around both sides of the legs without bunching. A release cut is made by using scissors to cut a Y-shaped slit in the fabric. The triangle between the arms of the Y is then folded under, so that only the napped outer surface of the fabric is visible. The fold is pulled under the chair and anchored to the wood on the underside of the chair seat. We repeated these steps on both corners of the seat where it met the leg.

As is always the case, whenever a piece of fabric is first attached to a chair back, or any piece, we pulled the fabric over the back of the seat and stapled it to the center rail on the back of the chair. Then the bottom of the fabric was pulled over the bottom edge of the back and stapled in the middle (at 6 o'clock, remember?). We used a pneumatic staple gun for this work and it was a real boon.

The fateful day was August 17.

Substituting for the regular lunch cook for the first time, the young Richard Boone had to learn an entire new repertoire: beef burgers, grilled cheese sandwiches (with ham or tomato), Texas Tommies, BLTs, and tuna melts. And then there was the deep fryer to contend with: cottage fries, onion rings, and flounder fillets. As he got the hang of it and his confidence grew, the young Boone felt that he could do anything and was up for any challenge. Then, he heard a voice from the other end of the lunch counter. The voice had a nasal yet authoritative New-York-by-way-of-Europe accent: "Hey, you with the face."

Boone spun around on his heels, grim-faced, and ready for anything. He was already upset because of having had to work the breakfast and lunch shifts and he glared angrily at the portly, bespectacled stranger.

"Come over here," said the voice behind the accent, "and let me get a good look at that ponnim...."

Thoroughly miffed, something told Boone that to hit would be wrong. Or perhaps it was the expensive suit, five-dollar Havana cigar, and the massive pinky ring on the stranger's left hand that swayed Boone from violence. He also thought he had seen the stranger somewhere before, but couldn't be sure where. The man held out his thick-fingered right hand and said, "The name is Louis B. Mayer. What's your name, kid?"

The onion rings were burning....

(A spring-loaded staple gun would do the job, but not as well.) We then fired staples in at center

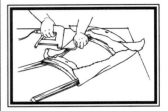

Attaching fabric inside chair back

points on the sides (at 3 and 9 o'clock), pulling tightly to eliminate inadvertent vertical pleats created when the top and bottom were pulled tight to staple.

We stapled all along the bottom at the outside back and then along the sides until we were about 2 inches from the top corners. We then stapled along the top until we were about 2 inches from the sides. There was excess material at both corners. At one corner we made two small folds, as follows: We pulled the excess material overlapping the side toward the center of the back and folded the excess material along the top over it, pulling straight down at each corner. These were small folds that would be hidden later by the material on the back, once attached. We folded the material similarly on the other chair back corner.

The curved cardboard was still in place on the inside of the arms, so we installed new batting and muslin over the cardboard and went on to cover the arms with mohair. Again, we used staples to anchor the mohair at the centerpoints on

Making fold at arm corner

Making final fold at arm corner

Stapling cardboard tack strip

Folding over fabric on outside arm panel

the top and bottoms of each arm, and at the centerpoints on each arm's edge. Then we stapled out from the centerpoints, ending about two inches from the corners—leaving enough room for us to fold and secure the excess fabric at the corners. We wanted these corner folds to be vertical (as with the back) and so pulled the fabric in from the side and stapled it at the corner. We repeated these steps at each corner and on the other arm.

To finish off the upholstery on the outside arm panels and chair back, we had to reassemble the chair. In keeping with its modular design, if you recall, the chair was assembled with nuts and bolts that went through the frame and were hidden by the fabric. Had we upholstered the outside back and arms first, we would have had a beautifully upholstered exploded chair sitting in pieces on the floor next to a large vase.

Once the chair was reassembled by bolting it back together we moved on to tack-stripping the remaining three fabric panels. Remember the original chair? Seemed so long ago, didn't it? The outside back and arms were a one-piece affair stapled directly to the frame from the outside. The staples were then hidden by decorative nails. We decided to use tack strips to achieve a lovely, even, sharp-edged effect, as typical of the Deco era as the sharp creases in Fred Astaire's trousers.

To achieve this sharp-edged effect, we used two kinds of tack strips: cardboard tack strips and aluminum tack strips. Cardboard tack stripping is purchased by the roll and is easily torn to size using your fingers or a pair of scissors. It is about ½ inch in width. We'll discuss aluminum tack strips shortly.

We cut a square piece of mohair that would cover the outside area of the chair's arm, plus an inch or so on all sides, and draped the fabric panel over the inside arm so that the underside of the mohair hung over the top of the arm by about an inch and a half. We put one staple in the center to anchor it in place and then lined a cardboard tack strip over the staple, making sure the upper edge of the strip almost met the top of the arm. We then anchored the strip over the fabric with a staple and worked out from the center to staple the strip and the underlying fabric at both ends. Every couple of staples along the way we flipped the material over the outside of the arm to make sure that the seam line created was straight and true. When it looked crooked or slanty we pulled the offending staples out, repositioned the tack strip, lined the fabric up straight, and restapled again.

We stapled all the way along the cardboard tack strip until we were about 2 inches from each top corner where the arm meets the chair back. Then we flipped the fabric over and pulled it tightly toward the bottom of the chair. (Remember to staple the cardboard tack strip along the top edge of the strip: When the fabric is flipped over and pulled down, the top edge of the cardboard may also be pulled down, creating an unsightly bulge.) With the mohair pulled tightly, we anchored it to the underside of the chair frame in the center. We continued tugging on the fabric and stapling along the bottom of the frame on either side of the center, anchoring staple, leaving a ½- to 2-inch unstapled space where the bottom corners intersected.

Now for the fun part: using aluminum tack strips to secure the mohair to the chair. These are ¾-inch-wide bendable strips with ¾-inch-long spikes protruding every 3 inches or so. The strips

Puncturing side panel fabric with aluminum tack strips

Folding back aluminum tack strip on chair

themselves are 30 inches long, but once bent back and forth several times, they can be snapped to the length you desire. (Did you ever notice that when bending metal back and forth to break it, it gets really really hot? Where is Don Herbert's phone number when we need it?)

With an aluminum tack strip cut to the same length as the side of the fabric, line the tack strip up along the back, side edge of the chair with the spikes facing toward you (away from the chair); position the tack strip vertically underneath the loose edge of the material overlapping the back.

With an excess of approximately 1 to 1½ inches of fabric at this vertical edge line the tack strip up underneath the fabric so that the tack strip's edge is flush with the edge of the fabric. Beginning from the top, push the spikes of the tack strip through the fabric. As you push each spike through, pull the fabric tight from the side so that the tack strip is straight. (If the tack strip is not straight, pull the spike out and do it again until it is straight. Any extra holes in the fabric will all be hidden later, so unless you've screwed up more than 2 inches' worth, you can respike without anxiety.)

Next, twist the tack strip and the spiked fabric so that the spikes face the outside back of the chair and line up along the vertical element on the chair frame. The outside fabric, held in place by the tack strip, should have a sharp crease and line up with the chair frame. The edge should not lap over the edge or be too far away from it.

Using a hickory mal-

Using mallet to hammer tack strip in place

let, we gently tapped the fabric-wrapped tack strip into the wooden frame, pulling tightly to the side as we hammered. We started at the top and banged all the way to the bottom of the chair and made sure that it looked wonderful. We then proceeded to attack the edges with vicious blows from the mallet to pound the tack strip and fabric flush to the chair.

A few words of advice: When using lighter fabrics, and even when using a rubber mallet, you may have to shield the fabric from the blows because the mallet could mark the fabric. Cardboard can be used as a shield between the fabric and mallet—just place a piece over the fabric and bang away. Styrofoam sheeting can also be used. The mohair fabric we used was tough, so we didn't bother with this detail.

Once the fabric was tack-stripped, we stapled the back, side fabric along the back of the chair, pulling the fabric as we stapled. To finish off the

Aluminum tack stripping being inserted into fabric at back edge

Aluminum tack stripping inserted in fabric at back edge

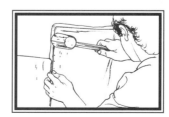

Using mallet to secure aluminum tack stripping along back edge

panel, we pulled the fabric tightly underneath the chair frame and ran a line of staples along the underside of the frame. We repeated the same tack stripping procedure on the other arm.

Once the side arm fabric was attached, we covered the back of the chair. We cut a piece of fabric the size of the back of the chair, plus 1 to 1½ inches more on all sides. We ran a cardboard tack strip along the top of the back over the underside of the fabric as we had done with the top part of the arms, and stapled the tack strip and fabric in place. We then flipped the fabric over, pulled down tightly, and anchored the fabric with a staple on the underside of the chair, as we had done with the arms.

With an aluminum tack strip cut to the length of the chair back's side, we spiked the edge of the upholstery with the sharp side of the strip, twisted it toward the frame, and used a mallet to pound the fabric-wrapped tack strip into the chair. We then followed the same procedure on the other side of the chair back. To finish off the job, the fabric on the bottom of the chair was stapled to the underside of the frame.

Attaching cambric (dustcover) to chair underside

The finishing touch was to attach the attractive, though largely useless, cambric, or dust-cover, to the underside of the chair to hide the springs and protect the chair from dust. We used a black square piece of cambric, folded it under at the edges, and stapled it to the underside of the chair. We cut notches in each corner and to achieve a neat, tailored crease we folded the cambric around the legs and stapled it in place.

Et Voilà!

En zee chair, it ees *fini!*

The technique we used on this chair of pulling fabric tightly and evenly all around is one you will use on nearly any upholstery project. And the muslin attachment process presented here is an easy dress rehearsal for any fabric attachment you may do. The tack strip attachment, however, will prepare you for a long stay at Charenton asylum (you might remember the play and film *Marat/Sade*).

The most expensive item in the completion of this chair was the fabric. It costs about $40 a yard, but thankfully no more than a yard and a half was used. The tack strips, cardboard, and staples cost a little more than $8, while the muslin and padding came to about another $10. Figure in the lacquer and stain (a quart of lacquer costs ten bucks, and the type of stain we used costs about twenty bucks for a quart, or $45 for a gallon) and you have a rather inexpensive project—except for the cost of sweat and strain experienced by TV's most colorful personalities.

Moderne chair "after"

ART DECO TABLE

First things first. In order for you to comprehend this project fully, we need to go over a thing or two.

Most French Deco or Moderne furniture is French-polished; that is, it is exhaustively finished using an age-old polishing technique that is done by hand. There is really nothing that compares to the beauty of French-polished furniture. French polishing is time-consuming and arduous, but it results in an incredibly smooth, glasslike surface with unparalleled reflective qualities. At the risk of sounding romantic, we believe that the effect and charm of this look is due to the relationship of the craftsman to the wood. French polishing is a touchy-feely process: the craftsman rubs shellac and pumice into the wood and increases its sheen with every successive step in the polishing process.

French polishing isn't something the average person normally undertakes—in other words, it's better done by masters in the fine art of French polishing (there may be ten in the whole wide world). French polishers put in a long day and rely on a hearty breakfast to sustain themselves. Before any finish comes in contact with the wood, they sand the wood extremely smooth. Traditionally, the pores of the wood are then filled with powdered brick, but today dry artists' paint pigments and powdered wood putty are mixed with water to create a pastelike fill. This paste is applied with a small pad made of linen and is rubbed in using small circular movements. The goal of rubbing in small circles is to grind the pores down even more than was done by sanding to create an even smoother surface.

Purists don't use a filler but instead dust the surface with powdered pumice and use a linen pad loaded, or saturated, with shellac. Rubbing in circles with pumice abrades the surface and "cuts" extraneous microscopic wood fibers on the surface. With this technique, the finish is applied and the pores of the wood are filled with the pumice at the same time. It's efficient, but the first method of filling and then shellacking is a lot easier. In fact, the purist's method is crazy—those doing it are truly and madly in love with their art.

If you have ever finished any kind of wood, you know that the first finish coat is absorbed immediately into the wood. Consider how fast thinned shellac applied with a pad to dry wood would be absorbed. The finisher's arm is going around and around in circles on the wood's surface, while he simultaneously squeezes the pad tightly and sweats profusely. One can only imagine how maddening this process was for French polishers. They must have ended up with biceps the size of Popeye's.

A shellac applicator is made from a square of linen with the four corners folded toward the center. A piece of wool (from a sock or sweater) soaked with shellac and wrung out is placed in the middle. The corners of the cloth are folded in again and the ends are twisted around until the pad is tight and firm, and about the size of a medium egg. The polisher's grip on the pad holds it together. When the pad needs to be reloaded after the shellac has been rubbed into the wood, it must be unfolded and more shellac poured on the wool center. Talk about needing a lot of free time to undertake this process! By the way, the French who originated the finish call the pad a "tampon," while the English refer to it as a "rubber." Giggle, giggle . . .

Remember, we're just skimming over French polishing to give you a feeling for what it's all about, and to scare you off from undertaking it yourself. We hope you are not trying to follow the steps presented here literally by tying a rag around an egg from the fridge in a completely lost attempt to fathom what is being said. The rag is tied to form the shape of an egg! The egg was used only to hint at the size of your pad. Save all eggs for your soufflés.

While French polishing is becoming a lost art due to the long hours it entails and the excessive toil it requires, there are many fine craftsmen who consider it the one true finish. These days, most French polishes are done on museum pieces, and to freshen up tired, old surfaces. This is done by reamalgamating the existing finish by applying a bit of ethyl alcohol to a felt rag and then moving the rag over the surface in continuous, graceful strokes to clean and brighten the surface. Most musical instruments in the string family such as violins, cellos, and double basses are cleaned and treated in this fashion. But the arrival of the cocktail hour, if you remember from a previous chapter, necessitated new and improved tabletop surfaces that were able to withstand the rigors of alcoholic beverages—especially whiskey, scotch, vodka, and gin (the evilest of liquors), which would eat right through shellacked finishes like the Wehrmacht cut through the Maginot Line.

Say So Long to Shellac
Shellac as a topcoat is beautiful, but forget about it and use lacquer instead. Lacquer is a very versatile finish, and while most lacquers are applied to furniture with spray guns inside commercial spray booths costing thousands of dollars, lacquers formulated for brushing are also available. Which brings us to our next project.

Our next project—a circular coffee table—was attained from the store Moderne, a great place where we hunt for projects for our shows, in Philadelphia. The finish was in poor shape and the table needed to be stripped. Even though the finish appeared to be badly scarred and scratched,

Art Deco table "before"

we were surprised to discover that all the marks were only in the finish and hadn't scarred the mahogany underneath. Whew!

Stripping Down
We stripped the piece in the usual fashion by using a paste paint remover, applying it with a brush by patting it on the surface (as opposed to brushing it on). The intention here was to leave globs of remover on the surface. The entire surface was covered this way using an inexpensive throwaway brush. We allowed the remover to sit on the surface and do its work (usually about 2–3 hours). Don't be impatient and start scraping the remover off the surface right after it's applied.

Once the remover had done its work we donned heavy rubber gloves and rubbed planer chips over the striped surface to absorb the

Materials List

- Paste paint or finish remover
- Planer chips
- Alcohol
- Lacquer thinner
- Paper towels
- 0000 steel wool
- Paint thinner
- Dark red mahogany dye
- Oil-based wood filler
- Horsehair clumps
- Naphtha
- Lacquer
- Aerosol, spray-on lacquer (5 cans)
- 2000-grit wet/dry silicon carbide sandpaper
- Tack rag
- 320- to 600-grit silicon carbide sandpaper
- Soft, lint-free cloths
- 4F-grade powdered pumice
- Powdered rottenstone
- Furniture wax or car polish

Tool List

- Throwaway foam paintbrush
- Heavy rubber gloves
- Stiff-bristled gong brush
- Respirator
- Sanding block
- Felt block (for pumice and rottenstone)

Applying planer chips to tabletop

excess remover. We rubbed and scrubbed until all the goop had been removed. Once most of the remover and softened finish had been removed this way, we brushed away the excess using the stiff-bristled gong brush.

Next, we created a fifty-fifty mixture of alcohol and lacquer thinner (called a solvent wash) and scrubbed it into the wood using 0000 steel wool. With the wood still wet from the solvent wash, we rubbed several more handfuls of fresh planer chips over the surface until the surface was completely dry. Remember that if you are removing a dark finish from an old piece, such pieces were often dyed or stained before they were finished, and old stains and dyes are pretty stubborn to remove. Don't be surprised if you can't completely remove the color from the wood. A hint of the old color often helps in achieving an attractive, warm glow in the new finish and

serves as a pleasing undercolor. If you want a light or natural finish, you'll have to work harder to remove the dye from the wood by following the directions outlined in Project 4 (page 67).

With a few exceptions, you should never sand furniture after it has been stripped. For one thing, sanding will remove coloring from the wood and cause horrible-looking light streaks caused by the lighter color of natural wood showing through the finish: If there are any "high" spots on the wood and the sandpaper travels over them they will become glaring, festering eyesores that won't go away even once stain is applied but will stand out as lighter spots on newly stained wood. The wood on our table was therefore left unsanded and only given a final wash with paint thinner (important for "fishy" reasons that we'll discuss later) and then left to dry. Use plenty of clean paper towels for this wash.

Staining and Filling

The person who owned the table wanted it stained, filled, and finished. He provided us with a dark red mahogany stain to apply and let us loose to refinish the table. (This stain really was more of a dye. Nowadays, companies market liquid dyes that are usually alcohol-based. These coloring agents inevitably become known as stains—a bit of a misnomer, but because people associate stains with wood, dyes often end up getting called stains.)

These penetrating dyes are methanol-based and are usually called non–grain raising because they don't raise the wood grain when applied, as water-based stains and dyes do. Methanol is very toxic and you should be very careful when using

> **TECHNIQUE TACTIC:**
> **HOW TO CLEAN FRESHLY STRIPPED SURFACES**
>
> Many paint removers contain paraffin wax to give them their pastelike texture. The wax has the habit of remaining engrained in the wood even after repeated washings with lacquer thinner or alcohol. For this reason, and to ensure the removal of grease and wax, paint thinner or mineral spirits (the same thing with different names) should be used to clean freshly stripped surfaces. Turpentine, another petroleum distillate, is the main ingredient contained in a lot of spray-on insect repellents. Turpentine is good for washing down surfaces, too, and it can be used in other interesting ways as well. We once encountered a store worker removing black scuff marks from the white ceramic floor tiles in his store with a can of spray insecticide remarking on how wonderfully it worked! "My mother used to scrub for hours to get these things up," he said.
>
> "Did you tell her about your discovery?" we asked.
>
> "She's dead," he said.

Applying dye to tabletop using paper towels

it. Always wear a respirator equipped with the appropriate filters, work gloves, and goggles. We poured about 6 ounces of the dye into a small container and applied it to the wood using paper towels.

Once the stain was applied, we wiped off the excess and allowed it a few hours' rest. When the stain was dry we proceeded to fill the wood pores in preparation for creating a final finish that would be as smooth as glass.

Filling the wood pores is the only way to level off a porous mahogany surface. Old-timers labored hard to fill the pores in wood by sprinkling pumice over the wood's surface and rubbing with linen pads for hours on end. But these days there's less time, so we used an oil-based wood filler designed for dark mahogany. If you fill the wood pores adequately at this stage you'll use less lacquer or varnish later when it comes time to apply the finish. Contrary to what many wood finishers believe, a pore-filled surface with less of a finish coat is as durable as an unfilled surface coated with more finish.

Thinning filler with solvent

Filler straight from the can has the consistency of ice cream. Actually, it's more like yogurt, or unrefrigerated peanut butter. It is too thick for filling purposes and you'll want to thin it by putting some in a container and adding a bit of paint thinner to it. Some companies sell solvents specifically designed for use with their own brand fillers, but these are really just common solvents that have been relabeled.

Stir the solvent into the filler until the two are emulsified and the mixture has the texture of Hershey's chocolate syrup (no, make that Bosco, or maybe CoCo Marsh with the push-pump).

Once the solvent and filler mixture has the right consistency, paint the filler onto the wood

Painting filler onto tabletop against the grain

across the grain. If you went with the grain you would not trap the filler in the pores—rather, it would be pulled out of the pores as you brushed. Therefore, make sure you brush perpendicular to the grain. If you're working on a large surface like a dining table, concentrate on filling small sections at a time, allowing the patches to dry, and then remove excess fill. A tabletop the size of our small Deco table, however, can be filled all at once.

Let the filler stand after it has been applied. When it has dried for about half an hour it will take on a dull, flat appearance. Don't wander off and get involved in a long badminton or mahjongg game: you don't want the filler to harden too much or you'll have to use chisel and hammer to remove the dried residue.

Rubbing off filler with horsehair

When the filler has a consistent flat appearance and there are no shiny wet spots, it's time to remove the excess filler, which can be done in one of two ways: You can use some burlap balled up in the hand and rub across the wood grain, or use our favorite method—wads of horsehair (that's "horsehaarr") to absorb the filler. Save horsehair remnants from old upholstery jobs for this job or go out on trash night and comb the better neighborhoods in your city for old (more than 30 years) upholstered chairs that have been tossed out. Another option is playing *Psycho* with a big knife to an old chair, or maybe hang around the racetrack and apprehend the truck on its way to the glue factory. You can also purchase horsehair from an upholstery shop. Pull horsehair out of chairs in handfuls the same way that Moe would pull out Larry's hair. (Isn't it amazing that when you mention Moe, Larry, or Curly everyone immediately knows who you're talking about?) Once you find a source for horsehair stuff as much as you can into a bag and slink away into the cold, dark evening. Neighbors will think you are absolutely mad but they will leave you alone. A dark hat is good for disguising your identity, but avoid wearing a woolen balaclava which, as we all know, is the international headgear for criminals. (Have you ever seen a police artist's rendition of a criminal suspect not wearing one of these?)

Take a clump of horsehair and rub it over the wood surface across the grain to absorb the filler, shaking it out as it becomes loaded with filler (like we all do sometimes). Use a new clump when the old clump becomes unusable, and don't even try saving this stuff. When it's been used, it's been used—toss it. Some people like to save little bits of sandpaper and we know of several furniture shops that save milk crates full of itty bits of sandpaper, which is a good idea if you're in the homemade emery board business and want to paste them onto used Popsicle sticks. Scraps of used sandpaper, like used horsehair, are basically unreusable.

Once all the excess filler is removed, you should be able to see a faint trace of residue crossing the grain perpendicularly (almost a smear) if you shine a bright light on the wood surface. This ghostly haze—a light film of filler—must be removed immediately by dampening some paper towels with naphtha and wiping the surface with the grain. Be very careful not to use too much naphtha. If the paper towels are too wet, the naphtha will flood the pores, soften the filler, and create a great big mess. After wiping, the paper towels should be the color of the filler, and there shouldn't be any smeary marks on the surface when you shine a bright light on it.

Spraying on lacquer using spray gun

Put on Your Topcoat

With deep-grained woods such as oak, two or more fillings may be necessary. But mahogany is a relatively closed-grained wood, and this makes a second fill

Spraying on aerosol lacquer

unnecessary. So, with the pores filled and the surface cleaned, we moved on to applying a new finish to the table. We allowed the tabletop to dry overnight after filling and washing it before proceeding to apply a lacquer finish.

When big furniture companies finish furniture with lacquer, they apply a lacquer "sanding sealer" after staining. Sanding sealers are specially formulated lacquers that raise the grain of the wood slightly so that the succeeding coats of clear lacquer will adhere better. Sanding sealers, however, have a milklike consistency and can obscure the natural appearance of the wood grain. They can also change the color of the wood if too many coats are applied. If you are attempting to create an unstained, natural finish, applying a couple of coats of sanding sealer and a couple of coats of clear lacquer should do the job. We promised the owner of this table that we would just shoot a clear lacquer onto the table after staining. We did this for two reasons: We didn't want the milkiness of the sealer to blanket the red mahogany color of the wood and obscure the grain. And two, he wanted us to do it this way because it was his table.

We used the same lacquer to seal the wood as we later used to topcoat it. Products called brushing lacquers are (surprise, surprise) lacquers that are formulated for brushing. Our advice is to use brushing lacquers on projects that are unstained. On stained wood, such as our table, the action of brushing on a lacquer would pull the stain and filler out of our tabletop, and the lacquer's solvent base combined with a brushing action would surely have done this deadly work with the very first drag of the brush. If this scenario had occurred, we would first have noticed red on the brush, and then this red stain would have in turn infected the entire contents of the lacquer supply when the brush was reloaded. We felt that using a professional spray gun connected to a compressor would give us the best and most even lacquer coating. But first a word from our lawyers. **Warning: We do not recommend that anyone use professional spray guns in their basements without the proper facilities and training.** Instead, follow the same directions for using spray-on lacquers in aerosol cans to finish wood outlined on page 47.

We filled the spray gun canister one-half full with clear gloss lacquer, and one-half full with lacquer thinner so the lacquer would flow smoothly through the spray gun's nozzle. If lacquer or any sprayed-on topcoat is too thick, the sprayed-on film will end up resembling the mottled skin of an orange, which explains why this effect is called "orange peeling."

Orange peeling can occur when a topcoat begins to dry before it has had time to flow out, or evenly settle on a wood surface. Varnish, for example, because of its slower drying properties, will flow out and level before it dries. Lacquers, however, will begin to dry seconds after they have been sprayed. For this reason lacquer thinner was added to speed up the flowout time. Before beginning we tested the spray on a scrap piece of wood, holding the nozzle about 12 inches away from the surface. If orange peeling occurred, we would have diluted the lacquer with more thinner. We also added six drops of silicone stop sealer, or fisheye flowout, to the

TECHNIQUE TACTIC: THOSE STUBBORN SILICONE DEPOSITS

If silicone deposits on a wood surface can't be removed even after thoroughly washing the wood with paint thinner and clean paper towels (providing you're working on a small surface) use a poultice made of clay to cleanse the wood.

Find workmen digging up a street and look into the ditch. Chances are you'll see lots of tar, rocks, dirt, and orange clay. If you can get a bit of the clay by trading a six-pack of beer, some Chiclets, or a Furniture Guys T-shirt with the foreman, you're halfway to ridding your tabletop of its silicone problem.

When you get the clay home, sift through it and remove as many stones as you can. Also have the table cleaned, sanded, and ready to go. Mix just enough water into the clay to make a smooth poultice. Then spread the poultice on the untreated wood and let it sit on the table overnight until dried. The poultice will open the pores of the wood and as it dries will absorb the silicone deposits therein. Once the clay is dry, peel it off the wood surface and wash the surface with water. Then sand the wood and proceed with your finishing project. Although we said earlier that you should never sand furniture after it's been stripped, this is an exception to the rule.

A few words of advice: Never apply a poultice to veneered pieces because you will destroy them. Also, poulticing is a last resort and should be treated that way. In most instances, a paint-thinner wash, some fisheye drops, and a coat of sealer shellac will do for eradicating nasty silicone problems, but we like to present you with as many obscure remedies as possible.

mix. These are additives mixed into lacquers, paints, and varnishes that prevent notorious puckerings in the finish that can occur when a wooden surface becomes impregnated with grease or silicones. Grease can come from anyone's hands, and silicones are contained in common spray-and-wipe furniture polishes.

A silicone problem can rear its ugly head after a coat of lacquer or varnish has been applied. Puckers or craters resembling halibut or hake eyes appear and stare at you in silent, ichthyological mockery.

Refinishers hate these craters and complain about them endlessly. To rid a piece of furniture of this problem they will charge you a pretty penny, even though the remedy is quite easy. Washing the piece well with paint thinner after it has been stripped will break up some of the silicone deposits. Keep using clean paper towels while washing to ensure that the silicones aren't just being redistributed over the wood surface. And be sure to add at least six drops of fisheye eradicator to the new lacquer or varnish. As a final precaution, shoot a coat of thinned shellac over the surface before any lacquering or varnishing takes place. Those fisheyes will go away as sure as Bob's your uncle—even if our uncles are called Vito and Benny.

Most good refinishers nowadays treat every

refinished piece as if it were fisheye-infected. If you come across a refinisher who moans and groans about needing more money to deal with a fisheye problem, show him this book and have him follow the simple (and cheap) remedy described above by highlighting the instructions in yellow.

We set up our collapsible spray booth (page 90) once again, and set the tabletop in the center upon a small stand so that it could be turned. The first thing we sprayed was the edge of the table, turning it until the entire circumference was wet with lacquer, but not so wet that it dripped (You would follow these same procedures if using a spray-on aerosol lacquer). Next, working from left to right (or right to left, if you prefer) we moved the spray gun to "lay on" the first coat of lacquer/sealer. This immediately brightened the wood and gave us a preview of what the finished product would look like.

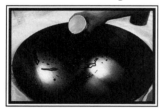
Preparing for wet sanding

Wet sanding with block

After the lacquered surface had dried for several hours, it was leveled or cut back by wet sanding it—a process involving sandpaper used with a lubricant. One of the best lubricants for wet sanding is naphtha because it allows the sandpaper to travel more easily over the lacquer-sealed surface, "cutting" the finish. Wet sanding is done to achieve a more level final finish and helps eradicate dust bumps and other blemishes in the wood. Water—especially soapy water—can also be used as a lubricant. But a water-based solution is less than ideal when used over the first coat of lacquer because if the sandpaper cuts through the thin lacquer finish, allowing water to penetrate the raw, unprotected wood below, the wood grain will swell. You'll have another problem on your hands and will have to wait for the next book for advice on solving that problem.

Use soapy water or naphtha as a final rub-out lubricant. For wet sanding this coat and any others, just pour the lubricant onto the surface and wipe it around with your hand. Ask for wet/dry silicone-carbide paper; it's usually available up to 2000-grit. It is the best sandpaper for use with lubricants because it has a glued-on backing that holds up better in wet circumstances. If you prefer sanding without a lubricant, you can use stearated silicone-carbide sandpaper, which is sold as no-load or self-lubricating sandpaper. Cut the sandpaper into quarters and wrap one piece around a cork or felt block.

Be careful when sanding the first, sealer coat of shellac or you may cut right through it. The object here is to only roughen the surface, not to break through the shellac and expose the wood. If you're refinishing a piece of furniture that has a lot of turned or carved element—spindles, finials, cartouches, or gadroonings (look these terms up because there's going to be a test at the end of the book)—don't, under any circumstances, sand these decorative parts because there is no way to avoid damaging them. You'll likely end up cutting into the finish too far and pulling off the finish and stain.

Applying second coat of lacquer

After wet sanding, we wiped the wood to remove all traces of lubricant and sanding residue using a naphtha-soaked rag, then we tack-ragged the surface (page 17) and sprayed on another coat of lacquer. Lacquer is a solvent-release finish, meaning that when the solvent in the lacquer evaporates, a glossy film of finish is left behind. The solvent released is lacquer thinner. As layer upon layer of finish is applied, all coats merge and meld and the film increases in thickness. To ensure maximum adherence of each coat without cutting through the coats too deeply, each coat of lacquer must be wet-sanded with finer and finer grits of silicon carbide paper. Sanding with finer grits ensures a smooth finish because you are removing microscopic imperfections in the dry film. Use 320-grit sandpaper for the first couple of coats. A finer grit, such as 400, should be used for the next couple of coats to eliminate sanding marks left behind by the coarser 320-grit sandpaper. Five-hundred-grit sandpaper should be used on the next coat and, finally, 600-grit sandpaper should be used on the second to last coat. Allow about an hour drying time between coats.

If you are using the felt block, by the time you get to the 600-grit sandpaper you will notice the sandpapers getting thinner and thinner. Because of its high grit and gentle cutting power, 600-grit sandpaper will not hold up well under wetness. The paper is very flimsy to begin with, and when it's wet, it can become as soft as tissue paper. By the time you get to the higher grits it only takes a few passes over the surface for the paper to tear. You'll know when the sandpaper should be discarded when you feel it cutting and then suddenly sticking to the surface. Stop immediately and throw out the sandpaper. Then wrap a fresh piece around the sanding block and continue sanding.

Rubbing-out supplies

After wet-sanding for the sixth and last time with 600-grit sandpaper and after the sixth and final tack-ragging, we sprayed on a final coat of lacquer and allowed it to dry for about a week. The longer you allow the finish to set up before rubbing it out, the better.

It is impossible to use any type of sandpaper on the dried finish because sandpapers are too coarse. To finish the finish, so to speak, we used a powdered abrasive. The two most often-used powdered abrasives are pumice and rottenstone. Pumice is pulverized, volcanic rock and comes in grades of 1F, 2F, 3F, and 4F. Rottenstone is decomposed limestone pulverized into a powder. Our supplies for this job included 4F-grade pumice, some naphtha, and a felt block. Pumice and rottenstone have been replaced in some refinishers' shops by more modern rubbing pastes, but we still advocate using the old ones.

We like the thrills associated with returning to the methods of yesteryear and request that you use these products because if you don't, all the guys who make little rocks out of big rocks, the guys with the small ball-peen hammers who break up the little itty-bitty rocks, and the people who bag the powders left behind will eventually be out of jobs. And would you be able to sleep at night if all these people lost their jobs?

Pouring naphtha onto surface

Spreading naphtha over surface

We poured the naphtha onto the surface and spread it around with our gloved hands. Next, we sprinkled the pumice over the wet surface. An oregano bottle is good for storing pumice: the little plastic cover with the tiny holes in it is perfect for sprinkling. Using the felt block we rubbed the naphtha and pumice into the wood surface, moving in long strokes parallel with the wood grain. We checked the surface for leftover pumice to make sure that we didn't accidently scratch the surface when we next wiped it clean; we wiped off all traces of pumice with a soft lint-free cloth soaked in naphtha.

Rubbing felt block over surface

When the surface had been cleaned off, we applied the final finishing abrasive of rottenstone. Rottenstone is only used with water and needs to be rubbed in using a new felt block. Apply water to the finish surface, spread it around, sprinkle on the rottenstone, and use the felt block to rub the rottenstone over the surface. When finished rubbing, wipe off all traces using a clean lint-free cloth and fix yourself a drink.

Polishing Off

You'll have done a good job if you can't feel any of the wood grain and the tabletop looks as sleek as glass. Depending on your tastes, some may like a dull satin appearance or a more shiny look. Using finer and finer sandpapers will give more of a satiny finish to a gloss lacquer.

After rubbing out with the rottenstone, we waxed and polished the surface with a car polish (yes, car polish). Simoniz brand car polish works really well if this is the path you take. If you visit the automotive store you can find a vast array of polishes, cleaners, and waxes to choose from and they all work on lacquered surfaces. Just apply polish with a wet cloth, allow it to haze, and buff it clean with a soft, lint-free cloth. If you have the patience and desire, you can use an electric polisher in conjunction with liquid- and paste-buffing compounds from your automotive dealer.

Our finished table was dazzling: Its pores were

Art Deco table "after"

filled and it was finished to a glasslike sheen. Ahhhh. We almost needed sunglasses to admire its radiant beauty.

The materials for this project cost about $100. The filler was the most expensive ingredient at about $50 a gallon. But you can fill a lot of wood with a gallon. The lacquer cost about $20, and the sandpaper and Simoniz polish about $10. And now Bob, the owner of the table, is happy (even though he won't admit it) and the table sits in glory on the second floor of his store, Moderne, across from the mohair chair we upholstered earlier, waiting for a buyer. The casual shopper, while impressed by the beauty of these pieces, has no idea of the fame and notoriety that accompanies their history . . . until now. If only Bob had been savvy enough to place a sign trumpeting "As seen on *le television.*"

Six

MARVELING AT MARBLING

(OK, Then You Think of Something Funny with Marbling!)

The technique known as marbling began appearing in early nineteenth-century America. Public buildings in the North and private residences in the South were being built in great profusion and drew on classical Greek designs. In order to capture the classical look and majesty of ancient buildings, marble was used in the construction of these nineteenth-century monuments to antiquity. But as with many grand schemes, budgets often dwindled and substitutes for expensive real marble had to be found. Artisans who could re-create marbling effects with paint (which they called "deceit") were brought in. Faux marble created with a brush became a popular finish on both interior and exterior columns, ceilings, archways, and picture frames. A thriving business in faux marbling lasted until after the Civil War, when postwar architecture and design began to stray from classical models and was replaced by Victorian excess. And then the Age of the House Painter was born.

In America, the idea of painting surfaces to resemble marble was considered novel, even though the technique had been used around the world for quite some time. In fact, American faux painters were often only copying Old World designs that were themselves copied from classical motifs. The act of painting something to have it resemble something else can be traced all the way back to the Mycenaeans about four thousand years ago.

At the time depicted by Charlton Heston and Stephen Boyd racing chariots in a stadium, marbling was being used extensively in Pompeii to beautify interiors. Because it was either impractical or impossible to lift huge hunks of marble up onto ceilings, it became easier to fake everybody out and create artificial marble surfaces with pigments and plaster. Many domed and vaulted ceilings were plastered, sanded smooth, and then "grained" with pigments made from pounded minerals and stones used to color the plaster. These lies angered the gods and . . . well, you know what happened to Pompeii.

Faux finishes continue to be used today, especially on walls and ceilings in restaurants, hotels, and bars. There are other types of faux finishes that can be performed on tin and metal surfaces to give them the look of rusted iron or oxidized bronze or copper. We know of one establishment that boasts of having originally restored copper ceilings when in fact the ceiling is made of tin and was sprayed with a bronzing lacquer colored with real copper dust. We should know because Joe did the work! Perhaps those types of finishes will be covered in the next book.

No New Tricks Here

During the Renaissance, too, marbling was a specialty technique, as it is today. But back then, no one had business cards, there were no home decorating videos, and no how-to shows. Faux finishers traveled around and got work by word of mouth: "I hear he needs marble—he's got a space . . . give 'em a visit." Faux finishers would mount a horse, ride over to the place, and present samples of their work. Like today, the door got slammed in their faces, but the expletives were different: "A pox on ye, rapscallion!"

In both rich and poor churches marbling was used in interesting ways. And did you know that even Michelangelo did faux? Not only did he work with real marble, but he knew how to paint it, too. Large portions of his Sistine Chapel murals consist of simulated marble.

During the fifteenth century the artist Paolo Veronese was going crazy because he had so much work creating depictions of architectural scenes on interior walls in private residences. He and his troupe of artists were practitioners of the art of trompe l'oeil ("fool the eye") and were always running out of business cards (cards had been invented by this time). Much of Veronese's works can still be seen at the Villa Barbaro in Maser, Italy. We once attended an advertised class on trompe l'oeil but when we got there it only *looked* like a class on trompe l'oeil. . . . The Romans were masters of the faux finish and made pottery using different colored clays to mimic the background and veins in hard stone. A millennium and a half later Messrs. Wedgewood and Staffordshire in England did the same thing with their china and everybody thought they had come up with a completely marvelous, new, and original idea. You get the picture—nothing is new. Except our show, that is. Everybody since antiquity has been doing marbling and everybody today still wants to do it. We hope that we can help you do it, too.

Project 8:

WHY DO A PAINTED FINISH?

Glad you asked that.

Painted finishes are a way in which you can transform a piece of unattractive furniture, a wood panel, or even plaster appliqués into something that looks pretty damn regal and splendiferous. Architectural features such as crown molding around a ceiling perimeter can be made to appear like the real thing, especially if ceilings are 14 feet high and you have to squint to see them. If you are a first-time marbleizer, begin practicing your newfound artistic talents on items that can't be examined closely—in short, start way up high. Marbling is usually done with brushes but the effect also can be achieved using canned spray paints! (Come see us when we appear in your hometown and we'll give you a demonstration. Then buy an official Furniture Guys T-shirt.)

Squishing

The simplest of all painted finish techniques can be called "squishing," in which a surface is coated with thinned oil paint and then covered with a sheet of thin plastic sheeting. The plastic is then pressed against or "squished" into the oil paint with open hands, and then is removed. The result is a marbled look. This technique is something a child of four could do with his eyes closed. The end effect of squishing can be compared to the appearance of the swirled interior of a Good Humor chocolate bar.

Stippling and Spattering

Stippling is a technique where thinned paint is patted or "stippled" onto walls and furniture with a brush or sponge, lending a textured appearance to the surface. "Spattering" occurs when paint is flicked onto a surface that has been painted with a contrasting color. This is an amazing type of finish that was aptly displayed by Bill Russell on the "Amazing Things with Paint" TV segment of our show, which was a takeoff on the wonderful world of infomercials. Like all painted finishes, vinegar-based paint has been around for ages. Books describing how to make and use this decorative finish are available at bookstores and public libraries or you can wait for our next book, in which we'll cover everything else that we couldn't cover in this weighty tome.

Speaking of amazing, a fake lapis lazuli finish (a deep blue effect named after the semiprecious stone) is quite marvelous. Azurite, another blue stone, is also a superb finish suitable for adding color to plain picture frames and small boxes. Oxidized bronze and tortoiseshell finishes are also nice options. None of these finishes, however, is as popular as the fabulous *marbre faux*.

What Is Real Marble?

In order to simulate real marble, you first need to understand what real marble is composed of, which is primarily limestone. (This is very different from lime Jell-O with miniature marshmallows and pineapple chunks suspended in it.) Marble is composed mainly of calcite or dolomite crystals. The crystalline texture of a marble slab is the result of extreme metamorphism caused by age, pressure, and heat. Marble can be polished and is therefore suitable for use as a decorative or ornamental stone. When you look at marble—whether it is black, green, yellow, white, or sienna—you do not see one color, or even two, but a variety of gradations and harmonizing hues

that are so varied they cannot be counted on all fingers and toes together. When you set your mind to painting or faking marble with paint don't think in black and white because there are grays, shades of deep indigo, and sometimes silver slivers in some marbles. The range of colors you want to create is almost limitless and it all depends on how carried away you want to get creating a marble finish (and how intent you are at driving all your loved ones insane with incessant chatter about marble accompanied by pictures of the marble).

Finding a Subject

To truly fake marble (so to speak) the item you select, or the structural elements of an item (the turned columns on a mantelpiece, for instance), should be something that has traditionally been made of marble. For example, it would be desirable to finish a mantel and marble its columns for a more elegant or decorative effect, since many mantels are indeed made of marble.

TECHNIQUE TACTIC: FILLING PORES

If the item you select for marbling is made of oak, you first must fill the pores of the wood in order to create a smooth surface. This can be achieved through the use of a commercial wood filler such as the one used in Project 7 (page 100), or by using plaster as a filler, as we did on the console table in Project 5 (pages 75, 77).

We have seen many instances where the wooden banisters on three-story stairways have been marbled, as well as bar rails, mantelpieces, and tabletops. Decorative effects on floors can be created with interlocking and crisscrossing patterns of different faked marbles—almost anything is possible. The major source of inspiration should come from viewing real marble. We bet you could walk anywhere in your city and find examples of real marble on the facades of old buildings, in the interiors of malls and galleries, and on fountains—just don't send us pictures.

What is it that attracts the eye when you look at marble? The shine? The crystalline color? No. It's the hypnotic effect of the stone that possesses us . . . the rhythmic feel of marble. This is what is so difficult to capture in faux marbling (never mind the difficulty of expressing it in words).

Building Your Self-confidence

Marbling can be the perfect solution when a solid color paint on the top of an old nightstand or dresser just doesn't make it. Despite what we have said above, the effect is not difficult to achieve, so don't let anybody tempt you to pay $125 for a course on marbling. That's not to say that if you wanted to become an expert there aren't good places where you can learn how. But with very little trial and tribulation you can achieve a fairly successful effect on the very first try. The dreaded angst that wells up from the very pit of the soul in many people when confronted with such an endeavor has to do with a lack of self-confidence. Some people just can't or won't ever attempt marbling. It's a fear of the unknown; they may feel foolish, incompetent, or convinced that they are clods without grace enough to pull a feather or brush across a surface to produce a line of grain. These are the same people who worry about time, color coordination, and which way the toilet paper should hang (down or over). We say you know you best and, by the way, the sun has only got about five million billion years left before it goes out, so you should start packing now. . . .

Walnut table "before"

See . . . It's Really Easy

The steps described here will come easily for adventurous, nonanal types. But please don't look at our graining and try to duplicate it exactly. Make your own lines—they'll be just as good as ours with some practice. There are a lot of folks who enjoy those artist how-to shows where the host displays, with amazing grace, how to paint an entire picture in a half an hour. There are those who set up their canvases and easels and try and duplicate exactly what the funny German guy's doing, mark for mark. But that ain't right. Instead of duplicating the line, take note of the effects that may be created and try duplicating the movement. Copy the technique rather than the results.

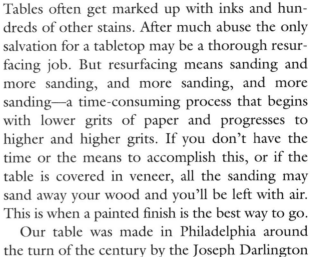

Tables make the best subjects for marbling. Tables often get marked up with inks and hundreds of other stains. After much abuse the only salvation for a tabletop may be a thorough resurfacing job. But resurfacing means sanding and more sanding, and more sanding, and more sanding—a time-consuming process that begins with lower grits of paper and progresses to higher and higher grits. If you don't have the time or the means to accomplish this, or if the table is covered in veneer, all the sanding may sand away your wood and you'll be left with air. This is when a painted finish is the best way to go.

Our table was made in Philadelphia around the turn of the century by the Joseph Darlington Co. It is made of walnut, with turned, fluted legs. This table was in almost perfect condition when we spotted it in an array of clutter at a woman's house after she contacted us to explain that her husband had been in the antique business and had died. She was trying to get rid of the furniture and thought we'd be interested in some of it. She had been watching our shows from the time they premiered on PBS in our hometown back in 1989.

Joe wanted the table immediately and had to have it. The top was scarred and stained with some ink and we could have easily resurfaced the wood and matched the color. But that wouldn't have been as exciting as watching us paint marble, would it?

The woman seemed a bit hesitant when we told her that we were going to prime the top and paint it to look like marble but we reassured her that the end result would look good, and when we offered hard cash for the table, her face lit up. She thought about the old lace pillowcases, the beach home, the new hat, and Ovaltine. We walked away, grunting, carting the table to the waiting truck, which had been ticketed for illegal parking and had several flyers for massage parlors (where boy and girl become boyfriend and girlfriend) and Olsen's meats.

The table was a wonderful candidate for marbling because it was constructed of solid walnut planks, had the thickness of a real marble slab, and had a great rounded torus molded edge. If we succeeded with a convincing marble finish, we could actually fool someone into thinking it was the real thing (unlike the soft drink, which changed for the worse when they screwed with the recipe a few years back).

Materials List

- 3 quarts of latex, semigloss house paint (one each of rose, sienna, and ivory)
- Naphtha
- Paper towels
- 220-grit garnet sandpaper
- Newspaper
- Masking tape
- Quick-drying primer
- Disposable latex gloves
- Water-based varnish
- 320- to 400-grit silicon carbide sandpaper
- 0000 steel wool
- Automotive wax polish

Tool List

- Sea sponge
- Feathers
- 3-inch-wide paintbrush (synthetic for latex paints)
- Tack rag
- Shallow pan (for dabs of paint)
- Disposable paint palette
- Long-bristled "blender" paintbrush
- ¾-inch bristle lettering brush
- Sword brush (also called knife brush)
- Paint sprayer
- Soft cloth
- Touch-up markers

Getting the Supplies

Our first stop was an art supply store. Sea sponges are necessary items for marbleizing.

Beware of cheap synthetic sponges. A real sponge is identifiable by the sand it holds: manhandle the sponge and if sand falls out you've got the real goods. Before using the sponge, however, be sure to rinse it out several times to rid it of sand.

Feathers are also required and art supply stores usually sell turkey feathers for about 80¢ or so per feather. You can use just one feather or a variety of sizes for all your colors. A little experimentation with these, and you will see how easy it is to make grain markings that resemble those in real marble. Large brushes (3 inches wide) are essential for applying foundation colors. You can buy a cheap brush for seven to ten bucks, or you can go all the way and get a brush with badger or fitch hair bristles for $20 and up. Just know what type you will be needing: if you're using oil paint you'll need to get natural bristle brushes. If you're going to use latex and acrylics, you will need synthetic, or nylon, brushes. Latex can ruin an expensive brush made with natural bristles. You have been warned. We'll cover the other materials you need when the project calls for them.

Paints

This brings us to paint. Marbling is usually rendered with oil-based paints because they are thinned with paint thinner and take longer to dry, giving you more time to futz with what you are doing. It is also possible to work with latex and acrylic paints. These paints are water-based and are what we used to achieve the rose-colored marble effect on this project. Our reasons for using water-based paints were threefold: First, we are limited in the amount of time we have to tape a show and oil-based paints need much more time to set up and dry before succeeding steps can be performed—and the less time spent waiting for things to dry, the easier the taping goes. To achieve the look of marble, a succession of layers and finish coats are needed. Drying times between each coat are required and we had to consider that the entire project had to be completed in a day and a half. Had we been working with oil paints, each layer would have taken overnight to dry and we wouldn't have had the time to attend to our other far-flung business interests (never mind factoring in the time for a load or two of laundry). By using water-based paints, we were able to cut drying times between coats to about 2 hours. The second reason for using water-based paints is that when acrylics and latex are used they can be varnished using the new acrylic polymers, or water-based varnishes that are now available. We wanted to try these out, so we could tell you in this book about the pros and cons of these types of finishes. The third, and final, reason on our list of reasons for using water-based paints and varnishes is that we enjoy the challenge of using them.

Sanding table surface

With any marbling job, the first thing that has to be attended to is the existing finish. If it is in good condition, free of lifting or buckling veneers, the entire surface should be cleaned by wiping it down repeatedly with naphtha and paper towels. Keep changing the naphtha and the towels, and remember to keep the dirty towels in a bucket filled with water so they do not spontaneously ignite.

Once the grime is gone, the surface should be sanded with 220-grit garnet sandpaper. This process roughs up the surface so that the new paint will bind to the surface. After sanding, dust off and tack-rag the surface in preparation for painting.

Taping newspaper skirt around table

Next, we taped a skirt of newspaper around the bottom portion of the table. This is done by opening a sheet of newspaper and applying masking tape to the edge so that half of the tape is on the newspaper and the other half can be applied to the underside of the table.

Before attempting any kind of painted finish, a surface needs to be primed. Priming is necessary

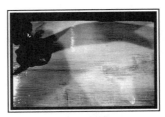

Applying primer coat

for two reasons: to improve paint adhesion and to enhance subsequent coats of colored paint which, when applied over the primed white surface, appear more vivid. Quick-drying white primers do just this kind of job. Always stir the can contents adequately because the primer may have been sitting on the shelf as long as the store manager has been sitting on his stool. If you ask nicely, the mean man at the paint store may even put the can in the paint-mixing machine for you. Use a 3-inch bristle brush if you're working on a large table like ours. If you're working on a smaller surface, use a smaller brush.

Apply the primer to the surface evenly, avoiding drippy globs. Move the brush straight back and forth. Quick-drying primers usually take about 30 minutes to dry and then need to be scuffed with a 220-grit garnet sandpaper, tack-ragged, and painted again.

While waiting for the primer to dry you'll need to prepare a few other things before moving on to the actual marbleizing. We used a shal-

Marbling supplies

low pan for holding dabs of acrylic paints. We also purchased a disposable palette at the art supply store. We named it Eugene after the actor Eugene Pallette, the wonderfully gifted fat man who played Friar Tuck to Errol Flynn's Robin Hood in the original 1939 film version of the story. These palettes are 11 × 14-inch bound pads of wax paper sheets used for mixing paints and are alternatives to the large circular thing with the thumb hole. Disposable palettes offer the same thumb holes for handling convenience but the wax paper can be peeled off and thrown out when the job is completed. A large table near the project is handy for putting your stuff on while you work. Other stuff you need for marbling may include: things like paint trays, wide brushes for "feathering" or pulling your painted

Blending paints

marble grain, various graining tools like 1-inch artists' brushes, feather(s), string. And the odd snack (the only kind we eat). Your modus operandi should be one of order, except that we are slobs. Don't be like us. Be neat.

With the primer dry, sanded, and tack-ragged we were ready to lay on our base or foundation color. We purchased three quarts of latex semigloss house paint: a rose, a sienna, and an ivory. These three colors

Dabbing paint on palette

were dabbed individually with brushes all over the tabletop. Then they were blended using a long-bristled paintbrush, commonly referred to as (you guessed it) a blender.

Stippling surface with sponge

We then placed small puddles of paint on the palette, wet a sponge, soaked up the colors with the sponge, and dabbed each of them onto the surface of the table separately and blended them together on the surface.

Stippling with sponge

This step, called stippling, is important because the foundation on which the marble patterns are made is being created. Irregularities in this coat mimic those in real marble. Blend all the colors evenly and try not to create marks that look as though they are impressions made by a sponge. It helps

Stippling with sponge

Spattering

to keep the sponge turning in your hand as you dab so that you are using all parts of the sponge and not only one side. This way the pattern on one facet of the sponge won't be repeated as you dab. Capiche? Get your hands dirty. If you want to save the manicure, buy a pair of disposable surgical gloves and put them on before you start.

Once the foundation looks satisfactory, wait for it to dry. If it doesn't look good, just wait until it dries and paint over it again. You have a lot more flexibility with a painted finish than with a regular varnish or lacquer finish, because if you screw up in the preliminary stages—namely, the painting of the marble—you can just paint over it and start fresh. Don't be nervous. Even Michelangelo screwed up here and there.

On top of the sponged-on stippling, we spattered. This is done by using a brush loaded with the darker paints in your repertoire (thinned with water if you're using latexes or acrylics, or with paint thinner if you're using oil-based paints) and a 4-inch-long stick, or the long handle of another brush.

Flick the brush end of the brush handle against the stick. If the paint has been thinned properly, little dots of paints will hit the surface of the table. Have two or three brushes loaded with thinned paint ready to go so you are not dipping the same brush into different paints like a callow beginner. You want variety in the speckles. The important thing to remember is to move around the whole table to

Graining with feather

avoid a large buildup of spattered paint on one part of the table. Waiting for the speckled paint to dry is optional. In our case, we immediately moved on to graining the finish.

With the speckled paint still wet we proceeded to start the preliminary graining in the finish using a feather and a ¾-inch lettering

Applying grain with lettering brush

brush. Try and visualize how the grain in the finish should travel. Look at real marble or pictures of it to see how grain patterns typically look. Marble grains may be random but there are also repeated patterns in nature. Separate the feather and dip one side into a puddle of dark-colored paint on the palette. To separate the feather, hold the stem (the quill part) and run your fingers down the length of the feather in the opposite direction. Then drag the edge of the feather across a length of the table, occasionally pushing it back over the area you have grained. Remember, when you are pulling a line of grain across the top surface with a feather, especially if the table has a molded edge as ours did, bring that line of grain over that edge and around it. This will create a realistic, three-dimensional effect designed to fool everybody. We then used a small lettering brush to add some more highlights with lighter-

Spattering again

colored paints along the edges of the grain marks made by the feather.

Once you feel you have a good amount of grain running in the proper directions, allow it to dry. You'll know if the graining is off course

because it will look it. In the accompanying pictures you can see the grain effect when we started, and then later as we continued with more spattering. You can grain over the top of the dried graining as much as you like until you get the effect you want; that goes for spattering and stippling, too.

The next stage was to drape a mist of color over the entire table. How was this achieved? You could continue spattering but the surface would dry feeling like the bumpy, scaly alien called the Horta in the old *Star Trek* episode "Devil in the Dark" (the one where Spock mind-melded with the alien). If we were working with lacquer, we could have shot a transparent layer or glaze on top of the marbling. We also could have used an electric airless sprayer, but both these options require setup time and cleanup time. And the last thing you want to do when you're creating something is to worry about cleaning something out of your nozzle (which can be painful) before it dries.

What we used was a $10 item purchased at a paint store. It turns any paint into a spray paint once the paint is thinned. These sprayers come with a glass screw-on bottle that attaches to a gas-charged propellant with a spray button (the kind of button you find on a can of spray paint). To deepen the salmon color of the marble finish, we poured a bit of the sienna-colored semigloss latex paint into the jar and then thinned, or diluted, it by adding some acrylic water-based varnish to make the paint transparent. The thinned mixture would therefore not mask or otherwise obscure the marbling that we had worked on for the better part of an hour under the hot studio lights. It would, however, heighten the reflective qualities of the finish and make it resemble polished stone.

Holding the sprayer in hand and pressing our thumb on the nozzle, we were able to walk all around the table spraying a fine mist of paint over the table's edges and top surfaces. Keep moving when doing this—if you stay in one spot too long the mist may build up, puddle, or drip over the edge. The change in the appearance of the finish

GLAZES

Glazes are created quite simply by applying a color in a clear vehicle. If you are using water-based paint you can use any number of water-based clear coatings; with oil-based paints you will have to use an oil-based varnish or polyurethane as your vehicle. Correct proportions are based on how deep you need the glaze to be, so experimenting will be necessary. One part of paint to five parts of clear "vehicle" will create a thinner glaze than a 1:3 mixture.

Brushing on glazes also can become a problem, especially when glazes are thicker and more embodied with paint. You will see brush marks in the dried film. Using foam brushes can markedly reduce this problem, or you can buy lots of those little spray bottles we mentioned earlier to apply the glaze (page 114). Electric airless sprayers are also available—check out the other options on the market today. Learning to produce and work with glazes is central to applying any decorative finish and we advise you to practice. We'll be going on a national tour to check up on your work, and woe betide if you mess up, people. . . . (Does anybody really know what "woe betide" really means and why nuns used to say it right before an open palm came in contact with the cheek?)

The layering of glaze with graining mimics the strata of real marble. Any number of effects can be achieved

Spraying glaze

through layering, but be sure that preceding finish work has dried properly before covering it with varnish. A clear-coated surface that has been sanded or cut back with a 320- or 400-grit silicon carbide sandpaper will produce a tighter bond between finish layers. Rushing your work may result in a finish that cracks, which can happen right away or over time. Cracking occurs when the outer coating dries to hard finish, while undercoatings remain soft. As the undercoats dry and contract, splitting and cracking inevitably occurs. Giving each coat a chance to dry completely prevents cracking.

As with any finishing project the final step is rubbing out the finish. You can't really abrade a water-based topcoat and have it come out feeling and looking the same way the console table did in Project 5 (page 73) because the table was finished with lacquer. However, minor surface bumps caused by dust can be removed using 0000 steel wool and water. Remember what we said earlier: some water-based finishes are not as impervious to ordinary tap water; it's a good idea to test a sample, that is, marbleize and clear-coat a piece of scrap wood while you are working on your project, applying the same finish every step of the way. When it comes time to rub out the project test the procedure on the scrap wood. If you screw up, you've only screwed up a hunk of wood.

Applying acrylic gloss varnish

should be very dramatic. We allowed the paint to dry while we had lunch.

We then proceeded to apply a coat of acrylic gloss varnish with a 3-inch-wide paintbrush and allowed this coat to dry.

Sanding, Graining, and Glazing—Yikes!

It took about 90 minutes for the varnish to dry to the point where it could be sanded. There is

Graining again using feather

no need to sand much, but a sand*wich* is good. Use 320- to 400-grit silicone carbide sandpaper to lightly scuff the surface and prepare it for the next step: paint and a clear topcoat. This is the same process as when coat after coat of clear finish is applied during any usual wood-finishing job (such as the rolltop desk project, page 49). After sanding and tack-ragging, we were able to apply more graining using feathers and brushes. When

ABOUT WATER-BASED FINISHES

Years ago, when nobody cared about the environment, most house painters used latex paint only on walls, preferring oil paint for all trim work. Latex was expensive to produce and there was no real demand for it. This situation enabled Salvatore, the ninety-four-year-old painter with the big overalls and too-small hat who had been painting with oils and turps from the time his father handed him a brush and pepperoni at age ten, to continue painting the interiors of closets, as well as your basic living rooms, dining rooms, and kitchens, with the same types of oil-based products. Salvatore and other painters his age often lunched on Jupiter, a short trip fueled by fume intake.

Nowadays, however, local and state governments have been cracking down on the amounts of volatile organic compounds—commonly referred to as VOCs—in products, in an attempt to allow our planet to breathe. Water-based is a bit of a misnomer for the new finishes because these finishes are in actuality solvent-based to some extent and usually contain polyurethane or acrylic, which is mixed in water. But they are called water-based to set them apart from the standard cans of lacquer, shellac, and varnish. Most of the water-based finishes on the market today contain acrylics, which are very hard and tough once they dry. This makes them similar to regular solvent-based polyurethanes. However, water-based finishes offer a poor barrier against water penetration and are less resistant to solvents and acids than oil-based products. This doesn't mean that they are bad finishes, only that they shouldn't be used for everything. A hot cup left on the surface will make a mark, and if you wash the surface with soapy water you may soften the finish. Water-based finishes definitely will not stop the wood from swelling and contracting as the seasons change.

On the upside, water-based finishes don't emit sickening fumes, which seems to be the biggest advantage of using these products, especially among those working in the wood-finishing business. (You should still keep the windows open when using acrylics, by the way.) Water-based finishes are extremely scuff-resistant, they do not yellow, and there is no danger of fire. And these types of coatings do not contain much solvent (compared to solvent-based finishes, that is) so less solvent evaporates and less air pollution is created.

But two of the biggest problems with acrylics are that they raise the grain of the wood and they dry to a dull finish—especially when applied to a dark wood or to wood that has been stained a dark color. Another big problem with acrylics is their inherent inability to be rubbed out with abrasives for a final wax and shine when compared to traditional solvent-based products.

Some water-based finish problems can be dealt with: You can decrease the amount of grain swelling by sponging the wood with water first and then sanding. Sponging and sanding the raised fibers two or three times with higher and higher grits will dramatically reduce the amount of raised grain. A few words of advice: Don't pay attention to any of the newer products that claim not to raise the grain of the wood—anything that is water-based *will* raise the grain of wood. Trust us, we called Don Herbert (TV's lovable Mr. Wizard) on this one. Staining the wood first with an oil-based stain can also decrease the amount of grain swell; just make sure the stain is completely dry before applying the water-based finish, otherwise the water-based product will not bond well. Grain swell can further be decreased by applying a very thin spit coat of shellac (page 46) before applying a water-based topcoat, as long as you sand the dried shellac spit coat before applying the topcoat.

Another problem with water-based finishes is their weather sensitivity. On warm dry days they will dry (or cure) quickly, but on cool or humid days you will have to wait longer. Creating air flow around the finished project with fans helps to decrease the curing period. But on cold days, forget it; any water-based finish will be affected below 65° F. And you know what, you'll get those dirty white rings left behind by wet glasses just the same as you would on a lacquered or varnished surface.

Care must also be taken when brushing on water-based finishes. Make sure that the finish you buy specifies on the can or label that it can be brushed on, otherwise it will foam up when applied. And you'll run back to the paint store screaming, "My poly foamed!" and the good man will tell you to add a bit of mineral spirits, glycerin, or even milk. You should pay attention to the manufacturer's advisories on the can of the product you purchase. If there is a problem with a varnish, or if a poly doesn't flow out to level (apply smoothly) properly, you can add 10 to 20 percent of distilled water to the product. Distilled water does not contain trace metals that can stain or spot the surface, but regular tap water might.

And speaking of metals and spotting, steel wool should never be used in the preparation of a piece that is going to be finished with a water-based product. If steel wool dust is trapped beneath the surface of a water-based coating the steel filaments will rust (oxidize) and spots will develop on the surface. The final

problem with water-based finishes—purely from a tactile standpoint—is that they can't be rubbed out to as smooth a finish as traditional oil-based varnishes or lacquers can. And rubbing out is what makes for a most elegant look.

These are some of the reasons why many say that water-based finishes do not work well on everything. They are the finishes of the future but these formulations are still being tested and refined. We think we are probably correct in saying most of the water-based varnishes and polys on the market today are immature—which is not to say they aren't good, but just that you should be aware, as with all finishing products, of their limitations and advantages.

applying paint with feathers, keep in mind that you can use the feather as is, or cut it into pieces. The feather can also be ruffled (who doesn't like ruffling a few feathers every so often?) to produce different types of markings. Stippling, graining, and spattering can be repeated until you are satisfied with the effect. You will know if you have too much graining if it looks

Graining using sword or knife brush

like there's too much graining—and you'll know there's too much spattering if your spattering is covering up your graining, and your glazing is hiding your spattering.

The sword, or knife, brush is an expensive little devil costing about $20, but when it is wet with paint, the tip is amazingly sharp and perfect

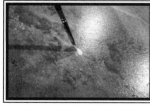

Graining using nylon ½-inch brush

for producing very thin graining. It creates a nice thin line or a fat line depending on how you employ it and can be used by itself or in addition to feathers.

A flat nylon ½-inch brush is also useful for cutting a sharp, clean line; just make sure you do not overload any of your brushes with paint.

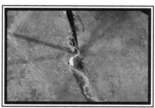

Graining using nylon ½-inch brush

When graining with a lighter color (as we did using ivory on top of the rose base) you may wish to intertwine that grain marking with a darker one applied earlier. In this case, all that need be done is to have someone tell you a very funny joke or story while you are graining. The vibrations from your laughter will result in the most natural interwoven grain markings you will ever see. Don Knotts has always been a natural at this.

Don't overload the surface with too many grain markings or the effect will appear contrived. The best results are achieved when you can create light and dark markings that can be enhanced by glazing the surface again. This is essentially what we did by spraying the mist, which was a pigment mixed in a clear acrylic varnish. Once the lighter grain markings had dried (about 90 minutes), we brushed on a clear coat of acrylic polyurethane. When the first clear topcoat had dried, we again created more grain markings and sponged on more salmon-colored

Rubbing out with steel wool

paint. Repeat this process over and over until the desired effect has been achieved.

The brand of acrylic polyurethane we used was particularly durable, and through previous testing we determined that a mild soapy solution could be used for the rub-out. We filled a bucket with water and squeezed some dishwashing soap into the bucket. Any color will do (but how come there isn't a red one?). We then wet a 0000 steel-wool pad and rubbed the surface in a back-and-forth motion with loooong stretching movements from one end of the table to the other. Steel

Padette for edges

wool is okay to use for a *final* rub-out since no further coats of finish are being applied. Avoid using steel wool *between* coats, as some filaments could be left behind to rust in the process.

Rubbing edge with padette

We rubbed with steel wool over the entire top once, wiped off all the water, and then buffed a second time with the soapy solution. The table edges were treated using the soapy water and small steel-wool padettes (page 57). We could feel the surface becoming som what smoother, although brushmarks could still be felt and (in a strong light) seen—the downside of using water-based finishes. Most of the time, however, any irregularities in the finish such as these won't be detected by even the most discerning eye.

Applying car wax

We wiped the table dry and proceeded to apply car wax to the table surface. There are many brands of car wax, and when car wax is properly applied on the right surface a fabulous shine can be rendered with a little elbow grease. For sleek finishes, such as lacquer or varnish, or on painted surfaces, such as our marbled table, car wax is ideal—and you can use what's left over on the Buick.

Simply wet the neat round sponge that comes with the wax with water and squeeze it out. Dig the sponge into the paste and

Buffing car wax

work it in until the sponge becomes totally impregnated with the paste (wear rubber gloves to protect your manicure).

Apply the paste in a circular motion, going from one end of the table to the other. Allow the wax to dry for about 15 minutes.

Automotive paste waxes will dry to a haze. Use a soft cloth or soft paper towel (avoid coarse ones like those that come from the metal-crank thing in the washroom) to buff the surface in a circular motion.

Once the top was finished, we peeled away the protective newspaper skirt taped around

Brushing dark lemon oil on carvings

SAMPLE JOKES TO TELL WHEN APPLYING GRAIN WITH A BRUSH

1. A guy's trying to cram a horse onto the subway train and the conductor starts hollering, "Hey, are you crazy? You can't bring that horse on the subway!"
   And the guy says, "But he gets sick on the bus!"

2. A doctor goes in to see his patient and says, "I've got some good news and some bad news. The bad news is we have to cut off your legs; the good news is the guy in the bed next to you wants to buy your slippers."

Wiping table underside with dark lemon oil

the table base and pro-ceeded to clean the table. We wiped all surfaces down with naphtha, remembering to toss all used naphtha-soaked rags into a bucket of water. We then applied a dark lemon oil to the existing finish. The lemon oil seeped into all the cracks and made the table base look bright and new. We

Using touch-up marker

could hear the finish thanking us. We used brushes dipped in lemon oil to clean the carvings in the table, and then buffed off all the excess oil with paper towels. We also used some new, dry brushes to remove any excess oil still embedded in the cracks and carvings.

We used touch-up markers to dis-guise cracks on edges and visible gouges in the wood. Just dab the

TECHNIQUE TACTIC: CAR WAX

Under no circumstances should you use automotive car waxes on porous surfaces, like oak, where the wood pores can be seen and felt in the surface. Using paste waxes on porous surfaces will clog the pores and this can be disastrous: White or yellow paste will dry in the pore openings and you will go absolutely mad trying to dig it out when you realize your folly.

TECHNIQUE TACTIC: TOUCH-UP MARKERS

Touch-up markers can be found in most well-stocked home centers. You can usually purchase them in sets of four, or buy them separately in colors limited to light brown, dark brown, red brown, and black brown. For the man or woman who must have everything, roll-up cases of fifty touch-up markers in a range of colors can be pur-chased from various woodworking supply houses. These super sets come in a nylon pouch organizer that closes with Velcro. When the case is opened the markers resemble a virtual Gatling gunbelt of touch-up ammo. You may, however, end up shooting yourself for buying these expensive markers. They cost around $125. Home-owners and do-it-yourselfers can get away with the set of four colors available at the home center.

our completed project pittance a table can be

Walnut table "after"

blemishes with the marker tips and they'll magically disappear. But remember to apply lemon oil first. If you do all your touch-up with the markers and *then* apply the lemon oil, you will remove the marker.

The final picture of proves that for a mere transformed from a worn and dingy item into a high-class piece of ele-gant art. The table cost $350 and the art sup-plies were provided to us by the wonderful folks at Taws Art Supply in our home town. If purchased, these mate-rials would cost about $150. Keep in mind, however, that when it comes to subsequent marbling jobs you won't have to buy brushes (only additional ones if you want them). Three quarts of latex semi-gloss paint came to $30, the acrylic poly was $12, and the car wax was $8. In total, minus the cost of the table itself, it would cost you about $200 to complete a pro-ject of this size. What are you wait-ing for, a written invitation? Put on the wild blow-out wig and paint yourself a happy grain.

Seven

MID-CENTURY MODERN FURNITURE,

or Hey, Look at Those Chairs Darrin and Samantha Have

The style referred to as Mid-century Modern can be chronicled more closely than any other line of furniture that came before it, mainly because, in the scheme of things, it is a most recent development—even if by "recent," we refer to its beginnings in the mid-nineteenth century.

Art and design historians are at loose ends where it comes to this period. They ask: "What the hell do you call the movement that comes after the one called Postmodern?" Post-postmodern? Post-neoclassical? Neoclassical Post?

Sounds like a cereal. Think about it.

But let's go back eighty years or so to Modern Times.

The last great wave we visited which crashed upon the beach of world style was the Art Deco movement, where traditional naturalistic decoration met industrial design and left us with one of two ways to go: a return to traditional representationalism—upholstery with flowers, a cabinet with a couple of carved nymphs (if you recall, the Decoists loved the odd nymph; angular and forward-moving, much like the hood ornament on a Pierce Arrow)—or to go totally nymphless.

We Declare by Manifesto!

The Mid-century Modern movement incorporated social politics into its ideology. The vehicle that the artists and designers of this era used to put forth their thoughts on the synthesis of art, technology, and ideology was known as the manifesto. A manifesto is not a soft drink or the Addams Family relative they never spoke about, but a declaration of principles over which a bunch of guys and gals who enjoyed one another's company labored endlessly to produce a reasoned statement proclaiming that everybody else stank and only they were good. It proclaimed in bold type: ONLY WE KNOW WHAT'S GOOD, NICE, EQUITABLE, AND, MOST IMPORTANT, MODERN.

Hmmmm, we haven't heard this before, have we?

The early part of the twentieth century was the golden age of the manifesto. Every new movement had to have one. The Arts and Crafts movement had one, the Mission folks—namely Gustav Stickley—had a monthly manifesto in the form of a magazine called *The Craftsman*. But with the growth of sociopolitical groups after the turn of the century, the manifesto industry entered its heyday. We have a Mister K. Marx of Berlin to thank for the legacy of modern manifesto mania. Every political movement, offshoot, splinter group, subdivision, what have you, just had to have its own manifesto.

Artistic types, staggering from their meetings, reeking of Gitanes and Beaujolais, muttering obscenities about the trade unionists, came up with the idea of having their own sacred manifestos on art and design. These manifestos synthesized political thought with the artists' own ideas about style and design.

The Futurists' manifesto, published in *Le Figaro* on February 20, 1909, decried the old edifices, cathedrals, and palaces and looked forward to an industrial future replete with hotels, ports, and stations—all of which they wanted to build: "The futurist city, dynamic in all its parts." (Just think of Fritz Lang's *Metropolis* and you'll get the picture.)

In 1917 a group of Dutch artists and designers led by Theo van Doesburg created a magazine called *De Stijl* (De Shteel). And—surprise, surprise—they had a manifesto, too! With times being what they were, they had the perfect reason for creating a new world of design: The old one had been reduced to rubble during World War I. To these artists, this new order would be pure and unencumbered by the old bugaboo of bourgeoisie symbolism. Yes, everything was going to be nice, neat, clean, and conscientious, and everybody would live and work together in cleanly designed buildings reminiscent of the angularity of the flat Dutch countryside. Everything would be in perfect harmony, and the world would be at last a nice place in which to live. (Meanwhile, somewhere in Austria, a funny-looking corporal with a postage stamp mustache was thinking, "Feet get cold in these trenches . . . the fastest way to France is a straight line across that flat Dutch countryside.")

Because the De Stijl was one of the most important movements in the eventual creation of Mid-century Modern design, we present you with the movement's entire manifesto:

There is an old and a new consciousness of time. The old is connected with the individual. The new is connected with the universal. The struggle of the individual against the universal is revealing itself in the World War as well as in the art of the present day.

The war is destroying the old world with its contents: Individual domination in every state. The new art has brought forward a

new consciousness. Time contains: A balance between the universal and the individual.

The new consciousness is prepared to realize the internal life as well as the external life.

What nonsense.

The representation of a stark linear landscape is very evident in the works of the best-known De Stijl member, Piet Mondrian. Mondrian spent a lot of time looking at the fields from his back window, which inspired the crisscrossing, interlocking colored shapes characteristic of his work, and boy, are we lucky. Had he been looking out his front window, we would be left with endless pictures of his dachshund, Schnitzel, chasing Lars the postman.

What's that? All this ranting and raving and we haven't even been talking about furniture? Well you know, furniture doesn't just appear one day. There are many things that bring about change, and furniture changes just like anything else.

If we were to name one major proponent of the De Stijl form of furniture design, it would be Gerrit Rietveld. Rietveld was the son of a cabinetmaker and apprenticed in his father's shop when he was eleven, during the height of the Arts and Crafts movement (see Chapter Five). Rietveld's father was that preindustrial type of cabinetmaker who had no need for the Arts and Crafts movement's high-minded contempt for simplicity. He had been simple for years—his work, that is. Rietveld the younger was himself unpretentious, nonelitist, and a true craftsperson. Much of his early work does have a distinct Arts and Crafts style with its simple rectilinear designs and solid, exposed construction. His quality of design evolved as he began studying architecture, and with the influence of the De Stijl dynamic of simplicity and angularity, he came up with some groundbreaking designs.

Rietveld's Red/Blue chair was, in essence, the three-dimensional representation of a Mondrian painting, incorporating the primary colors red, blue, and yellow along with black. All the parts of this chair are exposed and hide nothing from the viewer. You can see exactly how it has been put together. In this sense it is sculpture—no, architecture. If there is one aspect of modern design that stands out above everything else it is that all aspects of an object's design, inside and out—the very mechanism that makes a chair a chair, for instance—can be exposed and decorated, even if that decoration is pure color, and the very mechanics of the design can be appreciated.

One has to ask the question: does the chair function as a chair *and* as art? Now, while we may admire Rietveld's Red/Blue chair for its artistic and spatial qualities, we must say it is quite uncomfortable to sit on for long periods (if you strapped on some patio furniture pillows, however, you could sit real nice for quite a while). So that's it for his chair. On the other side of the room there's a sideboard. This can be said to be his true masterpiece.

Created in 1919, the sideboard plainly shows the influence of Arts and Crafts: exposed drawers, mechanisms, and battens (strips of wood). While critics decry this piece as inferior to the Red/Blue chair in design innovation, we take the opposite tack. We appreciate the fact that the sideboard plainly shows the influence of earlier designs, for what it lacks in sterling newness is compensated for by its place in the time line of furniture design. In simple terms, successful furniture design has always been an evolutionary—not a revolutionary—process. A piece of furniture must represent the artistic sensibilities of its maker and it must be made to be functional—if it don't function right, it's art, not furniture. Though Rietveld's Red/Blue chair is a masterpiece of design and is revolutionary in concept, it isn't furniture because it's not comfortable. It evolved not from chairs gone before it, but from art gone before it—Mondrian's art—and what it gained in art, it lost in function. Drawing its functionality from earlier designs, Rietveld's sideboard had this base covered. It expresses artistic advancement without sacrificing utility.

If these criteria brand us "bourgeois" by the members of the Manifesto for Lunch Bunch all we can say is, we have our own TV show.

The Petty Comfort of the Bourgeoisie

If there was one thing all these Modernist design collectives hated it was any design that smacked of being bourgeois, meaning anything that had come before what the Modernists created. This hatred was a cornerstone of the Bauhaus school of design, which began soon after World War I ended. Two of the main proponents of Modern International design were architects Walter Gropius and Le Corbusier (which was the pseudonym of Charles Èdouard Jeanneret-Gris, and which was affectionately shortened to "Le Corbu"). They decried the heavily ornamented designs of the past. Their architectural designs were always clean, spare, flat, and angular—perhaps much the same as their personalities.

Although the originality of their designs heralded a new era and was deeply influential on design even today, the dogma explaining their vision belongs in a sparse, clean, flat, and angular waste can. These designers felt that their designs foreshadowed an age when workers would labor in a happy utopia: happy craftspeople building white boxes, living in white boxes, and eating out of white boxes as the video screen glowed and cooed, "Big Brother is watching you." The working-class utopia populated with boxes for living, or *boîtes d'habitier* as Le Corbu referred to them, is a soul-destroying concept. Moreover, due to the unornamented nature of the International style, an entire working class of artisans skilled in ornamental decoration was wiped out. Stone-carvers, wood-carvers, gilders, and others whose art had adorned buildings for centuries were suddenly unneeded in this new world. Creativity by the masses, for the masses, became an outdated concept and became instead the exclusive province of the upper class.

Some utopia.

Breuer and Mies van der Rohe

The most important Bauhaus designers were Marcel Breuer and Mister "less is more" himself, Ludwig Mies van der Rohe. Breuer enjoyed using metal in his designs, and the advancements in the use of tubular steel during the postwar era allowed him to create a multiplicity of design and construction possibilities. Continuous lengths of tubing could be bent, turned, and twisted until they formed a unified skeletal shape for a chair upon which a simple sling of leather or canvas could be attached to support the sitter. This design was ably displayed in his Wassily chair, made for that great nutty artist Wassily Kandinsky. A further development in tubular steel chair design was the cantilever effect of a singular piece of tubing ending beneath the back of the chair, negating the need for any rear vertical legs.

Marcel Breuer's Cesca chair, with its singular tube frame and cantilever base, is a common sight in many kitchens throughout the world. The chair's structure itself acts as a spring, as the tensile strength of the tubular steel allows the chair to flex when somebody sits on it. With a woven cane seat and back and, more often than not, a dent or break in the woven seat because people like to use this type of chair as a ladder to change lightbulbs, this chair is almost ubiquitous. (We repaired a couple of these chairs on one of our shows.) If you're thinking about buying this type of chair for your dining pleasure, consider getting the seats and backs padded and wrapped with fabric.

A second technological breakthrough was the development of laminated wood, which we now call plywood. By laminating thin sheets of wood together, it was possible to create greater strength in the wood, while still allowing the wood to be bent or molded using steam into different shapes. The foremost designer of laminated wood furniture was an architect from Finland named Alvar Aalto. He developed a method of laminating and then contouring wood to create the skeletal structure for a chair. His designs found their way into average homes because of the inexpensive nature of the materials used—especially when compared to the polished steel furniture made by Le Corbu and his Bauhaus buds. Many of Aalto's designs and ideas, however, were inspired by the earlier work of Michael Thonet of Austria.

Thonet was a craftsman who, around 1830, began experimenting with new techniques for making furniture without using the traditional construction methods of joinery. The results of his experiments included using heat and water to bend thin strips of wood, which could then be laminated together and molded into any shape imaginable. This type of wood furniture was more readily accepted in the average home than the cold, twisted-pipe furniture of Mies van der Rohe, Breuer, and Le Corbu. For all their posturing about easily mass-produced furniture, their early work was all handmade and not produced in quantity until after World War II. In contrast, Aalto's designs were marketable due to their ease of construction and use of modern materials like plywood.

The developments taking place in wood and metal furniture designs allowed furniture makers a freedom they had never had before. Padding and springs could be eliminated; wood, if necessary, could be molded to fit the buttocks for chairs; plywood or metal could now be bent and shaped to support the back of the sitter. Before these developments, wooden frames had to be padded and covered for comfort. For the first time, hundreds of years of design orthodoxy could be ignored. That's not to say that cushions and springs were completely abolished, but they were only one of many alternatives in modern furniture-making.

The future was indeed for Modernist designers and furniture makers. They had the manifestos and the designs; all they had to do was wait for the post–WWI European industrial complex to rebuild itself to the point where all of their designs could be mass-produced for happy workers everywhere. There was one catch, however: Germany's industrial complex was being run by a funny little man who crawled up and out of a foxhole and branded the Bauhaus movement (and others like it) Socialist. (See, this is what happens when you leave your manifesto lying around; not only does the paper it's written on get wrinkled and torn, but any jerk can pick it up and read it.) Interestingly enough, just as the Bauhaus boys were escaping to America, the Fascists in Italy were beginning to like this variety of furniture—which heralded the beginning of Italian Modernist design. We consider this to be the beginning of the end for Adolf and Benito, culminating in a savage (though undocumented) whirlwind of a food fight at Berchtesgarten on Christmas Day in 1943: sauerbraten, braciola, Wiener schnitzel, provolone, strudel (apple and cherry), saltimbocca, bratwurst, sauerkraut, gnocchi. . . .

The vast majority of European designers had immigrated to America and made this wonderful country of ours the center of modern design. Their influence was felt internationally, with terms such as "Scandinavian Modern" entering into the furniture purchaser's vernacular. The natural materials used by Alvar Aalto became very popular in America, and "organic design" became the buzzword for designers of the late 1930s. Asymmetrical, biomorphic shapes—soft or curving shapes modeled after organisms—found their way into the designs of renowned Japanese artist Isamu Noguchi and laid the groundwork for our kidney-shaped table in Project 10.

In 1940, the Museum of Modern Art held a competition called Organic Design in Home Furnishings. Alvar Aalto and Marcel Breuer were among the judges at this competition and, right there on Fifty-third Street in New York City, the torch was passed from these two founders of the Modernist movement to Charles Eames and Eero Saarinen, whose winning entry was a groundbreaking plywood design. Eames and Saarinen replaced Aalto's plywood skeletal chair structure with larger sheets of plywood that were bent into a continuous three-dimensional form. In essence, the two designers had made a chair from a single sheet of plywood, perfectly designed to accommodate the curves of the human back and but-

---

VISIT ED'S MOM

If you are ever in northeast Philadelphia, you can see a wonderful copy of Mies van der Rohe's most famous design, the Barcelona chair (so named because it was created for the German Pavilion at the Barcelona Exhibition of 1929), at Ed's mom's house. This steel-and-leather masterpiece sits just inside the front door, functioning as the place where one places coats, packages, and groceries. Ed's mom will bid you welcome and invite you to nosh a little something with the words, "Come in, are you hungry? I have plenty. . . . "

After dessert—and after being told you're a scarecrow and you should "have some more of my apple cake because you're thin as a rail" (as she holds up her pinkie, which is supposed to resemble your profile)—you'll have the chance to see an excellent reproduction of a Wassily chair like the one we described earlier upstairs in the den.

---

tocks. This design, along with others they had entered in the contest employing the same concepts, set the stage for the postwar boom in mass-produced Mid-century Modern furniture.

The moniker "Mid-century Modern" refers to furniture produced from the 1930s through the 1970s with design routes springing from any of a range of Modernist movements, several of which we've just discussed. The label can refer to one-of-a-kind designer pieces, mass-produced knockoffs adapted from daring original designs, or any streamlined mass-produced furniture.

A post–World War II home-furnishing buying frenzy coincided with the rise of these easily produced pieces. The parlors of yesteryear were replaced with living rooms and dens; the new suburban homeowner had to buy sofas and chairs for two rooms instead of for a single sitting room. The creation of the den created a need for the lounge chair—a seating apparatus on which Pop could recline, unbutton his pants, and watch Gorgeous George saw the turnbuckle off a squared circle. Life in the den was a far cry from the situation in the parlor, where you drank tea and munched gingerly on a biscuit while sitting on a straight-back chair and staring at others in the room, carrying on what was quaintly called a "conversation." The den made conversation obsolete: The narcotic glow of the Admiral or the Emerson was all the company that was needed, or for that matter, would ever be needed again.

The den invited you to take your shoes off, elevate those feet, recline those backs, and relax—that is, unless you had naïvely joined any liberal group in the 1930s, had sung any folk songs, or had curly hair and glasses (read: looked like Ed).

Shortages of material during wartime had kept the seminal designs of many Modernist designers from reaching the public until 1946. Meanwhile, in the early 1940s, the Hans G. Knoll Furniture Company had been established by Hans Knoll. His father, Walter Knoll, had manufactured furniture in pre-Hitler Germany designed by the Boys from the Bauhaus—not to be confused with *The Boys from Brazil,* whom they hated (just as we hated the scenery-chewing performance of Gregory Peck in the movie, complete with comic-opera mustache and hair color courtesy of Kiwi shoe polish). Anyway, while Hans Knoll was preparing for the postwar boom he knew would come, he hooked up with designer Florence Schust, who had attended the Cranbrook Academy of Art with Eero Saarinen and Charles Eames. After the war, these designers and others worked for Knoll and set about designing some of the most influential furniture this side of Dodge City.

In 1947 Saarinen's first design for Knoll was produced: the Grasshopper chair with matching ottoman. It used Scandinavian-style bent plywood construction and featured a one-piece semireclined seat with back. This chair became immensely popular and was in production for almost twenty years; the last ones were produced in 1965. Naturally, with success came that most sincere form of flattery: imitation.

Imitation has its limitations, however, and in order to fend off the inevitable copyright suits, knockoffs of famous designs had to be altered to some degree. Witness, if you will, our next project, the Cricket chair. The seating element is basically the same as that of the Grasshopper, but the legs and arms are drastically different in that they are not made from bent plywood but from three pieces of wood connected in such a way as to suspend the body of the chair above the floor. So while our Cricket chair rips off the basic look of Saarinen's design, the technologically innovative elements used in the construction of the Grasshopper chair have been trashed.

Project 9:

MID-CENTURY MODERN CHAIR

Michael Gladfelter is the proprietor of the store Mode Moderne in Philadelphia, which specializes entirely in Mid-century Modern furniture. When we went to him looking for projects for our TV show, he led us to our chair. Structurally, the chair was in great shape, but the fabric, which may have been original, was tattered, saggy, and very discolored (basically a grime-tinted, disgusting swamp green). The arms and legs were riddled with surface scratches

Mid-century Modern chair "before"

of contact with sweaty, hairy forearms. That's the trouble with lounge chairs: bodily fluids mixed with Piels and Lucky's rapidly wreak havoc on the finish. The color of the wood led us to believe it was oak. We soon discovered, however, that it was bleached walnut, darkened over the years. Michael also supplied us with fabric for the chair, an aqua sharkskin he had been saving for some time. This was a good thing, because we didn't have enough money to buy any fabric.

Materials List

- Roll of burlap webbing
- Burlap
- Foam (if necessary)
- Dacron
- Fabric
- 2-ounce nylon thread
- Chemical paste remover
- Planer chips
- 0000 steel wool
- Lacquer thinner
- Denatured alcohol
- 80-, 220-grit garnet sandpaper
- Hydrogen peroxide bleach
- 400-grit finishing paper
- Clear shellac
- Clear gloss lacquer (brushing or spray-on)
- Automotive paste wax
- Soft cloth
- 2 aluminum tack strips (36-inch long)
- Cardboard tack strips
- Cambric

Tool List

- Staple puller
- Pliers
- Pryers
- 2 pairs of channel-lock pliers
- Scissors
- Staple gun
- Button maker (or button kit)
- Tape measure
- 8-inch upholstery needle
- Cabinet scraper
- Metal file
- Sharpening stone
- Burnisher
- Clamps
- Dust mask
- Respirator
- Protective eyewear
- Heavy rubber work gloves
- Wire brush
- Plastic or earthenware container for mixing bleach
- Nylon bristle brush
- Apron
- Tack rag
- Rubber mallet

Removing fabric from back

The chair was constructed in three pieces: two leg/arm pieces, and a one-piece seat/back section. Four bolts and nuts connected the leg/arms to the back, and in order to remove the legs from the seat we had to remove the bolts. To get at these bolts, we had to first remove the fabric from the chairback (this is completely different in human anatomy) with staple pullers, pliers, and pryers, as we did on the throne chair in Chapter Two. We removed each staple along the top and bottom of the outside back. We then removed the metal tack strips holding the sides of the outside back to the frame. We also removed a sheet of muslin from underneath the outside back fabric that helped to define the shape of the outside back.

Removing bolt with channel-lock pliers

Under the muslin we noticed that the wooden frame of the chair consisted of some crosspieces and a loosely woven system of burlap webbing, which maintained the slingback shape of the chair. There was a reason for the looseness of the webbing: if the webbing and fabric had been pulled tight, the deep curve in the seat would have disappeared.

Holding bolt with channel-lock pliers

So the webbing and seat material had been left loose. The question then becomes How can the fabric be left loose this way without having the end result appear baggy and wrinkled? The answer is: buttons. We discovered that the button thread of the old buttons on the chair had been stapled to the crosspieces of the chair frame, holding the loose arrangement in shape. We cut these threads and the buttons flew across the room and disturbed the sleeping pussy on the TV set whose name is, ironically, Buttons. (Later, fabric-covered buttons would be sewn on the outside fabric with the thread pulled through the seat cushion and stapled tightly to one of the wooden crosspieces. The tautness of the thread pulls the button tight against the fabric and eliminates any slackness in the upholstery material.)

The bolts holding the chair together were also visible and we used two pair of channel-lock pliers (one clamping the inside bolt and the other clamping the outside bolt) to loosen and remove them.

Attaching webbing

With the arm assemblies removed we were able to proceed to refinishing the arms and removing the remaining inside back/seat fabric. Under the fabric we found an enormously entertaining and ingenious system of padding that led us to believe it had been upholstered at least once in the past by an insane person. Underneath the full-length sheet of foam we uncovered a white, tattered child's quilt, followed by a pink fuzzy bath mat (without its matching toilet seat cover or the Scarlett O'Hara toilet paper cozy). Apparently, the deeply troubled people who had attempted the job were psychotic shut-ins surrounded by cats and *Life* magazines from the Truman era (they even remembered to leave a piece of Dacron in the chair—a bona fide artifact of the 1950s). The more upholstery jobs you do, the more you will be astounded by the items you find embedded in old furniture. The wearing of protective gloves is definitely recommended for the skittish.

After discarding these aberrant innards (except for the foam padding), we had to strengthen the webbing system. Most of the straps were in good shape, so they did not need replacing. Some of

Attaching webbing

Burlap-covered webbing

the cross webbing was tattered, mainly in the seat area, which takes the most punishment.

We cut some new straps from a roll of webbing and wove them through the existing vertical straps, making sure the new webbing was loose enough to retain the sling shape of the seat. But we had to be careful that it wasn't so loose as to leave the buttocks grazing dust bunnies on the floor.

Once the webbing had been repaired, adjusted, and stapled in place, we covered it with a full-length sheet of burlap, folded its edges over the chair frame, and stapled it in place.

Fun, Foam, and Fabric

We were able to reuse the sheet of foam we found inside the chair, but we turned it over so that its less worn side was facing upward—oh, the joys of recycling. If the foam is decomposing or crumbling, or if it smells like Uncle Sid and his Optimo Admirals, you'll want to get some fresh stuff from an upholstery supply store.

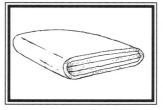

Covering foam with Dacron

We placed a brand-new piece of Dacron on top of the foam (this process is sort of like making a sandwich) that was cut large enough to cover the seat/back and wrap around the sides at the top and bottom edges of the chair seat/back frame. The Dacron holds the foam in place, provides additional loft in the seat, and pads the sides of the frame, while giving the chair more rounded edges. Also, when fabric is placed over the Dacron and pulled extremely tight, the

Dacron and padding together will protect the fabric from the sharp edges of the wooden chair frame and prevent excessive wear, especially where the chair frame curves severely.

We pulled the Dacron around the sides of the chair frame and made sure it lapped over the sides of the chair to cover the back edge of the frame. We then stapled the Dacron in place.

Pulling fabric over edges and making fold

With the webbing in place, the burlap sheet covering the webbing, the foam in place, and the Dacron covering secure, we were ready to cover the chair with fabric. Luckily, only two pieces of fabric were needed for our chair: one large, full-length piece to cover the inside back and seat, and a second piece to cover the outside back.

The inside back piece was generously oversized, with about 8 inches of overlap on all sides. We laid the piece across the chair, making sure the pattern (such as it was) was running straight across the chair. Next, we pulled the fabric around the top of the chair—where your head would rest—and stapled the fabric to the outside of the back. The first staple was placed directly in the center of the frame, approximately 2 inches below the top edge. We then stapled outward away from the center on each side of the center staple. At about 4 inches from each edge we stopped stapling to take up the excess fabric by making folds at the chair edges. We made a crisp vertical fold right at the edge of the fabric by gripping and pulling the fabric on the side under the fabric on top and then pulling it straight down where it could be stapled to the underside and back of the chair. For a neat-looking fold

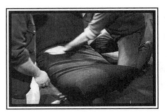

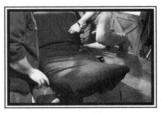

Pulling and stapling fabric to frame back

job, make sure that excess fabric is not bunched under the fold. We then stapled from the fold back toward the center staple to complete the row of staples that we had fired into the fabric along the frame.

When each corner had been neatly folded, we pulled the fabric tightly around the chair, pulling the fabric over the chair on both sides and stapling it to the frame at the back. This was accomplished by first stapling along the fabric near the top of the chair for about 6 inches down one side, and then along for another 6 inches down the other side, working toward the bottom to achieve maximum tension in the fabric. Pull really hard to achieve the high tension. Another challenge was to make sure that the pattern in the fabric ran in a straight, even fashion and wasn't being pulled crookedly in the process.

Bring On the Buttons

It became necessary to pull extra hard on the fabric where the frame curved. (You'll be thankful for the Dacron padding protecting the fabric from the hard chair edge when you do this.) With the top and sides stapled, we had to pull the fabric down and under the front of the seat, stapling it first at the center point on the front of the chair. Here the procedure is the same as the one used on the back. Staple in the center and work outward toward each side, stopping about 4 inches from each edge to make folds in the corners. These folds don't have to be so pretty because no one is going to see them under the seat—we made them pretty and neat because, well, that's the kind of guys we are: It would have bothered us to do them any other way!

Despite all this pulling on the seat/back fabric, we noticed that horizontal wrinkles had been created across the stretched fabric. They could have been eliminated by pulling on the fabric vertically (toward the top and bottom), but we didn't want to eliminate these particular wrinkles. If we had pulled hard enough vertically to rid the fabric of these wrinkles the fabric would have been stretched so taut that it would have lifted up and away from the deepest part of the seat. This would have changed the shape of the chair seat considerably and the fabric would have ripped the moment someone sat down. Obviously, this wasn't the scenario we wanted. There is one easy solution for eliminating wrinkles like these, and that is by using buttons.

Ah, buttons. They straighten out wrinkles, keep foam from moving around, add a decorative touch, and can even be used to make a face. We love buttons—but what kind of buttons are needed for this project, and where do you get them, you may ask? Well, you have to custom-make them, especially if you want them to match your fabric.

There are two ways to make your own covered buttons: You can buy a professional $150 button maker, which will make a button in seconds that will never come apart, or you can go the cheaper route and purchase the $2.98 button kit pack from a fabric or notions store that will hardly, probably, maybe, never, ever come apart.

We used the expensive button-making machine because we had never shown it on our

TV show before, and we didn't have to pay for it. Whatever method you use for making your buttons, you have to start out the same way. Buttons are made from three components: the cover or front of the button, the back of the button or shank, and the fabric you want to cover the button with.

After you cut the fabric in a circular shape with enough excess to pull around and stuff into the back of the cover part, then choose your assembly method. If you've sprung for the button machine, which can be purchased at an upholstery supply store, you also have to purchase the appropriate-size die for the size of the button you need to make.

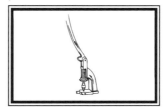
Button-making machine

We placed the fabric-covered button face-down in the die, then slipped the button into the receptacle of the button-making machine, making sure the excess fabric was folded up and inside the hollow button top. Next, the shank part of the button was placed on top of the button top, and the large lever on the machine was pulled down like the lever on a fancy orange-juice squeezing machine.

The pusher element on the machine pushes the shank portion of the button into the hollow covered part, trapping the fabric, crimping it closed, and giving you a button. Sounds like fun, right? At times we have also used a simple button-making kit, which comes with the button cover, shank back, and a "pusher" part, which is a bottle cap–shaped piece of metal that, when placed over the shank back, has to be pushed down manually. You can't push this down with your bare hands; the instructions that come with the kit recommend using the flat end of a spool of thread to do it. We positioned a pair of upholstery shears over the "pusher" right where the nut held the shears together and used them to push down hard until we heard the button snap together. Do not attempt to hit the pusher with a large mallet or hammer; you won't achieve uniform pressure and you'll end up with a sloppy-looking button, if you don't ruin the button completely.

By now, if you're reading and making buttons at the same time, you probably have lots and lots of buttons, 'cause we sure do. Once the buttons are made, you need to attach them.

Our chair, as we found it, had six buttons. Three buttons ran toward the top of the inside back at about shoulder height where the frame took a slight bend. The other three buttons were placed at the severest bend in the seat, right where your you-know-what would go.

To line up the buttons, place a tape measure across the width of the chair, find your center-point, and make a mark. Then determine two more points that are equidistant from the middle mark and the chair sides—you do the math!

With an 8-inch upholstery needle purchased at the upholstery supply house where you got the fabric and button maker, thread the needle with 2-ounce nylon thread—the stuff Hemingway used to catch marlin with. Cut a generous amount of thread and thread it through the shank of the button; pull it through and even up the ends of the thread, then thread both ends of thread through the eye of the needle. Working with the pointy end (so many people get this part wrong), push the needle through the center mark that was made on the inside back. With sewing buttons, as with stapling fabric, you always start with the center. Push the needle all the way through the inside back. Since the outside back hasn't been installed yet, the needle can be pushed through the fabric and underpadding and retrieved on the other side, where it can be tied to a crosspiece on the chair frame. We pulled the thread just tight enough so that the button dimpled the fabric surrounding it. We had to leave enough slack in the fabric, however, to permit dimpling around the two other buttons that would be inserted on each side of the center button. Don't ever pull the first button so tight that the dimpling takes up all the excess fabric. You don't want the fabric that taut because then the button holes themselves may start to fray, or the holes will get so big they will swallow the buttons, and then only a surgical excavation of the chair will retrieve them.

Once the button dimple was the desired depth—say, the depth of the cleft in Kirk Douglas's or Cary Grant's chin—and, after tying off the thread, we stapled the thread to the chair's crosspiece to ensure that it was very secure. We repeated this process with all five remaining buttons, making sure that we had SDD, or Symmetrical Dimple Depth, for each. (Asymmetrical Dimple Depth, or ADD, is the scourge of upholsterers everywhere.)

Bleaching and Finishing of Arms and Legs

We spoke of the bleached blond effect earlier. But how does one achieve the look? With bleach, of course, but there are a few steps that have to be gotten out of the way before you can bleach. The first big step is to strip the thing. Don't even try to bleach something that hasn't been stripped first.

The old finish on the flats of the wooden leg/arm pieces was scraped away with a cabinet scraper. These tools are flat pieces of carbon steel that are sharpened when they become dull by using a file, sharpening stone, and a burnisher. When used properly they can remove old brittle finishes faster than anything, though be warned: they are not good for everything. On table surfaces and delicate, soft woods, these tools can scratch, gouge, and badly scar the wood. Well, the tool itself can't mar surfaces, but the person using it can. In this respect, cabinet scrapers are a lot like guns. Be careful with these tools; practice using them first.

When cabinet scrapers are bought new, they are already sharpened but they will quickly dull with use, and when they do you need to know how to sharpen them.

The rounded, or curved, scraper works well

130

on rounded areas. And all four sides of the flat scraper can be sharpened. Using a metal file (you can lock the scraper into a vise for stability), travel the length of the scraper edge, and feel for the file cutting the scraper metal as you go along. A few passes will do. When the steel of the scraper edge is moved across the tine "cutting lines" of the file, you will feel a resistance, which means the file is creating a new edge on the scraper.

Scraper and file

With the scraper edge filed, use a sharpening stone to continue sharpening the scraper. Sharpening stones typically have one coarse side and one smooth side; use the coarse side first. Squirt a little general-purpose oil or water onto the stone and hold the scraper perpendicular to the stone. Move the scraper back and forth along the stone about eight times. Then lay the blade flat, and with your fingers placed on the side of the blade, pull the blade across the stone to cut the "burr" created by the sharpening stone.

Scraper blade on sharpening stone

Repeat this procedure on the opposite scraper blade by turning the scraper over and "cutting the burr" on the other side. With both sides of the scraper rubbed, sharpened on the rough side of the sharpening stone, and deburred, you are ready to use the smooth side of the sharpening stone. Repeat the same steps on the smooth side of the stone, and deburr the scraper blades. The process is the same, and only the wood will know the difference.

Once you have finished using the stone, it is time to "turn your burr"—which is exactly what Raymond Burr's friends used to do when he snored at night. This is achieved through the use of a burnisher, which can be purchased at most art supply stores, where they are typically sold to those who do gold leafing. There are many types

of burnishers, but the best are those that are rounded like the one shown here. The idea is to pull the burr to an angle through turning. Simply lay the scraper flat on the edge of a table,

Turning burr using rounded burnisher

hold it with one hand, position the burnisher perpendicular to the flat scraper, and pull it back and forth across the edge. You achieve the "turn" in the burnish by holding the burnisher at a 45-degree angle (or thereabouts) and pulling it along one edge out toward you. You should be able to feel the sharpness of the turned edge with your fingertips.

You've done it! Now when you hold the scraper in your hands and bend it gently, bowing the blade away from yourself, and scrape it along a wood surface, you should create fine shavings.

We secured the legs/arms to the tabletop on our work surface with a couple of clamps and drew the scraper over the flat surfaces to

Scraping chair legs

remove most of the finish, turning the pieces over and resecuring them as needed to scrape all the flat surfaces.

By using the scraper first, you save on the amount of paste chemical remover you'll need to apply to the wood later and minimize your exposure to the smell of remover fumes. Always wear a mask when scraping wood, and a respirator equipped with appropriate filters when working with chemical removers. You should also be sure to wear protective eyeware because most old finishes are brittle and have the tendency to fleck off during refinishing.

Because old finish always remains in the pores of the wood, after scraping we applied a paste remover to the wooden chair pieces and let it sit for about 15 minutes, softening the wood in the process.

The next step was "the chips treatment." Wearing heavy rubber work gloves, we began

Rubbing planer chips on wood

rubbing handfuls of chips over the remover as we did on the throne chair (page 30). (In actual fact, Christopher King, our great assistant for our TV show, undertook this step. Thanks!) When the paste remover had been removed by the chips, we washed down the wood by

Scrubbing wood with wire brush

rubbing with 0000 steel wool soaked in a mixture of lacquer thinner and denatured alcohol (one part lacquer thinner to one part denatured alcohol), and then scrubbed the wood with a wire brush.

We then sanded the cleaned wood by hand,

Sanding wood

going with the grain using 80-grit garnet sandpaper, because we needed to really open up the wood to allow the bleach to enter the wood when it was applied. If the wood is not clean, the bleach will only bubble on the surface and you will waste a goodly amount of bleach in the process. So sand, sand, sand. . . . A good test of whether the wood is ready for the bleach is to sprinkle a bit of water on the surface when you think it's clean enough. If the water soaks right into the wood, then it's clean; if it beads, roll up your sleeves and continue sanding.

We couldn't use just any bleach to bleach the wood. Only hydrogen peroxide bleach would do the job. This is the strongest and most potent form of bleach. It removes unsightly stains and will also remove all traces of color from the wood until it resembles the pallor of *American Journal*'s Nancy Glass. These bleaches are sold as kits containing an "A" and a "B" bottle. Half the contents from each bottle are combined in a

plastic or earthenware (not metal) container before being applied with a nylon-bristle

Applying hydrogen peroxide with nylon brush

brush. Natural-hair brushes will get eaten away by the bleach—impatient readers will probably use natural-hair brushes anyway, but don't say we didn't warn you when you're looking into a pail of bleach and bristles. When bleaching wood, make sure that you wear protective work gloves, an apron, and goggles. If peroxide gets in your eyes you'll be in a world of shellac!

You should see and hear the bleach foaming up as it enters the wood, but don't be afraid. This means the peroxide is doing its thing. Once the bleach is applied, allow the wood to dry overnight and then, wearing a dust mask, sand the wood lightly with 220-grit finishing sandpaper. The peroxide's water base will have raised the grain of the wood so you'll need to "cut" the raised wood fibers before proceeding with the final finish.

Once the wood has been bleached it will be devoid of color. This is a look that was popular in the 1950s—it was chic and showed up in everything from wood furniture to Marilyn's hair. After the sanding was completed, we tack-ragged the wood to remove the dust and proceeded to apply a wash or spit coat of clear shellac (page 46). We allowed the shellac to dry and then sanded with the used 220-grit sandpaper from the previous step. It's a good idea to save worn sandpaper to use when you don't want the sandpaper to be too coarse or too smooth (is this technical stuff or what?).

We used a clear-gloss lacquer for the final finish because it dries fast and because lacquer is the clearest finish you can buy. Varnish would have changed the color of the wood slightly, because most varnishes have a tinge of amber. We applied four coats of spray lacquer (waiting for each coat to dry and sanding between coats with 400-grit sandpaper). If you don't want to spend the time required to build up layers of lacquer coating with spray-on lacquers, you can paint on just a couple of coats of brushing lacquer, sanding between each coat.

Spraying on lacquer

Sanding lacquer

Buffing lacquer with padette

When the last coat of lacquer had been applied we buffed the surface with 0000 steel-wool "padettes" (page 57) to achieve a bright shine and the silky smooth feel of a baby's ass. Spray-on lacquers dry faster than brushing lacquers because the lacquer is drastically thinned so that it can be pushed out of the tiny hole on the button that the finger pushes by the hydrofluorocarbons or whatever "safe" propellant they are using these days. They dry fast, and up to six applications can be applied over a three-hour period. Also, because canned spray lacquer is thinned so much, more coats are needed to really build up a film of what can indeed be called finish (not Norwegian or Scandinavian).

Brushing lacquers demand more drying time because they are thicker, and even though can labels often say a piece can be recoated an hour after application, I would wait two. On a nice day where the humidity is low and the air is crisp, three coats can be applied in a ten-hour period. Lacquer is a solvent-release finish, which means after it has been applied the solvent, namely the lacquer thinner, evaporates into the air leaving behind a dry film which can be re-dissolved in its own solvent or succeeding coats of the same finish. So it is best to have the previous coat good and dry, since the next coat of lacquer you will be applying can and *will* meld and eat into the finish, ultimately becoming one coat (with a matching vest).

We applied a car paste wax to the legs/arms of the chair with the dampened circular sponge that came with the wax. Car wax will create a tremendous shine. We allowed the wax to dry to a haze, and then buffed away the residue with a soft cloth. What could be easier?

Attaching the Arms and Legs

With the leg/arm assemblies bleached and looking lovely (which is also the name of

Putting wax on sponge

Applying wax with sponge

Buffing away residue with cloth

Pegs marking bolt holes

L'Oreal's new hair conditioner) we had to reattach them to the chair before applying the final fabric panel to the back. If you recall, the leg/arm assemblies of our chair were bolted on the inside of the chair frame. The nuts holding the leg/arms on the chair must be tightened from the inside before the fabric back panel is put on.

When the frame of the chair was wrapped with the new material earlier, the holes where the bolts went were covered. We therefore had to create some holes in the new fabric by shoving a narrow blade on a pair of scissors through the fabric where the holes for the bolts on the wood were and twisting the blade to create an adequate hole. We placed a couple of wooden pegs in the holes to mark where the bolts would go so we wouldn't lose track of where the holes were under the fabric. We inserted the bolts where the pegs were and tightened them with a pair of locking pliers to secure the leg/arm assemblies in place.

And Now for the Back

With the leg/arm assemblies bolted into the chair, we were able to proceed to putting on the back fabric panel. This panel is not any different from other back panels except where alterations had to be made in the bend where the chair frame curved at shoulder height. We also needed to use two full-length (36-inch) aluminum tack strips along the back edges.

We positioned a cardboard tack strip across the top of the back, just as we had done with the deco chair (page 95). (This chair was much easier to reupholster than the deco chair, however, because its edge was flat and straight across. The deco chair, if you remember, was curved.) We then laid the fabric with the "pretty" side down on the inside back of the chair and cut it, leaving two inches hanging over the top of the chair. We fired a staple into the centerpoint of the fabric where it lapped over on the top edge and into the outside frame of the back. We then placed a piece of cardboard tack strip cut to the width of the chair length and placed it across the overlapping fabric, stapling the strip in place along the upper edge of the cardboard tack strip. With the fabric secured under the tack strip at the top of the chair, we flipped the fabric over so that it hung down over the back. The line across the top of the chair should appear straight if you did the job properly. If the fabric appears to have dipped in the middle of the seam, you may use a smaller piece of cardboard tack strip to bolster the offending area by stapling the strip right over the top of the existing strip.

With the outside back hanging over the back, we pulled the bottom tight at the centerpoint on the chair's bottom frame and placed a single staple to anchor the fabric in place there. This process created tension in the fabric panel at the top and bottom and allowed us to attach aluminum tack strips along the side edges of the chair without inadvertently pulling the fabric to

Begin piercing fabric with aluminum tack strip at the top corner

Piercing side fabric edge with aluminum tack strip

one side or the other.

We lined up the tack strips, spikes facing up, along one of the outside edges of the frame, pulled the fabric over the strip, and carefully pushed the "spikes" through the fabric one spike at a time, pulling the fabric as we spiked it to avoid making wrinkles. Once the fabric had been spiked along the entire length of the fabric, the tack strip with the spiked fabric was rotated toward the chair frame so that the spikes faced the frame along the outside back edges.

Using our trusty rubber mallet, we banged the aluminum tack strip carefully halfway into the frame. We took care here because the tack strip had to travel over the bend in the frame and we wanted to encourage the tack strip to conform to this bend. Done hastily, the fabric may have bunched and we would have been left with bumpy wrinkles—who was a distant relative of one Gabby Hayes. We repeated the process on the other side of the chair and then pulled the bottom tight and stapled the material along the edge of the fabric panel to the underside of the frame.

As with every upholstery job, the last thing that had to be done was to apply a cambric, or dust cover, to the underside of the seat, which we stapled neatly around the perimeter of the bottom of the chair.

This project cost less than $100 to complete, and would still have cost less than $100 if we had had to pay for the fabric. The bleach, lacquer,

Mid-century Modern chair "after"

and car wax all cost about $25. The chair was returned to the furniture showroom where it came from, this time wearing a price tag of $600, though we last heard the proprietor of the store was thinking about keeping it for himself. So there you have it: a bastardized copy of a classic chair, refinished and reupholstered by your favorite funny, er, uh . . . bastards.

Project 10:

MID-CENTURY MODERN TABLE

Well, we're still in the 1950s with the last project in this book. Behold a simple, amoeba-shaped coffee table, the likes of which may have decorated one of your relatives' den or rec rooms. The owner of this particular specimen bought it at a flea

Mid-century Modern table "before"

market, paid someone to do a faux malachite finish on it, and then sold it.

Five or six years later, while at an auction, the owner happened upon the same table and purchased it. This was a perfect project because it was like us: simple.

Materials List

- Chemical paint remover
- Planer chips
- 0000 steel wool
- Denatured alcohol
- Lacquer thinner
- Mahogany veneer (small piece)
- Vinegar
- Veneer glue
- 220-grit garnet sandpaper
- 320- and 400-grit silicon carbide sandpaper
- Paint thinner
- Hydrogen peroxide bleach
- Sanding block
- Krazy Glue
- Wax paper
- Tack rag
- Paper towels
- Methanol
- Shellac
- Quick-drying varnish
- Automotive paste wax
- Soft cloth
- Spray paint (optional, for legs)

Tool List

- Nylon-bristle household scrub brush
- 4-inch flat paint stripper
- Gong brush
- Rubber or latex gloves
- Respirator
- Dovetail saw
- Goggles
- Small brush, like a toothbrush or a brass brush of similar size
- Veneer roller
- Clothes iron
- Upholstery needle
- Razor blades
- C-clamp
- Cabinet scraper
- Wire brush

Scraping paint from table

Scrubbing with planer chips

Brushing clean with gong brush

Stripping

If you don't know the proper steps for stripping by now, you should be beaten, or worse, be made to go back and reread this entire book. Using a brush, we applied paste paint remover to the tabletop and allowed it to sit until the old finish crackled and bubbled. This took about 15 minutes. Then we applied a second coat of remover right on top of the first, remembering to pat the coats on, rather than wipe the remover over the surface as if we were painting it.

Once this step had been completed and the stuff was ready to come off, it was time to scrape and use planer chips (page 15) to remove the softened paint. (The hands of our faithful assistant, Christopher King, who now resides on the Emerald Isle with his mum and family, are shown scraping the surface with a 4-inch flat paint scraper, and then using planer chips to clean off the softened paint. He also used a lot of exotic Irish profanities in the process.) We then used a gong brush to brush the surface clean. We like to practice safe stripping: Always wear rubber gloves and an appropriate respirator when undertaking this job.

We then proceeded to wash the stripped mahogany veneer table surface, scrubbing it with a 0000 steel-wool pad soaked in a 1:1 mixture of denatured alcohol and lacquer thinner.

Venerable Veneer

With the paint removed and the surface washed of excess paint, we noticed that a small repair needed to be done on the edge of the table: A chunk of the veneer had been chewed away and

Applying glue to veneer patch

Applying glue to table

Inserting patch into table

Veneer roller

needed to be replaced. We used a small dovetail saw to cut the section of worn veneer away along the grain (because the grain on the edge band that ran around the table was perpendicular to the floor, it was easy to cut the damaged section away neatly).

We also cut a patch of mahogany veneer to fit into the section we had cut out. (Many types of veneer can be purchased by mail order from Albert J. Constantine in the Bronx, New York. You can buy huge sheets of exotic cuts, or itty bitty bags of veneer pieces for small touch-ups.) It's important to clean the open wound where the veneer has been cut out of the table. Use a 1:1 solution of vinegar and water to clean the area and allow the area to dry.

Whenever old veneer is cut and peeled off a tabletop there's always going to be a residue of dried glue. Older furniture was usually assembled with hide glue, which is soluble in water; the vinegar in the solution allows the solution to "cut" better. Scrubbing with a small brush such as an old toothbrush, or with a small brass brush that resembles a toothbrush, and abrasive pads works great for removing this type of residue.

If the table is newer, or let's say you need to replace a piece of laminate (which is always adhered using contact cement), you would have to use a solvent called methyl ethyl ketone, or MEK for short. This solvent is nasty and must be used with a respirator, goggles, and gloves. It

may take a while before the old stubborn stuff begins to soften, so be patient.

Once the area to be patched had dried after washing, we applied a new veneer glue to the patch and to the spot on the table where the patch was going to fit and then waited for 15 minutes or so until the glue felt tacky (but not wet). Confused? Well, you see, unlike other glues, veneer glues work after they dry. You coat both surfaces and allow them to dry. Then, you cover each surface with glue again. This process ensures that all areas are adequately coated. You will be able to touch your finger to the glue when it has become tacky but will find that it will not stick to your fingertip. All you have to do then is insert the patch into the opening and press; the glued surfaces will meld and become one as pressure is applied. This is when a veneer roller comes in handy: Roll it over the patch, applying pressure as you do so.

There; your repair is complete.

Applying bleach with nylon brush

Bleaching

You will notice there is a difference in color between the existing veneer and the patch. The patch is a lot darker than the table veneer, but this is normal. You will never be able to find a piece of veneer that matches exactly . . . well, we should never say "never"—Sean Connery came around again, but that film was no *Goldfinger* or *From Russia with Love*. Still, it was better by far than any of those Roger Moore jokes (c'mon, even Connery's *Thunderball*, the worst of his Bond films, was superior to any that came after he had left the series . . . and don't get us started on Timothy Dalton or Pierce Brosnan).

For the look we wanted to create on this table, which was a deep red, we knew that we had to use an aniline dye (page 45) and that our canvas had to be as light as possible to take the true color. That meant we had to bleach the wood.

Once the table had been cleaned (washed down using a 1:1 lacquer thinner/denatured alcohol solution), it was sanded well and scrubbed with a household scrub brush, a Tampico brush just like what Grandma used to clean her floor (of course nowadays you'll find them made out of nylon), and paint thinner. Remember what we said in the Mid-century Modern chair project: in order for the bleach to work, the wood has to be absolutely clean, otherwise it will not enter the wood and will only bead up on the surface. So it pays to go those extra few cleaning steps.

We cleaned the wood again by rubbing it with 0000 whole steel-wool pads soaked in clean lacquer thinner, going with the grain. You know you're getting the wood clean when the lacquer thinner doesn't get too dirty from scrubbing. Once the table was dry, we washed the wood one final time with paint thinner, allowed that to dry, and then sanded the tabletop with used 220-grit garnet sandpaper, sanding with the grain to open the pores of the wood before bleaching. We dusted off the surfaces and proceeded to bleach the tabletop.

We mixed a cup of "A" bleach with the "B" bleach in a glass bowl and applied the bleach to the surface using a nylon brush, just as we did when we bleached the wood for the chair in Project 9 (page 130).

The bleach entered the wood and began to foam. If you're real quiet, you can hear it working, kind of like the famous snap, crackle, and pop of the breakfast cereal, but more deadly: SSSS . . . SSSS . . . and SSSSS.

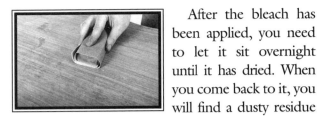

Sanding with wood block

TECHNIQUE TACTIC:
SUCCESSFUL SANDING STRATEGIES

When sanding bleached wood, be careful not to use too coarse a grit of sandpaper. Also take care not to sand too much or too hard; go over the wood with light, even strokes. Remember that when you bleach something you are not bleaching the entire thickness of the wood but only the surface to a depth of about 1/16 of an inch or less. If you break through the thin bleached surface, the original color of the wood will show through as streaks or spots.

Using iron on damp cloth to repair split veneer

Inserting razor blades in split veneer

After the bleach has been applied, you need to let it sit overnight until it has dried. When you come back to it, you will find a dusty residue that is nasty if you get it in your eyes. Wear goggles and an appropriate respirator. A simple dust mask will do you no good here. Hydrogen peroxide bleach dust, just like Liza, is an eye, nose, and throat irritant, so wear protection. Using a new piece of 220-grit garnet sandpaper wrapped around a wood block, we sanded with the grain, and then dusted off the surface with a rag.

Often, after bleaching veneered surfaces, you will find that the surface has lifted, buckled, or split, which is what happened to the table surface in this project. The bleach lifted the veneer because the bleach is water-based and the veneer was attached with a water-based hide glue. In our case, the veneer split and was raised a bit in two places.

What had happened? Well, to be honest, we had laid on too much bleach in an effort to lighten the wood as much as possible. This is fine to do as long as you know how to remedy resulting problems as they arise. After a single application of bleach, the wood appeared uneven, so before it

Inserting glue under split veneer

had dried completely (overnight), we applied more bleach and kept it wet for a good 2 hours. This activity, while keeping us busy off the set between takes, left us with a wonderful little quick-fix tip to show you.

A first attempt at remedying the problem by placing a hot iron over a damp cloth to reactivate the old hide glue failed. We were therefore forced to resort to open heart surgery. We slid two razor blades into the open wounds. Then using an upholstery needle (or some other long, sharp instrument) we lifted the split, removed the razor blades, and injected some Krazy Glue into the opening. We conducted the same surgery on the second split.

C-clamp on repaired veneer

Once both splits had been filled with glue, working fast, we laid a sheet of wax paper over the splits (this is important so that the wood and glue do not bond), a block of wood on top of the wax paper, and clamped the whole mess tightly using the ever-popular C-clamp. Once the glue had dried (if you use carpenter's glue for the job instead of Krazy Glue you need to wait overnight for the glue to dry or the splits will reopen), we removed the C-clamp and peeled off the wax paper. A small bit of wax paper had adhered to the spot which we were able to remove with a few passes of a cabinet scraper (page 130). Then we were able to proceed with our refinishing job.

Staining Simplified

We sanded the entire table with a 220-grit garnet sandpaper, dusted

---

TECHNIQUE TACTIC: DRYING TIME

Wood glues need at least 24 hours of *clamped* drying time. Using epoxy, as we did, enables clamp removal in 5 or 10 minutes—in TV, time is everything. If we don't tape, schedules are thrown off and everyone gets bitchy and unhappy. Although we had carpenter's wood glue on the set, we couldn't possibly do the repair with it. We would have had to wait 24 hours for it to dry, so we used a tube of Krazy Glue and got the job done quickly.

Mixing aniline dye powder

off the table surface, and then tack-ragged it (page 17). With everything in order, we were ready to dye the bleached wood with an aniline dye. We discussed anilines in Project 4, on the pine hallrack (page 68). To refresh your memory, aniline dye stains are sold in powder form and have to be dissolved in a solvent. For a standard stain you would use one ounce of powder to one quart of solvent. Though these dyes are sold in water-soluble, alcohol-soluble, and oil-soluble forms, the most popular are the water-soluble types because they are the most lightfast, meaning that the color will remain true the longest. You can use hot or cold water to mix them, and a bit of methanol alcohol to bring out the real color of the dye—the label directions will tell you the amounts. If you really want to be compulsive about it, use distilled water, as the minerals and various salts in tap water can alter the intensity of the dye's color.

We selected a brilliant red, mixing an ounce of powder to a quart of water, plus a shot of methanol. What's a shot? About a half a cup. Wearing rubber gloves, we applied the dye with a soft brand of paper towels, such as Bounty (we don't get a penny for endorsing this brand, by the way). Paper towels will not leave a lint residue the way a rag might. The dye penetrates the wood and colors it. The red we used was as red as any red you may have seen before on TV, except for the whites of the eyes of Dean Martin in the 1970s when his show was on top.

Once the dye had been applied to the entire surface, we wet some paper towels with plain methanol and wiped the surface again, which removed some of the red in the process. This also gave us an idea of how the color would appear when we later coated the surface with a clear finish.

The dye is dry when the surface appears flat in color, indicating that the water in the dye has evaporated. You will notice that if you touch the wood a residue will come off on your fingertips. What's more, if you were to resort to applying the ubiquitous spit coat of shellac (page 16), you would find the shellac turning red when you brushed it on. You could, however, apply a spit coat if you sprayed it on (page 69). This is why we went straight for a quick-dry, oil-based varnish to coat the dyed surface; it could be applied without fear of pulling the water-based red coloring out of the wood. When the dye dried, we sanded it lightly with 400-grit silicon carbide finishing paper before varnishing.

varnish should be rubbed out afterward, which will produce a satiny smooth feel in the surface. A satin varnish looks fine but will remain a bit rough to the touch. Satin varnishes can be rubbed with steel wool to produce the same tactile quality as gloss varnish. We used a satin varnish for our project.

If the wood is new and fresh, you may want to consider first applying a "cut" coat of varnish as your sealer coat. This is one part varnish mixed with one part paint thinner. This will penetrate the wood and dry a lot faster than your succeeding full-strength coats. If the wood has been recently stripped, you can start off with a full-strength coat of varnish; just be sure to follow the rules for silicone infection (see the section on cratered finishes in Project 4 [page 72]).

Follow the same directions for rubbing out and polishing described for Project 3, the rolltop desk (page 56), for details on doing this.

We then spray-painted the legs on the table black. We could have removed them for the job, but we didn't.

Waiting for Varnish

Varnish is looked upon as the slowpoke of finishes because it takes a while for it to set up, or dry. Polys dry faster, as do lacquers and shellac, but there are also quick-drying varnishes that cure and are ready to recoat within 2 hours. They will say "quick dry" on the label.

When it comes to varnish, you first need to decide whether you want to use a gloss or satin varnish. Gloss

Varnishing table

Applying varnish   Spray-painting legs

Mid-century Modern table "after"

GUIDELINES FOR SUCCESSFUL VARNISHING

There are more people who want to know about brushing varnish than we care to tell you—this, and how to get white rings off of finished surfaces. Well, there is no mystery to brushing varnish, just common sense. Follow the steps below for a problem-free varnish job. Our table presents the chance to practice this concise routine for producing a masterful varnish finish.

1. Do not apply varnishes in cold conditions, inside or out—say, below 60° F.

2. Any sanding and dusting off should be done in a different room from where you will be applying the varnish.

3. Make sure your brush is fresh and clean.

4. Hit the brush bristles against your hand to remove any loose hairs before starting the job.

5. Make sure you can see the surface clearly and that you have a reflected light source.

6. Brush gently so as not to create too many air bubbles.

7. Don't wear fuzzy sweaters while brushing. If you feel the need to wear these, wait until later to varnish.

MORE GUIDELINES FOR SUCCESSFUL VARNISHING

1. Make sure your piece has been cleaned and tack-ragged.

2. Fill a clean container with enough varnish to complete the job.

3. Varnish all pieces that can be done horizontally first.

4. Dip the brush into the varnish and tap the "loaded" bristles against the side of the can. Do not scrape—this creates bubbles. Apply the varnish in long strokes across the grain and with the grain but always finish off brushing *with* the grain. This is called "tipping off." Hold the brush almost vertical with the bristles, just touching the varnished surface, and drag the brush from one end to the other.

5. Allow the varnish to dry overnight, unless it is of the quick-drying variety, in which case an hour or so should do.

6. Sand the dried surface with a 320-grit silicon carbide finishing paper. Some people advocate using 0000 steel wool but this in itself will not remove dust that has dried in the film.

7. Dust the surface off with a rag and tack-rag it.

8. Apply a second coat of varnish, as described in point 4.

9. After drying overnight, sand with 400-grit silicon carbide finishing paper; additionally you will find rubbing with soapy water and using a 500-grit wet/dry sandpaper will produce an exceptionally smooth surface. Wet/dry sandpaper is paper that can be used with a soapy-water solution that acts as a lubricant. It can also be used dry.

10. After the third coat of varnish has been applied and allowed to dry, wet-sand the surface with a 600-grit wet/dry sandpaper and clean it off with a soft cloth, and then apply a paste wax. A paste wax is fine for most woods. Car wax can be used on those surfaces where the pores have been filled and the finish applied (so that the surface is smooth to the touch) to render a mirrorlike finish as in the Moderne table.

Varnish Rx

Certain problems may arise when you apply varnish. In fact, some people stay away from varnishing because they are actually afraid of the stuff, saying that they heard somewhere that it was very difficult to apply. Here is a checklist of problems and solutions:

SYMPTOM	DIAGNOSIS	TREATMENT
Varnish begins to pucker and spread	Silicone infection	Use a fisheye flowout (page 72). A wash coat of shellac before varnishing will also seal an infection—and these days, double protection is good.
Varnish will not dry or remains tacky	1. The varnish is old. If a can of varnish on your shelf has been closed and opened several times, not only will a skin form on the top surface that will have to be cut open but each time this happens, some of the dryers are lost. This results in a bad varnish that will not dry.	Use new varnish, not something that's been on the shelf for a few years.
	2. Cold also prevents varnish from drying properly.	If it's too cold out (below 60° F), varnish in a heated area with a small fan blowing to circulate air.
	3. If all traces of remover are not washed away, they will prevent proper drying.	The surface must be washed again with lacquer thinner and then given a final rinse with paint thinner.
After the varnish has been applied, tiny air bubbles become visible	You're brushing wildly. Take your time and don't scrape the brush across the rim of the can.	If the bubbles in the dry film of varnish remain, sand down the surface using 320-grit silicon carbide sandpaper just to smooth it out and then apply a second coat thinned with paint thinner. The addition of thinner will allow the varnish to "flow out" better.

Although varnish can be sprayed with an electric airless sprayer, with conventional spraying equipment, or with the newer HVLP (High Volume Low Pressure) flow systems, the cleanup time is a real pain in the you-know-what.

Listen to your buddies and stick to the brush.

Afterword

Well, you made it to the last page. Are you beat? Need a vacation?

Ready for splinters and fumes and the heartache of setting up your very own finishing and upholstering environment? You are?

Yeah, you need a vacation all right!

You know, since we started writing this book, a lot of things have happened to us. We have the only how-to show to ever win a Cable Ace award, for instance. In 1994 we were nominated for Best Informational or Documentary Hosts and beat out Jodie Foster, who had narrated a Bette Davis special; Jack Perkins and Peter Graves, who alternate hosting *Biography;* and James Burke, who does that *Connections* thing—and we won! How about that?

We were nominated in 1995 and 1996, too. We didn't win, but hey, they say you only have to win once, right?

We still got to meet a lot of famous people at the awards party, like Jean Stapleton, Shelley Duvall, and Walter Cronkite—who beat us in 1997 in the host category, by the way—and our good buddy Jon Voight, all of whom were pretty much just a lot of ordinary people like us, hobnobbing and eating shrimp. We smiled a lot and kicked any food that had fallen from our plates under whatever table we were standing next to, without anybody noticing. And other than that—

oh, yes, and the fact that they are all so much better known than we are, and make so much more money, and wear finer clothes, and know lots of really important people in Hollywood—we felt a definite kinship. Jeffrey Tambor even asked Joe if more trays of the chicken satay kebabs would be coming out soon. Ed had to explain that we were not part of the kitchen catering staff.

We were on *Good Morning America, Maury Povich,* and lots of local TV stations across the country and in Canada. We had a bit part (all of twenty-one seconds) in one of the worst movies ever: *Double Dragon* (look for us in the first ten minutes of the film, where we are shown on TV doing a commercial as "Earthquake-Jack Salesmen of the Future" just before the evening news!). Not to mention all the nice meals we enjoyed, traveling the country and throughout Canada doing our personal appearances, when we've had the good fortune of meeting great people like *you,* who have become our fans over the years. Guess you could say *we* bought the dream, huh? Did *you* buy the book? If you did, thanks; if not, don't smudge the pages and put it back—someone else may want it.

In any case, we thank you.

Good night, everybody!

Resources for Supplies

Here's a list of where you can obtain many of the supplies used for the projects in the book:

A. Brood and Sons
727 S. 4th Street
Philadelphia, PA 19147
(215) 925-0776
For fabrics of all kinds, this is the place we go. The fabric we used on the throne chair project in Chapter Two came from Sam and Lou at A. Brood and Sons. They've appeared on a few of our shows as well. You'll never meet two nicer guys. Tell 'em we sent you.

Constantine's
2050 Eastchester Road
Bronx, NY 10461
(212) 792-1600
(800) 223-8087
Constantine's stocks finishing materials as well as upholstery supplies. It also stocks a wide variety of veneers and veneering supplies.

The Gryphin Co., Inc.
3501 Richmond Street
Philadelphia, PA 19134
(800) 482-1886
The folks at Gryphin specialize in wonderful historical paints, going to extremes at times to make exact color matches to ancient chips of paint.

We've used their paint for a variety of projects on our shows over the years. Ask for Nick and tell him we sent you. (Ask him to stand up on his desk and shout, "To be or not to be!")

Mohawk Finishing Products
Route 30 North
Amsterdam, NY 12010
(518) 843-1380
(800) 545-0047
Supplies for all types of finishing, upholstery, and touch-up needs. It sells mostly to the trade, but do-it-yourselfers can call for a catalog and a salesman will be at your door before you can say "horsehaar!"

Specialty Environmental Technologies, Inc.
4520 Glenmeade Lane
Auburn Hills, MI 48326
(800) 899-0401
These are the folks who developed the orange stripper you've seen us use on the show so many times: Citristrip.

Star Chemical Supplies
360 Shore Drive
Hindsdale, IL 60521
(708) 654-8650
(800) 323-5390
Sells supplies to the professional trade.

Index

How to Reach Us

To contact The Furniture Guys, write:

The Furniture Guys
P.O. Box 53240
Philadelphia, PA 19105-3240

Web site: www.furnitureguys.com